Pets and Mental Health

ABOUT THE AUTHOR

Odean Cusack, a freelance journalist whose specialties include animals and the environment, earned her baccalaureate in psychology from The University of the State of New York and did graduate work in zoology at Temple University and Rutgers University.

Cusack's serious writing began in 1980, when she founded Signature, the Mensa special interest group concerned with animal rights and the environment, and edited and published the group's newsletter, *Signature News*, which was widely distributed throughout the animal rights and welfare community. Her articles have appeared in such publications as *Omni, Orion Nature Quarterly, Pure-Bred Dogs American Kennel Gazette, Dog Fancy, Today's Animal Health, Woman's Day, Lady's Circle,* and *Guideposts* magazines, as well as Philadelphia-area and national newspapers. *Pets and the Elderly: The Therapeutic Bond*, which she coauthored with Elaine Smith, was published by The Haworth Press in 1984.

Pets and Mental Health

Odean Cusack

The Haworth Press
New York • London

The Haworth Press, Inc., 10 Alice Street, Binghamton, NY 13904–1580
EUROSPAN/Haworth, 3 Henrietta Street, London WC2E 8LU England

LIBRARY OF CONGRESS
Library of Congress Cataloging-in-Publication Data

Cusack, Odean.
 Pets and Mental Health / Odean Cusack.
  p. cm.
 Bibliography: p.
 Includes index.
 ISBN 0-86656-652-X. ISBN 0-86656-801-8 (pbk.)
 1. Pets — Therapeutic use. 2. Psychotherapy. 3. Mental health.
I. Title.
RC489.P47C87 1988
'616.89' 14 – dc19   88-9671
                                                              CIP

CONTENTS

CHAPTER 1

Pet-Facilitated Therapy:
An Introduction

What is man without beasts? If all the beasts were gone, men would die from great loneliness of spirit, for whatever happens to the beast also happens to man. Whatever befalls the earth befalls the son of earth.

—Chief Seattle of the Duwamish Tribe, State of Washington, Letter to President Franklin Pierce, 1855

The terms *human-animal bond* and *pet-facilitated therapy* are relative newcomers to the scientific literature, but the concepts they encompass have been with us for centuries.

James Harris of the Montclair Veterinary Clinical Hospital in Oakland, California, defines the human-animal bond as "that physical, emotional, intellectual, and philosophical relationship that occurs between a person or family unit and an animal."[1]

In our society the most common of these relationships and the ones we are most familiar with are undoubtedly those between people and their pets. However, the human-animal bond is not confined to urban domestic animals, nor is it necessarily an outgrowth of our pet-loving society.

One of the earliest archaeological indicators of the human-animal bond was uncovered in 1976 by Simon Davis of Hebrew University, who excavated a human skeleton in a tomb in northern Israel. Clutched in the hands of the skeleton were the remains of a puppy, suggesting to Davis that the relationship between the two was an affectionate, not a dietary, one. Probably the first animal domesticated, the dog has occupied many roles in human society. Davis's

1

poignant find, estimated to be approximately 12,000 years old, suggests that its early, and possible its best, destiny was as man's friend and companion.[2]

The terms *pet-facilitated therapy*, *animal-facilitated therapy*, and *adjunctive pet therapy* refer to the use of animals (usually pet or companion animals) as aids or accompaniments to more traditional therapies. Again, although the terms are of recent vintage, the concepts have historical antecedents.

The first recorded historical use of animals as institutional adjuncts was in 1792 at the York Retreat in York, England. Founded by a Quaker merchant, William Tuke, the York Retreat included animals as part of the living environment and encouraged patients to care for them. A forerunner of positive reinforcement programs, the York Retreat stressed positive, rather than punitive, means to control behavior.[3] A writer of that era remarked that an animal not only provided pleasure to the patients, but " . . . [it] sometimes tends to awaken the social and benevolent feelings" as well.[4]

Bethel, a multibased treatment facility in Bielefield, West Germany, was originally founded in 1867 for the treatment of epileptics, but eventually expanded its treatment base to care for other disorders as well. Dubbed "an institution without walls," Bethel incorporates farm animals and a wild game park in addition to traditional pet animals and a highly successful equestrian program.[5]

Formal use of animals as therapeutic aids in the United States began at the Pawling Army Air Force Convalescent Hospital in Pawling, New York. The Hospital utilized farm animals and small reptiles and amphibians from the nearby forest, and encouraged their patients, who were recovering from fatigue as well as physical injury, to interact with them. Patients organized frog jumping contests and turtle races, which inspired a competitive spirit and provided an educational experience.[6]

In 1953, however, a shaggy dog named Jingles paved the way for more extensive use of animals in psychotherapy. Jingles belonged to psychiatrist Boris Levinson and happened to be in the office with him when a mother and child arrived unexpectedly for an appointment not scheduled until many hours later. Levinson, a pioneer in pet-facilitated therapy, noticed that the youngster, previously withdrawn and uncommunicative, interacted positively with the dog.

This breakthrough enabled Levinson to treat the youngster, and eventually contributed to his recovery. Jingles acted as an intermediary between the child and Levinson, and enabled the youngster to develop trust in the therapeutic milieu. With the publication of Levinson's article describing his experience, pet therapy formally began.[7]

Much of Levinson's subsequent work stressed the importance of pets to children both in the home and in a therapeutic environment, but he also recognized their value to adults, particularly the elderly, as well.

During the 1970s Sam and Elizabeth O'Leary Corson* were researching dog behavior at Ohio State University Hospital. The kennels were in earshot of the adolescent ward, and several of the young patients broke their self-imposed silence and asked to play with the dogs. The Corsons selected the most withdrawn patients for a pilot project to ascertain the effects of interacting with the canines. Forty-seven of 50 participants showed improvement, and many eventually left the hospital.[8]

The Corsons extended their work at the Castle Nursing Home in Millersburg, Ohio, and obtained similar results. Interaction with the animals promoted self-reliance and increased responsibility among the patients, many of whom had been almost entirely unmotivated in these areas. The animals also facilitated social interaction between the residents themselves and between the residents and the staff.[9,10]

The value of prescribing a pet for an otherwise lonely individual has been recognized by many in the field. Levinson reports the case of a 72-year-old man who, although recently widowed, declined to live with his son:

> During the week he was alone it soon became evident that he was not eating enough to stay healthy. He and his wife had a cat, but it died about a month before his wife did, and he had

---

*The works of Boris Levinson and the Corsons are classics in the field. Because they are so well-known, they are not discussed in detail in this book, which is concerned primarily with more recent research. The reader is encouraged to consult the bibliography for extensive listings by these pioneers.

not the energy to replace it. The son came to the shelter to get a cat for his father, in the hope that the animal might relieve the old man's loneliness. . . . .His father [was] delighted with the pet . . . with the result that the man ate more than formerly. By the end of the first week an elderly lady who lived next door had made friends with the cat and through it with the man.[11]

Marcel Heiman often practiced "zoo therapy" — prescribing pets for individuals who, for various reasons, could not live with other persons but were too anxious to live alone comfortably. Heiman reports one case in which a parakeet was placed with a woman who had a long clinical history of social estrangement, irrational fears, and semi-psychotic episodes. The patient found that when she was irritable with the pet, it responded that way to her, and she learned that her unrealistic demands upon others contributed to her maladjustment. Eventually, she was able to discontinue therapy.[12]

The late Michael McCulloch, psychiatrist and former vice president of the Delta Society, the multidisciplinary organization for investigation into the human-animal bond, was one of the first professionals to evaluate formally the influence of pets in a person's life. By questioning his patients about pets past and present while establishing a history, McCulloch found unexpected and revealing insights into their mental health:

I look at pets as a window to psychodynamics, as a way toward understanding a lot of the developmental things that occurred in the past. People often talk freely about relationships with pets, and you can see tremendous insights. And I do it as an assessment of what the current support is for a patient as a diagnostic tool. You can get someone to chronologically draw out the level and intensity of dependence on pets over a lifetime and begin to look at what was happening at certain times. A pet often mirrors some of the conflict level.[13]

McCulloch was also one of the first psychiatrists actually to prescribe pets:

Prescription of pets is a very tricky situation, and you need to be very cautious and sensitive to the social, economic, and psychological status of an individual. There are many situations where pets can be used without requiring full-time ownership.

The therapeutic value is self-evident. Research is showing animals have tremendous value in promoting humor, laughter, and play, and in promoting a sense of importance. They make people feel significant.[14]

McCulloch practiced what he preached. After leaving his dog one weekend with his father, who is hard of hearing, he asked his mother to notice how much his father laughed with the pet. The following weekend he took the dog away, once again asking his mother to notice. His father laughed four times as much with the dog.

"Animals do not emphasize or force you to look at deficits you may have," said McCulloch. "The dog didn't care if my father was hard of hearing. In the presence of a pet, my father felt whole."[15]

The exact number of animals now used in a clinical or therapeutic environment is not known, but some surveys suggest that the number is significant. In 1970 Philadelphia psychologist Ethel Wolff prepared a survey for the American Humane Association and reported that 48% of the institutions she surveyed used animals in some capacity.[16]

In 1972 Levinson randomly surveyed members of the Clinical Division of the New York State Psychological Association. Of those who responded to the questionnaire (319), 39% reported familiarity with the use of pets in psychotherapy, 16% had used pets at one time or another, and 51% recommended pets to their patients for home companions. Dogs were most frequently used, followed by cats, fish, hamsters, birds, and turtles. Emotional and social isolation, schizophrenia, and desensitization of phobias were the more frequently mentioned problems amenable to pet-facilitated treatment.[17]

In 1973 Rice, Brown, and Caldwell questioned members of the American Psychological Association and found that of the 190 respondents, 21% reported some use of animals or animal content in therapy. The areas with the greatest clinical use of animals were the Northeast and mideastern United States.[18]

Phil Arkow, writer and humane advocate currently affiliated with The Humane Society of the Pikes Peak Region in Colorado Springs, Colorado, remarked that in 1977 he knew of only 15 humane societies utilizing animal therapy programs and eight U.S. university research projects investigating them. In his 1982 overview edition of pet therapy, he references 75 humane society programs, 44 academic projects, and numerous miscellaneous programs; he has also edited a comprehensive new volume on the subject.[19,20]

Articles about the human-animal bond and pet therapy have appeared in numerous national magazines, as well as science and animal publications. Anecdotal accounts illustrating the bond and applications of pet therapy are regularly featured on local news programs and even such prestigious network offerings as "Sixty Minutes" and "Nightline."

"When the first paper on 'dog as co-therapist' was presented in 1966, the researcher was laughed at in unison," psychologist Aline Kidd recently told a meeting of the American Association for the Advancement of Science.[21] Although there is still considerable skepticism within the scientific community, no one is laughing anymore. The evidence is overwhelming that animals make us happier, healthier, and more sociable, and the research has just begun.

NOTES

1. Editorial. (1983, fall). PAW/Latham radiocasts. *The Latham Letter*, p. 10.

2. Miller, H. (1979, April). Cro-Magnon's best friend. *Dog World*, p. 24.

3. Bustad, L. K. (1980). *Animals, aging, and the aged*. Minneapolis: University of Minnesota Press.

4. Levinson, B. M. (1969). *Pet-oriented child psychotherapy*. Springfield, IL: Charles C. Thomas.

5. Bustad, L. K. (1981-2, winter). Bethel—An institution without walls. *The Latham Letter*, pp. 4-5.

6. Bustad, L. K. *Animals, aging, and the aged*. op. cit.

7. Levinson, B. M. (1962). The dog as co-therapist. *Mental Hygiene*, *46*, 59-65.

8. Corson, S. A., Corson, E. O., Gwynne, P. H., & Arnold, E. L. (1977).

Pet dogs as nonverbal communication links in hospital psychiatry. *Comprehensive Psychiatry, 18*(1), 61–72.

9. Corson, S. A., & Corson, E. O. (1978). Pets as mediators of therapy. *Current Psychiatric Theories, 18,* 195–205.

10. Corson, S. A., Corson, E. O., O'Leary, D., DeHass, G. R., Gwynn, P., Arnold, E., & Corson, C. (1976). The socializing role of pet animals in nursing homes: An experiment in nonverbal communication therapy. Columbus, Ohio: Ohio State University, Department of Psychiatry.

11. Levinson, B. M. (1972). *Pets and human development.* Springfield, IL: Charles C Thomas.

12. Heiman, M. (1965). Psychoanalytical observations on the relationship of pet and man. *Veterinary Medicine/Small Animal Clinician, 60,* 713–718.

13. McCulloch, M. (1984, October). Personal communication.

14. Ibid.

15. Editorial. (1983, fall). Profiles. *People-Animals-Environment,* p. 9.

16. Wolff, E. (1970). A survey of the use of animals in psychotherapy in the United States. *American Humane Association Report.*

17. Levinson, B. M. (1972). *Pets and human development.* op cit.

18. Rice, S. R., Brown, L. T., & Caldwell, H. S. (1973). Animals and psychotherapy: A survey. *Journal of Community Psychology, 1,* 323–326.

19. Arkow, P. (1986). *Pet Therapy: A Study and Resource Guide for the USe of Companion Animals in Selected Therapies* (4th ed.). Colorado Springs, CO: The Humane Society of the Pikes Peak Region.

20. Arkow, P. (Ed.) (1984). *Dynamic relations in practice: Animals in the helping professions.* Alameda, CA: The Latham Foundation.

21. Editorial. (1985, March 24). Pets as co-therapists; idea gaining respect. *Los Angeles Times.*

CHAPTER 2

The Human-Animal Bond

Anyone who has ever owned a pet will readily verify the benefits of associating with furred, feathered, or finned friends. Animals are fun to be with and comforting to hold. Their antics inspire humor and a sense of carefreeness, a return to childhood with its buoyant spirits. Caring for pets encourages nurturance, responsibility, and adherence to a daily schedule. Pets enable owners to reach outside themselves and to put aside fears of an uncertain future. Pets live in the immediate moment, and interacting with them makes us keenly aware of the present with all its joys and idiosyncrasies.

Pets provide unconditional love and acceptance; they offer spontaneous affection and undying loyalty. They are a shoulder to cry on, a trusted confidante, a port in a storm. They are the temporary respite from our daily woes and an unending source of delight and surprise. For the majority of pet owners, the research findings linking animal ownership with health and happiness come as no surprise. Most of us felt this intuitively all along. In a sense, animal-facilitated therapy is an indicator that science is catching up.

The benefits that pet owners themselves describe appear in the literature along with some new and provocative findings. Pets provide their owners and companions with distinct physiological, psychological, and social benefits.

PHYSIOLOGICAL BENEFITS

According to research conducted by Erika Friedmann and colleagues at the University of Pennsylvania, pet ownership appears to have a positive impact on recovery after serious illness. The researchers studied the effect of pet ownership on patients recovering from hospitalization for myocardial infarction (heart attack) or severe angina pectoris (pain caused by lack of oxygen to the heart). Fifty out of 53 pet owners were alive 1 year after hospitalization compared to only 17 out of 39 persons who did not own pets. The finding was independent of the health status of the subjects. The researchers also considered that healthful walking of a dog could provide the definitive factor and eliminated dog owners from the sample. The results were the same.[1]

Was the increased survival rate the result of the pet's effect on the owner's physiology or are there distinct psychological differences between pet owners and nonowners that may have contributed to the finding? To address this problem, Friedmann and colleagues designed a large-scale study, the first of its kind, to assess the psychological and physiological status of pet owners and nonowners. The subjects were 309 students, of whom 140 currently owned pets, 102 had owned pets at one time, and 67 had never owned a pet. The subjects were tested for anxiety, depression, Type A (coronary-prone) behavior, androgeny, sensation seeking, mood, resting blood pressure and heart rate, and health status. Variables other than pet status included race, residence, sex, and living situation.

The researchers found no significant differences between current pet owners, former pet owners, and nonowners on the physiological and psychological measures. The single most important determinant of pet ownership in this study was residence type. Apartment dwellers were less likely to own pets and more likely never to have owned them than people who lived in houses. Pet owners did score higher on the vigor scale than nonowners; however, when residence type was included, no significant difference between owners and nonowners was revealed.

Says Friedmann:[2]

> On the basis of the present study we suggest that pet owners and non-owners do not differ in personality. Thus, our findings do not support the hypotheses that observed health differences between pet owners and non-owners are a result of psychological differences.

The precise reasons why animals enhance postcoronary survival are not clear. Pets require care and foster a sense of being needed. Concern about the care of the pet could provide an incentive to get well and keep living. Friedmann surveyed 100 hospitalized pet owners and found that the majority of them were concerned about their pet and kept in telephone communication with the pet's caretaker or the pet itself.[3]

Caring even for a pet other than a dog provides moderate exercise, which is important to heart patients. And interacting with and talking to pets of all types — petting a dog, stroking a cat, even gazing at a tank of tropical fish — reduces blood pressure.[4] The effect can be present with strange pets, but it is most prominent when there is a bond between the dog and its owner.[5] (See Chapter 6, Stress and Anxiety.)

This is one area where the pet therapist has a distinct advantage over the human therapist. Talking to pets lowers blood pressure, but talking to people raises it.[6]

PSYCHOLOGICAL BENEFITS

Pets provide an unlimited source of love, affection, and companionship, and these aspects of pet association are cited most frequently in the literature. Our relationships with our fellow humans may be deep and fulfilling, but they are subject to whims, moods, other obligations, and pressures of everyday life. The pet, however, is always there, always loving, and always willing both to give and to accept affection. Unconditional and nonjudgmental love and affection are the most frequently cited benefits of pet association.

Lyle Vogel and his colleagues at the University of Minnesota conducted a survey of pet owners to identify the most advantageous aspects of pet ownership. Results indicated that pet owners themselves cite companionship (71%), love and affection (53%), pleasure (39%), and protection (36%) as the major advantages of pet ownership.[7]

Certainly these elements are present in our relationships with humans as well as animals, but their all-encompassing definition makes them difficult to evaluate scientifically.

Psychiatrist Aaron Katcher has identified four elements of the human-animal bond that relate to the larger concepts of companionship, love and affection, pleasure, and protection. These are safety, intimacy, kinship, and constancy. Each is a major factor in psychological health and well-being.[8]

The concept of safety is not synonymous with protection. Certainly, animals — particularly dogs — have braved gunfire, nature's rampages, even scorching infernos to protect or rescue their masters. Every year dog and, more recently, cat heroes are honored for remarkable actions. It may be anthropomorphic to consider such behavior "brave" or "valiant": that it has on occasion saved human (and other animal) lives cannot be denied.

But safety is as much a perception of security as an actual physical state. In these turbulent times, a late-night walk on a deserted city street is enough to provoke a shudder whether or not an actual threat exists, and a companion dog, particularly a large and aggressive type, would considerably ease a palpitating heart and sweaty palms. But more significantly, if we should encounter a stranger during this nocturnal jaunt, we would feel less uneasy if we were accompanied by a dog.

Randall Lockwood of the State University of New York asked two groups of subjects to interpret ambiguous line drawings of social interactions. One group of drawings included an animal; the other did not. His findings indicated that the animal's presence caused the social scenes to be viewed as less threatening and improved the perceived character of the people associated with them.[9] "Unless the animal is labeled vicious or dangerous," explains Katcher, "a person or face coupled with a dog is perceived as safer, more benign, more approachable, and less dangerous."[10]

Although we usually feel safe and comforted by our close human associates, generally they have earned our trust. Animals automatically are perceived as the good guys and trigger a sense of security in our minds.

Intimacy is characterized by both touching and talking, and even when there is no physical contact between the dog and owner, both parties tend to orient toward one another. People talking to their dogs lower their voices, sometimes affecting a different pitch. Their body language is open and accessible. The dog, of course, responds with rapt attention.

Unlike intimacy between humans, which requires some prior understanding, intimacy with an animal can be achieved instantly and can be expressed at times when such displays toward a human would be highly inappropriate. We can indulge our feelings for an animal far more freely than we can our feelings for another person.

Intimacy between humans is contingent upon the willingness of both parties; intimacy with a pet is solely at the whim of the pet owner. Sharon Smith of the University of Pennsylvania studied pet dogs within the home, and observed that no matter what the human members of the family were doing, the dog always made itself accessible. It was ready and willing to be played with and petted, and was far more attentive to the family members than they were to it. Furthermore, Smith observed no loss of attachment if the family members simply chose to ignore the pet for a time.[11]

The ability to achieve intimacy easily with an animal no doubt contributes to their effectiveness as cotherapists. Says Irwin Rothman,[12] a veterinarian turned psychiatrist in private practice in Philadelphia:

> The prohibition of physical contact between doctor and patient in orthodox psychoanalytical treatment is a practice one questions if he has had experience in animal care. It is my impression that absence of touch in treating mental patients is counterindicated by sufficient data on animal training, experimental animal behavioral studies, including primates, and also studies of humans who have been deprived in early life of adequate human physical contact. The slowly passing and much more mourned good old family doctor who was less proficient in technical knowledge but was able to show warm interest in his patients and their families, certainly was not reluctant to give us a pat on the back or a friendly hug when he thought it was necessary. Touching very sick, emotionally regressed patients is a modality that has been too much ignored. When properly indicated, physical touching may be valuable in gaining the patient's attention and to offer new hope in living.

They may not be human, but pets are definitely kin. A question-naire distributed by the University of Pennsylvania found that more than half of the families queried regarded their pets as "family." In fact, more than 48% considered their pets "people" rather than animals. The position of a pet in the family is like that of a child, says Katcher, a favorite child, considering the number of dogs per-mitted to share their owners' beds. "With the present child-rearing practices in the U.S.," he remarks, "most children are kicked out of the parental bedroom rather early in life if they were ever given a position there at all. There are undoubtedly more people sleeping with their dogs and developing an EEG sync with them than with their young children."[13]

The fourth element identified by Katcher is constancy. A pet can be replaced by another being physically and emotionally similar to itself because it is consistent in its behavior and relationships; al-though anyone who has lost a beloved pet will readily point out that another animal takes the former pet's space and not its place. No matter how similar in appearance or temperament, animals are as individual as humans; no two are exactly alike; each has a distinct personality. But the new pet will fill the identical role of the former pet. Constancy is perhaps the most striking difference between peo-ple-people and people-pet relationships.

The pet will remain a perpetual "child" in the family. It does not grow up in the sense that human children do. Children change phys-ically and psychologically as well; they will alter their feelings, discard cherished attitudes, and occupy a number of roles as they grow and mature. Most parents have at one time or another yearned for a particularly pleasant period in the child's life to "last for-ever." Love and deep friendship carry with them the assumption that the relationship will endure with no change in feeling, inten-sity, or behavior. Constancy is highly sought and idealized, but the human condition makes it virtually impossible to attain.

Animals, however, do not change in the way that humans do. As Katcher points out, in spite of advancing years, animals are never expected to grow up. Neotony, the presence of infantile characteris-tics in adult animals, is highly valued in certain breeds of dogs that are bred to emphasize their tiny bodies, high domed foreheads, and huge, soulful eyes. But animals in general remain infantile; they do

not learn to speak, make no efforts to conceal their bodily functions, and do not develop moral character. The attention we give to
the animal, says Katcher, maintains it in its present condition. It is
not expected to change; neither does it expect us to change, although if we do, it will not damage our relationship with us. [14]

Says anthropologist Joel Savishinsky:[15]

> It is significant that the modern therapeutic jargon . . . "the
> empty nest syndrome" is itself a faunal metaphor: the cure is
> to adopt a pet and become a born-again parent. Psychologi-
> cally, the quality of pets as "perpetual infants" eternally inno-
> cent and dependent, underscores their childlike identity. The
> pets who are child-substitutes not only stand in for the children
> we do not have, they also stand — as our own children do — for
> the children we ourselves once were. By parenting the pets
> who represent us as we once were, we relive our own child-
> hoods. The pet is simultaneously an animal, a child, and our
> own infantile selves.

The pet is, therefore, as constant as death and taxes. It loves and
will receive love without judgment, without condition, without
change. The pet will not leave home to get married, go to school, or
find new employment. The pet owner has a constant companion in
every sense of the word. And, if the pet is replaced, the new pet will
fulfill the precise role of the former one. The pet-owner relationship
can reach the age-old ideal: the love that lasts forever.

SOCIAL BENEFITS

In contrast to the stereotypic image of scores of animals surrounding a misanthropic recluse, statistics indicate that less than 5%
of the 48 million dogs and 7% of the 27 million cats that are kept as
pets in the United States are owned by people who live alone. More
than half of the pets in this country live in family groups that include children.[16] And research indicates that animals promote social
relationships between people whether they are in an institutional
setting or simply strangers on the street. In fact one Swedish study
mentioned meeting people as one reason for obtaining a dog.[17]

The social-lubricant effect of a pet has been observed both formally and informally. The animal acts as an icebreaker, facilitating social relationships between people. Robert Andrysco conducted a pet therapy project with his dog Obee at the Westminster Thurber Retirement Community in Ohio. As part of the project he rode the elevator alone for 10 weeks, then rode it for 10 weeks with Obee. "No one talked to me 'til I brought the dog," he said, "but eventually the conversation began about the dog." Andrysco then rode the elevator for an additional 10 weeks to determine the longevity of the effect and found that the social ties prompted by the dog remained. Obee proved to be an effective social catalyst, although after the initial breakthrough, his presence was no longer required to sustain the effect.[18]

Clark Brickel studied the effect of 2 cat mascots on an elderly institutionalized population. Among other findings, he noticed that the cats prompted a sense of camaraderie among the patients and that the affection and tenderness expressed towards the cats carried over to other patients and staff as well. By interacting with the cats, the patients were able to interact more positively with each other.[19]

An animal not only promotes conversation within the members of a community, but can prompt interaction between strangers, thus encouraging new friendships and associations for the pet owner.

Peter Messent of the Animal Study Center of the United Kingdom observed social interactions among 8 persons who were walking with and without their dogs in Hyde Park. When with their dogs, the walkers experienced some sort of interaction from passersby on 22% of the walks, compared to only 2% when not with their dogs. Messent later studied the interactions of persons walking their normal route and time of day. He found that on average, the walkers had 3 spoken interactions per walk, 1 of which involved extended conversation; the tendency toward a lengthy talk was enhanced if the other participant also had a dog.[20]

One possible explanation for the social-lubricant effect of a pet is that intimacy is easily achieved with an animal. It is not always considered proper to address a stranger, but it is perfectly acceptable to talk to his dog. Additionally, since persons associated with animals are perceived to be more benign and safer, the passerby might feel less threatened and more apt to strike up a conversation.

The pet owner or walker is someone you would like to know, and the pet is a perfectly safe way to begin the acquaintance. "Next to the weather," says Jean Veevers, "a pet may be almost the most neutral subject of conversation."[21]

Messent[22] offers some other explanations:

> James Serpell did a questionnaire study of 42 dog owners and 32 non-owners in Cambridge, England. He found relatively few differences in opinions on their own personality between the two groups. The most significant result was that female dog owners perceived themselves as more attractive than non-owners. Serpell suggested this finding might be due to an unconscious perception that the increase in social interaction described by Messent is a response to their own physical attractiveness. Alternately, it is possible that social interaction with a pet indirectly induces feelings of increased attractiveness by generally improving one's self image.
>
> Dufour in France compared dog and cat ownership attitudes between a relatively prosperous suburb of Paris and a modern new development outside Paris — Cretail. Among the findings was that the ownership of a pet in Cretail was seen as a significant help in overcoming some of the deprivation and alienation experienced in this living environment. A dog or cat was said to assist, for example, by helping to establish territory for the owners where the physical architecture did not allow for this outside of their own house or apartment. Therefore, though pet ownership is lower in cities rather than the country, and in apartments rather than houses, for those who do have pets, their role may be especially valuable psychologically.

However, Kidd and Martinez have uncovered at least one group that does not appear to benefit from pet ownership: men who belong to human service clubs. The researchers tested 99 male and female subjects, including 64 pet owners and 35 non-owners on the well-being and self-acceptance scales of the California Psychological Inventory. In comparing owners vs. nonowners, male and female owners vs. nonowners, and cat owners vs. dog owners, the researchers reported only one significant difference: male nonowners scored significantly higher than male pet owners on the well-being scale. Upon reviewing the data, the researchers found that one half of the nonowners but only one fourth of the pet owners belonged to multipurpose service clubs characterized by close human bonds. When members of these clubs were removed, there was no significant difference between owners and nonowners.

The researchers point out that the majority of their sample was business owners and professional people and that in this particular strata the needs of companion, friend, and confidante filled by the pet may be satisfied by human-human bonds. "Pet ownership would be less beneficial than it is to other groups and, in some cases, a liability, subtracting time and energy from human interactions," they say.[23]

This finding, however, is directly contradicted by a survey conducted by the Pets Are Wonderful Council that links former and current pet ownership to career success. The organization surveyed the chief executive officers at Fortune 500 companies and found that far from being a liability, pet ownership was perceived to be a significant asset. Ninety-four percent of the respondents reported having a dog or a cat during childhood, and credited pet ownership with helping them develop such character traits as responsibility, empathy, discipline, and compassion that contributed to their later success. Pet ownership was prevalent among the executives; 75% owned a cat, dog, or both. Interestingly, this greatly exceeds the national average of households owning a pet, which in 1983 was 53%. Dogs were the more popular pet, appearing in 90% of the pet-owning executives' homes, but 30% of the pet owners had at least one family feline.[24]

Perhaps the significant factor in the two groups is the service club. Men who belong to this type of organization participate in its activities in their leisure time, time that might otherwise be spent with a family. Yes, a pet might be a liability to such individuals; but so might a wife and children, who would take time away from their service pursuits. Executives, on the other hand, might be more disposed to spend their leisure time with their family, of which the pet is an important member.

OWNING A PET
IS GOOD FOR YOUR HEALTH

Pets promote responsible living, encourage laughter and a sense of humor, provide their owners with fun and entertainment, and are a valuable social support, all factors that contribute to well-being, reduced depression and anxiety, and thus a longer, more healthy life.[25]

Using the Purpose in Life test and the Health Opinion Survey, two measures of healthy positive attitudes towards one's self and health, Roseanne Wille compared 60 pet owners to a random sample of other subjects. She found that pet owners scored significantly higher on both tests and also that pet owners who described their pets as family members or companions scored higher than those who did not.[26]

Some individuals may take better care of the pet than themselves, but this in itself may be a health benefit. Scottish education expert Dorothy Walster tells a story of an elderly woman who refused to keep her room at an adequate level of warmth. Then she was given a pet canary and promptly relented when she learned a warm environment was essential to the health of her new pet. Thus the pet bird helped her avoid hypothermia, the abnormal lowering of the body's temperature that is a major problem for the elderly in cold climates.[27]

But are pet owners actually healthier than nonowners? To date, no large-scale demographic survey exists to answer that question. However, a small-scale survey of 488 households in rural northern California may offer a few clues. The researchers found that cancer was reported less frequently among elderly adult pet owners than nonowners. Frequent diarrhea among children younger than 5 years of age occurred more often in homes without pets than in homes with pets. Interestingly, hypertension was reported more frequently by pet owners than by nonowners, which the researchers say indicates more awareness of this condition. Also, adult pet owners reported more headaches than non-owners. But far fewer elderly pet owners reported a heart condition than did nonowners. More families without pets reported asthmatic members, which could show avoidance of pets by those with this condition. And, in less affluent areas, school-age children with pets had significantly more sore throats than those without. In affluent sections, however, the incidence was the same.[28] Since pet animals can transmit certain throat infections to humans, physicians recommend that families whose members have recurring sore throats should have their pets checked by a veterinarian. Presumably, more affluent families are more likely to seek frequent veterinary care than families of lesser means, who have to stretch their earnings. The correlation between incidence of sore throats and affluence may reflect this tendency.

Although intriguing, these findings do not answer the eternal chicken-or-the-egg dilemma. Particularly in the case of the elderly, it may be that unwell individuals do not get pets either because they are unable to care for them or because they fear for the pet's eventual fate. As researchers recognize the value of the pet-owner bond the future large-scale health surveys will include questions on pet ownership, just as they now include questions on exercise, diet, and life-style.

WHAT DR. DOOLITTLE SAID

Finally, although much of this chapter has examined the differences between animals and people, Stuart Hutton,[29] a social worker in the United Kingdom, has postulated that the reason social workers are so effective is that they act like animals. "Many of the purported beneficial attributes of companion animals are identical, or at least parallel, to the essence of the casework relationship as practiced by the 'old school' of social worker," he says.

Both social workers and companion animals:

1. break down barriers and establish meaningful communications (even if they are nonverbal communications)
2. allow people to experience the feeling of their being someone "of worth"
3. allow/enable people to learn and experience a variety of things by example and practice

4. can teach selflessness by example or responsibility, caring, and loving
5. are in a position of semivoluntary servitude
6. can be involved in healing the emotional traumas of everyday living
7. are at times friend, confidant, and companion (sometimes therapist)
8. are often an adjunct to other therapists
9. have little to offer in the way of therapeutic handouts such as drugs
10. have roles that are often ill-defined, which opens up opportunities to fit in to almost any situation
11. allow people to experience the feeling that someone cares about them
12. often start from a baseline of where people are now (behaviorally and psychologically) and gradually manipulate towards a better quality of life for both parties
13. are nothing to some, something to many, and all things to a few
14. despite ambiguity, are generally perceived to be sometimes beneficial/functional or therapeutic by the individual, family, or society
15. tend to help people use their own inner strengths to help themselves
16. are talked with, talked at, and confided in often with an expectation of tolerance, understanding, and very little backchat
17. have a cathartic effect, enabling people to get things off their chests, releasing repressed emotions
18. have the ability to keep the deepest of secrets
19. tend to have the ability to form and establish relationships quickly
20. are sensitive to peoples' feelings and emotions, thus recognizing those occasions when they are not needed or wanted as well as making the most of those occasions when they are

Says Hutton:

> The similarities between the social worker and the companion
> animal in this regard will be readily apparent to those involved
> in trying to understand the dynamics of the human/companion
> animal bond. [Since] animals were in families before social
> workers came into being it is social workers that act like ani-
> mals in these situations rather than the other way around. . . .
>   There are also many and varied differences between social
> workers and companion animals: people might be lucky to see
> a social worker on a regular basis once a week for an hour,
> whereas companion animals could be available for 24 hours a
> day when necessary.[30]

Or, as Dr. Doolittle might say: "Why can't we be more like the
animals?"

REFERENCES

1. Friedmann, E., Katcher, A. H., Lynch, J. J., & Thomas, S. A. (1980).
Animal companions and one-year survival of patients after discharge from a coronary care unit. *Public Health Reports, 95,* 307-312.

2. Friedmann, E., Katcher, A. H., Eaton, M., & Berger, B. (1984). Pet
ownership and psychological status. In R. K. Anderson, B. L. Hart, & L. A. Hart
(Eds.), *The pet connection* (pp. 300-308). Minneapolis: University of Minnesota
Press.

3. Friedmann, E., Katcher, A. H., & Meislich, D. (1981, October). When
pet owners are hospitalized: Significance of companion animals during hospitalization. Paper presented at the International Conference on the Human/Compan-
ion Animal Bond, Philadelphia, PA.

4. Katcher, A. H., Friedmann, E., Beck, A., & Lynch, J. (1981, October).
Talking, looking and blood pressure: Physiological consequences of interaction
with the living environment. Paper presented at the International Conference on
the Human/Companion Animal Bond, Philadelphia, PA.

5. Baun, M. M., Bergstrom, N., Langston, N. F., & Thoma, L. (1984).
Physiological effects of petting dogs: Influences of attachment. In R. K. Anderson, B. L. Hart, & L. A. Hart (Eds.), *The pet connection* (pp. 162-170). Minneapolis: University of Minnesota Press.

6. Friedmann, E., Katcher, A. H., Meislich, D., & Goodman, M. (1979).
Physiological response of people to petting their pets. *American Zoologist, 19,*
327.

7. Vogel, L. E., Quigley, J. S., & Anderson, R. K. (1983). A study of

perceptions and attitudes towards pet ownership. In A. H. Katcher & A. M. Beck (Eds.), *New perspectives on our lives with companion animals*. Philadelphia: University of Pennsylvania Press.

8. Katcher, A. H. (1983). Health and the living environment. In A. H. Katcher & A. M. Beck (Eds.), *New perspectives on our lives with companion animals*. Philadelphia: University of Pennsylvania Press.

9. Lockwood, R. (1983). The influence of animals on social perception. In A. H. Katcher & A. M. Beck (Eds.), *New perspectives on our lives with companion animals*. Philadelphia: University of Pennsylvania Press.

10. Katcher, A. H., Friedmann, E., Beck, A., & Lynch, J. (1981). op. cit.

11. Smith, S., (1983). Interactions between pet dog and family members. In A. H. Katcher & A. M. Beck (Eds.), *New perspectives on our lives with companion animals*. Philadelphia: University of Pennsylvania Press.

12. Rothman, I. (1970). Animal Communication. *Voices* (special issue).

13. Katcher, A. H., Friedmann, E., Beck, A., & Lynch, J. (1981). op. cit.

14. Ibid.

15. Savishinsky, J. S. (1983). Pet ideas: The domestication of animals, human behavior, and human emotions. In A. H. Katcher & A. M. Beck (Eds.), *New perspectives on our lives with companion animals* (pp. 112-131). Philadelphia: University of Pennsylvania Press.

16. Beck, A. (1983). Animals in the city. In A. H. Katcher & A. M. Beck (Eds.), *New perspectives on our lives with companion animals*. Philadelphia: University of Pennsylvania Press.

17. Veevers, J. E. (1985). The social meaning of pets: Alternate roles for companion animals. In M. B. Sussman (Ed.), *Pets and the family* (pp. 11-30). New York: The Haworth Press.

18. Andrysco, R. M. (1983, February). Personal communication.

19. Brickel, C. M. (1979). The therapeutic roles of cat mascots with a hospital-based geriatric population: A staff survey. *The Gerontologist*, *19*(4): 368-72.

20. Messent, P. R. (1983). Facilitation of social interaction by companion animals. In A. H. Katcher & A. M. Beck (Eds.), *New perspectives on our lives with companion animals*. Philadelphia: University of Pennsylvania Press.

21. Veevers, J. E. (1985). op. cit.

22. Messent, R. (1984). Correlates and effects of pet ownership. In R. K. Anderson, B. L. Hart, & L. A. Hart (Eds.), *The pet connection* (pp. 331-340). Minneapolis: University of Minnesota Press.

23. Kidd, A. H. & Martinez, R. L. (1980). Two personality characteristics in adult pet-owners and non-owners. *Psychological Reports*, *47*, 318.

24. Pets Are Wonderful Council. (1985, summer). Survey links career success with childhood pet ownership. *Family Pet*, 14(2), p. 2.

25. Cusack, O. & Smith, E. (1984). *Pets and the elderly*. New York: The Haworth Press.

26. Wille, R. (1982, spring). Rutgers report on pet ownership and health stresses value of H/CAB for healthy population. *The Latham Letter*, pp. 10-11.

27. Walster, D. (1982, summer). Pets and the elderly. *The Latham Letter*, pp. 1,3,14-16.

28. Franti, C. E., Kraus, J. F., Borhani, N. O., Johnson, S. L., & Tucker, S. D. (1980). Pet ownership in rural Northern California (El Dorado County). *Journal of the American Veterinary Medical Association, 176,* 143-149.

29. Hutton, J. S. (1982, November). Social workers act like animals in their casework relations. *Society for Companion Animal Studies Newsheet 3.*

30. Ibid.

CHAPTER 3

Why We Love Our Pets:
A Naturalistic/Psychoanalytical
Approach

Although relationships between humans and animals are universal and centuries-old, until relatively recently the importance of this
bonding has been ignored by the scientific community. "Pet-keep-
ing is too common and too cute," suggests Katcher as one explanation, "and cute isn't considered good science."[1] Leo Bustad,[2]
founder of the People-Pet-Partnership Program in Pullman, Washington, offers an example of the negativistic attitude too prevalent
in the scientific community.

> A social scientist visiting from one of the best known universi-
> ties in the Midwest was reviewing her data from a research
> project on the support network in the lives of the elderly.
> When asked about pets, she indicated they deleted all refer-
> ences to animals or God as irrelevant in their study.

Another reason for the lack of speculation about pet keeping is a
historical tradition that relegates animal life to a lesser and lower
status than humans. Interaction with pets might be pleasant or
amusing, but it should hardly be taken seriously.

Not surprisingly then, traditional psychology has had little to say
about the human/animal bond or the implications of pet therapy.
Obviously we love our pets, and what is becoming increasingly
obvious is that doing so reaps enormous benefits for us. But why
are we so attached to other species that do not look, act, or communicate the way we do? Why are we willing to lavish considerable

25

time and money to make them part of our intimate family, as valued as — if not more valued than — our human kin? In our search for answers, we can approach pet keeping from two perspectives: learning theory discussed in the next chapter and the naturalistic/psychoanalytic approach.

ANIMALS AS SYMBOLS

Animals are important to us because they represent that part of the natural environment that we have largely lost. They are our primitive selves, as expressed in dreams, fantasy, and our spontaneous relationships with them. In these relationships we can regress to another level, a more spontaneous, more natural, freer, less civilized or restricted affect. By relating to animals, we can once again become part of nature and thereby heal many of the rifts in our souls caused at least in part by our more civilized life-style.

Animals roam freely through our dreams, and although pet keeping may have been largely ignored by the early psychoanalysts, the importance of these faunal symbols was not. Sigmund Freud, the eminent Viennese founder of modern psychoanalysis, certainly recognized the pervasiveness of the animal symbol in the human psyche, and animal symbols figure prominently in many of Freud's classic accounts of dream symbolism. Predatory animals, such as cats, and most particularly the snake, represented male sexual prowess, whereas smaller animals and vermin represented children.

Of the relationship between children and animals, Freud wrote:[3]

> The relation of the child to animals has much in common with that of primitive man. The child does not yet show any trace of the pride which afterwards moves the adult civilized man to set a sharp dividing line between his own nature and that of all other animals. The child unhesitantly attributes full equality to animals; he probably feels himself more closely related to the animal than to the undoubtedly mysterious adult, in the freedom with which he acknowledges his needs.

The importance of animals is particularly evident in the dreams of children. In *The Uses of Enchantment*, Bruno Bettelheim suggests that children identify with the animals they find in fairy tales and in this way work out many of the psychological problems associated with growth and maturation.[4]

Robert L. Van de Castle, of the University of Virginia School of Medicine, analyzed the dreams of 457 children and found that more than 60% of the dreams of 4-year-olds involved animals. By the ages of 15-16, only 9% of the dreams involved animals. The most common dream animals were dogs and horses. These species, along with birds and cats, figured prominently in the dreams of 4,000 college students.[5]

Comparing the animal dreams to the non-animal dreams among the college students, Van de Castle found:[6]

> Much more aggression, particularly physical aggression appears in dreams about animals, and the dreamer is more likely to be the victim of the aggressive act. The most frequent emotion in animal dreams is fear or apprehension . . .
>
> Animal figures in dreams frequently symbolize unacceptable unconscious impulses that the dreamer is fearful will break through into overt expression. Animal figures in dreams seem to represent the primitive "animal" side of human personality that is repressed in waking life in order to function as a rational "civilized" person.

Carl Gustav Jung, the Swiss-born mystic and erstwhile disciple of Freud, advanced the theory of a collective unconscious that contains memory traces not only of our earliest human ancestry but of our nonhuman past as well. Within this richly imagined landscape dwell the archetypes, "primordial images" or "universal thought forms" such as the Mother Earth, the hero, and God. Some archetypes have assumed such importance that they have become systems within the personality; these include the self, the persona, the public personality or mask, the feminine anima and the masculine animus, and the shadow or dark side of our nature, which harbors primitive instincts.[7]

Says anthropologist Joel Savishinsky:[8]

> In Jungian terms, pets are an embodiment of the "shadow"
> the half-tamed demon of our persona that we will all have to

live with and try to integrate into ourselves if we are to be whole. These qualities of the pet may be part of the challenge and curiosity that impel both civilized and primitive people to invite in strays, adopt wild beasts, and tame them; in this way, we capture their wildness but instead of eradicating it, we make it a part of our all-too cultured and orderly lives. Taming and relating to such pets and incorporating them into our lives are therefore not simply ways of "getting back in touch with nature". They are ways of reconnecting to our own natures, making our peace with culture, and making ourselves more complete as people. Since the ability to tame wild animals is a quality often associated with shamans, saints, and other holy persons, pet keepers may enjoy not only a sense of power in their ties to their animals but a sense of sacredness as well.

GENETIC TEMPLATE
OR CULTURAL TRANSMISSION

Are we genetically predisposed to react to animals in a certain way, or have we accepted cultural attitudes handed down to us from one generation to the next? Did those ancestors who kept pets experience an increased survival advantage and thus ensure the perpetuation of that trait?

In the Jungian schema of the collective unconscious what we inherit are not memories but a predisposition to react to the world in a certain way. For example, we are predisposed to be afraid of darkness and snakes because our early ancestors found the night a time of danger and venomous snakes no doubt took their share of prehistoric peoples' lives.[9]

However, our seemingly innate aversion to reptiles might just as easily be the product of cultural transmission, passed along as learning and lore from one generation to the next, just as, for example, our information on edible and poisonous plants is.

Katcher, who as a psychiatrist has pioneered the research into pets as physiological relaxants, suggests:

. . . the presence of undisturbed living organisms exerts a calming effect because the sight and sound of undisturbed animals and plants have been a useful sign of safety for most, if not all, of man's evolutionary history. We know that infrahuman primates use the flight behavior of other animals with more acute senses as signals of danger, like the approach of a leopard.[10]

Katcher, however, does not regard this as an ability drawn upon a primitive racial memory. Instead he suggests that our language and symbolic media have historically used these indicators as signs of safety and thus undisturbed serene nature has persisted to present times as an illustration of peace.

Although Jung's collective unconscious has always held more allure for dramatists and philosophers than psychologists, the concept of innate universal attitudes towards animals is an intriguing one, particularly when mythology persists in spite of scientific evidence. The wolf, for example, has an almost universal image as a hound of hell, yet documented cases of its attacks on humans are rare, and involved rabid animals. Even though most experts credit a wolflike animal as the ancestor of our domestic dog, beliefs of the wolf's savagery persist both in those cultures, such as our own, that have largely exterminated the species and in those far fewer groups, such as certain American Indian warrior clans, that have revered the animal. The whale is another example of a species that has been devastated because of misconceptions about its nature. It has taken well into this century for us to perceive the gentle, intelligent leviathans as anything more than a source of perfume oils and pet food. Many of our grandparents didn't even realize that whales are mammals and not fish.

It's safe, if somewhat simplistic, to suggest that the earliest demarcations of the animal kingdom fell along practical lines. Animals that were liked, or at least not disliked, were those that had no potential to harm the primitive human. "Bad" animals were those that posed a threat or danger, like the previously mentioned snake. Interestingly, Stephen Kellert's attitudinal survey of perceptions by people in the United States found that as a group predators were less liked than prey animals.[11] Much of the animal symbolism in myth and literature supports this attitude, even though, aesthetically, large predators are among the most magnificent species known. Unlike a poisonous snake or insect, however, which is a clear and present danger in any area it inhabits, arguably most large predators never posed a serious threat to human welfare. Why then, has the myth persisted? How did it start in the first place if not as an instinctive memory trace?

Certainly anyone who has seen a wolf pack, or any large predator for that matter, bring down and devour its kill could easily surmise that these creatures were nothing to fool with. A whale, by its sheer size, could be presumed a threat. Additionally, what the whale and wolf have in common is their role as supreme predator of their ecosphere; that is, these respective species are at the top of the food chain in their environments, and as such, they are in direct competition with humans for food and habitat. As our history of human warfare tells us, we readily ascribe all sorts of exaggerated negative characteristics to our competitors.

We can look at our relations with animals in still another way. The way our ancestors interacted with animal species may have had distinct survival advantage and resulted in more descendants who possessed these traits. For example, individuals who feared or avoided snakes may have been favored during evolution, whereas humans who felt an attraction or fearless disregard for the reptiles may have had their family tree prematurely truncated. (Research by psychologist Aline Kidd found that snake owners, as a group, are ". . . relaxed, informal, novelty-seeking, changeable, unable to tolerate routines, unconventional and somewhat unpredictable." Kidd also makes the observation that these individuals may be risk-takers and enjoy the stimulation of possible danger, since some of them also owned pet tarantulas and black widow spiders.)[12]

The earliest wolf dogs were presumed to be camp followers, feeding on the scraps and refuse of the hunt, and many of these dogs and their pups were no doubt slaughtered themselves when game was scarce. But someone in that dawn of human history looked at a furry cub and was drawn to it. Perhaps he or she stroked its fur and found it pleasant or was moved by the helplessness of the little creature, and decided that this animal would be spared and adopted into the human family. This individual may have been the first humane advocate, and was no doubt rewarded for such compassion. These earliest primitive dogs surely alerted their human companions to danger and saved more than a few lives, and our ancestors surely learned very quickly that for a few scraps of meat or hide, they were gaining a trusty sentry system and skilled trackers of game. Human clans with companion dogs, thus, had survival advantage over those who did not. And as evolution was selecting pet keepers, pet keepers were selecting pets. Pups were chosen not only because they were good watch dogs and hunters, but because they showed a willingness to be domesticated and to bond with a human companion.

PETS AS SURROGATES

Pets are surrogates when they take the place of people. Usually, in these cases they have been endowed with human characteristics, that is, anthropomorphized. "To some extent," says Veevers, "almost all interaction with companion animals involves some anthropomorphism, and can in some way be construed as a surrogate for human relationships."[13]

Veevers is no doubt correct. The questions then are: If animals are stand-ins for people, is that all they are? and Is that necessarily bad?

Freud, who let few aspects of the human experience escape his scrutiny, had something to say about the pet-owner bond but virtually nothing to say about its meaning. About Jo-fi, his beloved Chow Chow, who may even have napped in his clinical waiting room, he wrote:[14]

Affectionate without ambivalence, the simplicity of a life free from the almost unbearable conflicts of civilization, the beauty of existence complete in itself and yet, despite all divergences in organic development [there is] that feeling of intimate affinity, of an undisputed solidarity . . . a bond of friendship unites us both. . . .

Freud certainly recognized the bond and accepted it with unbridled, almost naive enthusiasm. Unfortunately, this appears to be as far as he goes on the subject.

In psychoanalytical terms, the love and affection lavished on a favored pet is a displacement for the love felt toward a child or spouse. Displacement occurs when the original object choice of an instinct is unavailable or inaccessible. To relieve the tension produced by the instinct, a substitute object must be found or the instinct must be repressed. The enormous popularity of toy breeds with neotenized features adds substance to this theory. Freud would not be surprised to hear that many pet owners refer to their charges as "my child," or "my baby," because this is the role that the pet is actually playing.

But if the pet is simply a human substitute, why do the majority of pets live in multihuman households; that is, with owners who have at least one significant other in their lives? Several possibilities arise. The pet is an appropriate object choice in situations where the human object is not appropriate or accessible. For example, caressing, petting, and affectionate tactile behaviors (which Freudian theory would see as dilutions of sexuality) cannot always be directed toward a spouse or child for a variety of reasons. Yet it is always socially permissible to lavish physical affection on a pet. Katcher speaks of how easily and immediately intimacy can be achieved with a pet. We can hardly greet human strangers with pats, hugs, and caresses; we can, however, greet their dogs that way. We can also look at the human quest for variety in sensuality to be sublimated through the human/animal bond. Sublimation is defined as the diversion of the expression of an instinctual desire or impulse from its primitive form to one that is considered more socially or culturally respectable. Certainly, kindness and affection toward animals is considered a higher cultural achievement than indiscriminate promiscuity.

The social lubricant effect of the animal, which has been reported so often in the literature, fits quite well into this theoretical construct. Acceptance by the pet opens the door to interaction with the owner. It's as if, by its friendly demeanor, the animal is saying: "I like this one; it's okay to make friends."

Pets can function as human surrogates in a number of roles. As friends and confidantes, pets are especially important for children and adolescents (see "Pets and Children," and Chapter 9, "Pets and Adolescents") because the youngster risks no betrayal or ridicule by expressing the most intimate thoughts to the pet. Animals can be vitally important for the fringe groups of society; prisoners, the physically challenged, and the mentally ill. Gee and Veevers point out that pets fill an important role for the elderly widowed. They can function as a surrogate mate, absorbing much of the time and emotional energy previously invested in the late spouse.[15] Koller observes that the pet, which always requires care and attention, can prolong parenthood for middle-aged and elderly parents.[16] The pet may even reverse the traditional role and play the part of parent for a child whose human parents are in the process of divorce or separation. In this case the pet is the one parent the child can rely on.[17]

Even if our affection for pets were nothing more than the sublimation of drives we cannot express toward other humans, it would be a positive expression because sublimation is essentially progressive and integrative. However, there are many indications throughout this book that pets function above and beyond the human role, in a realm that is special and unique to them. In a sense, a pet is an idealization, a perfect entity that seems to react correctly to every situation, to respond to every mood. A pet may be a reflection of its owner's every need and whim, yet it still manages to retain an individual identity. And perhaps most important, pets seem to bring out the best in us. If there is a capacity for affection, compassion, for empathy or tenderness overlooked by our human fellows, a pet has an uncanny ability to ferret it out. Kidd once remarked that ". . . nobody would marry a man who does not like cats or dogs." After becoming acquainted with the research, I'm sure many of us would agree.

PETS AND THERAPY

"Plants and animals in out environment are like parts of our body," says Bustad, who is dean of the College of Veterinary Medicine at Washington State University. "If we eliminate them, we destroy part of ourselves. People must remain in contact with and relate to the environment throughout their lifetime to remain healthy. A strong people-animal-plant bond is critical to a healthy community."[19]

Speaking at a seminar at Green Chimneys, a therapeutic farm milieu for physically and mentally disadvantaged youth, Levinson[20] remarked that much mental illness is caused by:

> . . . our feeling anxious and powerless in our effort to be scientific. We are no longer entitled to feel, but have to think and evaluate. There is nothing to hold onto and hold sacred.
>
> We've alienated ourselves not only from our own inner beings but also from our natural allies — animals. And we end up going to therapists who have sprung up around us like weeds.
>
> While stroking his pet, a person often reveals his innermost feelings as well as experiences a loving acceptance that many never receive from another human. There is no pressure for the person to change himself, so there is no need to comply with or to rebel against this pressure.
>
> In addition to this link with our inner selves, a pet unites us with nature and with the universe.

Says anthropologist Savishinsky,[21]

> The use of pet animals in therapy is a reversal of the process of domestication. It was the human domestication of animals and plants that made our modern civilization possible. Nowadays, when confronted with a patient who cannot function in daily life, we place him in therapy in order to civilize him — make him capable of functioning in our culture. When a pet animal becomes the vehicle by which this socialization occurs, then it is the animal who domesticates the man, rather than the reverse.

According to Savishinsky, animals are less challenging than people and thus allow clients to improve their relationship skills in a nonthreatening way. They may also, however, represent the animalistic facets of the psyche that individuals have difficulty accepting and integrating into the whole self. "From this perspective, pet keeping can be an ongoing dialogue with the animal underside of this psyche and thus be a way for people to make ourselves whole," he says.

Western culture, argues Savishinsky, is alienated from nature and surrounded by civilization. The parts of nature we retain are cultural artifacts surrounded by boundaries and fences. Instead of living with nature, we are outside it looking in. Our pets are elements of nature that we have taken inside our culture. However, he continues:[22]

> . . . Western pets are more like strangers in a strange land, naturalized citizens cut off from their own roots and rooted instead in our needs.
>
> The contrast between culture and nature is recognized in all societies, but the gap between them is emphasized more by some people than by others. Totems, rituals and myths mediate between culture and nature and cultural categories keep these two ideas distinct and in their place. But pets actually bridge and embody both of these realms. My pet theory about pets is that their ambiguity as cultured, nonhuman creatures who share our intimate lives allows them to mediate in this manner. In keeping pets, we combine the conscious and the unconscious in the same way that we do when observing rituals, telling myths, and respecting categories. The bonding and reconciliation of culture with nature that pets symbolize is one of the most important of these meanings, and it is not less effective for the subtle way it works on us. We are not only the sole species that makes symbols; we are also the only creatures who keep other animals as pets.

SUMMARY

The naturalistic/psychoanalytical approach to the human/animal bond is certainly intriguing, and speaks to those of us who have felt a lifelong affinity to other species. Our attraction seems natural and spontaneous; obviously our interactions with animals answer some intrinsic need deep within us.

But not everyone is even superficially attracted to animals. How is it that some of us have this yearning, and some of us do not? Nor are attitudes toward animals (with a few exceptions) universal. For example, many cultures butcher species adored as pets in the United States, and one doesn't necessarily have to visit the Third World to see this. Consider how many of our unwanted horses wind up on European dinner tables as a delicacy. No amount of marketing has made horsemeat an acceptable dietary staple in the United States.

But the strongest objection to the numerous concepts that can be grouped within naturalistic/psychoanalytical theory is that they are largely untestable. We cannot verify the existence of and individual unconscious let alone a collective one. Hypothetical constructs such as the shadow and the animal bridge between the conscious and the unconscious are destined to remain hypothetical. It is very easy to explain all pet-owner relationships as a sublimation or substitution of human-human relations, but is that really what is happening? And if it is so, why is our physiological reaction to pets so different from what is to humans?

The next chapter reviews learning theory, which looks at the human-animal bond in another way.

REFERENCES

1. Katcher, A. H. (1983, November). Animals and the human psyche. Paper presented at the Symposium on Perceptions of animals in American culture. National Zoo, Washington, DC.

2. Bustad, L. K. (1983, March). Placement of animals with the elderly: Benefits and strategies. In R. L. Lee, M. E. Zeglen, T. Ryan, & L. M. Hines (Eds.), *California Veterinarian* (Suppl.) p. 361.

3. Freud, S. (1938). Totem and taboo. In A. A. Brill (Trans.), *The basic writings of Sigmund Freud* (p. 904). New York: Random House, The Modern Library.

4. Bettelheim, B. (1977). *The uses of enchantment.* New York: Vintage Books.

5. Van de Castle, R. L. (1983). Animal figures in dreams: Age, sex and cultural differences. In A. H. Katcher & A. M. Beck (Eds.), *New perspectives on our lives with companion animals*. Philadelphia: University of Pennsylvania Press.

6. Ibid.

7. Lundin, R. W. (1972). *Theories and systems of psychology* (p. 273). Lexington, MA: D. C. Heath.

8. Savishinsky, J. S. (1983). Pet ideas: the domestication of animals, human behavior and human emotions. In A. H. Katcher & A. M. Beck (Eds.), *New*

perspectives on our lives with companion animals. Philadelphia: University of Pennsylvania Press.

9. Hall, C. S. & Lindzey. G. (1970). *Theories of personality* (p. 47). New York: John Wiley & Sons.

10. Katcher, A. H., Segal, H., & Beck, A. M. (1984). Contemplation of an aquarium for the reduction of anxiety. In R. K. Anderson, B. L. Hart, & L. A. Hart (Eds.), *The pet connection* (p. 178). Minneapolis: University of Minnesota Press.

11. Kellert, S. R. (1979). *Public attitudes toward critical wildlife issues*. Washington, D. C.: U.S. Government Printing Office (Number 024–020–00–623–4).

12. Kidd, A. H., Kelley, H. T., & Kidd, R. M. (1984). Personality characteristics of horse, turtle, snake and bird owners. In R. K. Anderson, B. L. Hart, & L. A. Hart (Eds.), *The pet connection* (pp. 200-206). Minneapolis: University of Minnesota Press.

13. Veevers, J. E. (1985). The social meaning of pets: Alternative roles for companion animals. In M. B. Sussman (Ed.), *Pets and the family* (pp. 11–30). New York: The Haworth Press.

14. Freud, S. (1936, 1937). Letter to Marie Bonaparte (HRH Princess George of Greece), 12/6/36, 8/37. In *The letters of Sigmund Freud* (p. 434). New York: Basic Books, 1975.

15. Gee, E. M., & Veevers, J. E. The pet prescription: Assessing the therapeutic value of pets for the elderly. Cited in Veevers, J. E. (1985). op. cit.

16. Koller, M. R. (1974). *Families: A multigenerational approach*. New York: McGraw-Hill.

17. Schowalter, J. E. (1983). Clinical experience: Use and abuse of pets. *Journal of the American Academy of Child Psychiatry, 22,* 68–72.

18. Kidd, A. (1981–1982, winter). Mills College psychology professor explores aspects of H/CAB. *The Latham Letter*, p. 18.

19. Bustad, L. K. (1980). *Animals, aging and the aged*. Minneapolis: University of Minnesota Press.

20. Levinson, B. M. (1983, summer). Green Chimneys Seminar of plants, pets, people presents fresh perspectives. *The Latham Letter*, p. 15.

21. Savishinsky, J. S. (1983). op. cit.

22. Ibid.

CHAPTER 4

Why We Love Our Pets:
A Learning Theory
Perspective

LEARNING THEORY AND SOCIAL ROLES

"Theories arguing for an innate attraction to animals and their symbolic vitality are conceptually attractive," says Clark Brickel "but learning theory offers an alternate perspective which is less complex, more precise, and contains a high degree of practical application in explaining human behavior."[1]

Brickel postulates two central concepts: (1) we perceive animals as emotional wards and (2) the learning of this perception is rooted primarily in the family.

Although our interactions with animals are generally positive, they are not the result of any innate love or hate of any particular species. We learn that certain animals (pets such as cats and dogs, for example) are to be loved, and other animals, (snakes, certain predators) are to be feared or avoided.

What appears to be an instinctual love of animals by young children is instead, according to Brickel, a learning process that begins almost immediately and reflects the value that society places on animals. "By the time most children have reached the age of two the idea that pets and other domesticated animals represent a rewarding, uniformly positive experience is firmly engrained," he says.[2]

Parents teach children to love animals, he says, through the processes of classical, observational, and operant conditioning.

Classical Conditioning

The concept of classical conditioning involves substituting one stimulus for another and was developed not by a psychologist, but by Ivan Pavlov, a Russian physiologist whose studies of digestion earned a 1904 Nobel Prize. Pavlov observed that his subject dogs salivated (unconditioned response) not only when food (unconditioned stimulus) was placed in their mouths. They also salivated (conditioned response) when they saw the dish, when they heard the attendant's footsteps, and eventually when they heard a bell, a buzzer, or a metronome (conditioned stimuli). All that was necessary to evoke the conditioned response, in this case salivation, was to pair the neutral stimulus with the original unconditioned stimulus, in this case, food.[3] The unconditioned response and the conditioned response are usually similar, though not necessarily identical as they are in this case.

Once conditioned, a stimulus can be used to create additional conditioned stimuli, and a chain of learning occurs. Parents, initially neutral stimuli, soon become powerful conditioned stimuli to their infants since they are associated with all manner of rewarding, emotionally positive stimuli, such as food, warmth, and affection. But more important, parents can then influence the emotional investment in other stimuli. Animals become conditioned stimuli in two ways: through the symbolism of the nursery and through interactions with a pet.

Explains Brickel:

> The child's home — its place of protection, nurturance and security — is definably stamped with the imprimature of the animal kingdom. The developing child, having encountered a menagerie of animal figures in the home, learns to associate them with parents and home and feels comfortable around them.

Additionally, he points out, family members involve animals in play and fantasy, both verbally and tactilely. Stuffed toys become active loving companions. These actions not only prepare the child for positive interaction with a family pet, but also encourage the development of anthropomorphism.

The second more direct level, says Brickel, involves the child's interaction with pet animals in the home. Since the initial contact with the pet is usually closely supervised by the parent, the pet is associated with many of the positive qualities of the adults, particularly the pleasant aspects of touch and warmth.

Observational Learning

A second manner in which a child can learn to value animals is observational learning or modeling; that is, a child can learn from watching others that a pet is a valued and loving being, interaction with whom brings immense pleasure. Modeling occurs in the home as children watch their parents play, cuddle, care for, and talk to their pets. But children without pets in the home are still provided with strong models of animal worth through the mass media, which not only regularly feature "human interest" stories of positive owner-pet relations but also show advertising that endorses the concept that a pet is a valued being whose love and health one should wish to maintain. The effectiveness of this form of learning has been demonstrated by Bandura and colleagues in various studies in which children who previously avoided dogs began to approach the animals after watching other youngsters happily playing with them.[5,6] In another study subjects overcame their fear of snakes by handling them.[7]

Operant Conditioning

The third form of learning to influence the child, says Brickel, is operant conditioning, the learning process we associate most with behaviorist B. F. Skinner. Operant behaviors are those in which the individual acts upon the environment. The frequency of these behaviors depends upon reinforcement, which is a manipulation that alters the probability of whether or not that behavior will occur in the future. We are all familiar with reinforcers: positive ones include food, pleasure, and praise — things that make us feel good — and these strengthen behavior when they occur. Negative reinforcers can be pain, discomfort, and emotional distress, and these strengthen behavior when they are removed.[8]

Children's behaviors toward animals are reinforced not only by the adults in their environs but by the animals themselves. A child who pets an animal will be more inclined to do so again if the animal responds with affection and interest and the animal's owner reacts with praise and approval. On the other hand, if a child's approach results in a scolding from an adult and/or a scratch or bite from the pet, the youngster will be less likely to attempt the interaction again. As the child matures, adults no longer intercede. The maintenance of the human-animal bond is dependent upon ongoing relationships with animals.

Eventually, since animals have been associated with so many positive reinforcements they become unconditioned stimuli that can automatically arouse pleasant responses. And strangers and objects, previously neutral stimuli, paired with animals are benefited by the association. "These occurrences encourage maintenance of the human-animal bond through role-taking," says Brickel.[9]

Roles within a society, he notes, are an individual's link to society at large, and involve expected behaviors that incur both duties and privileges. In addition to these behaviors, social role carries an assumption of self-value and an expectation of how others will value us. The more we engage in meaningful social role activity, the more positive affirmation we receive about our self-worth.

Brickel explains:

> . . . interacting with animals comes to represent a functionally meaningful activity, allowing for the assumption of first (family-oriented) or second (extra-family centered such as friend, leisure pursuit, etc.) roles. Maintenance of the human-animal bond is therefore assured. Animals become the tabula rasa upon which the person inscribes, through activity, roles necessary for self-enhancement. Persons who are dissatisfied with their roles or undergo role conflicts experience manifestations of anxiety. Therefore animals additionally take on a therapeutic stance in presenting opportunities for "trying on" new roles and working out role conflicts.

Children, who usually occupy the lowest rung on the power ladder, can reassert their mastery over their environment by bossing the pet around or teaching it a trick. The pet is ever-willing to occupy a number of roles, so the child can test his particular role, say as parent or teacher, with no fear of rejection or failure.

In adolescence, role-playing and animal-related activities are more utilitarian in nature. Since much of adolescence involves a quest for identity, the animal becomes a source of emotional support, and animal activities help define the growing self. Additionally, although family members, peers, and the community may all change in attitude, animals do not. "They provide emotional anchors during the tempest, giving comfort and solace through their stability," says Brickel.[11]

Adults can perceive their pets in any way they wish, as child surrogates, as status symbols, as friends, as confidantes. For the elderly person who is experiencing a loss of role and a weakened self-image, interacting with a pet can reconstitute old roles and assert new ones. The pet can be a surrogate family, spouse, child, responsibility, or a "therapeutic distraction." "In general," observes Brickel, "activity with pet animals abridges negative consequences of old age, enhancing the probability of successful aging."[12]

Brickel's model is an attractive one in that it offers a lean, uncluttered explanation for human/animal interaction that at least in part can be tested scientifically. Research from both the United States and Britain linking adult pet preference to childhood pet ownership supports a family learning theory.

Kidd sampled 223 subjects and found that cat-owners had fewer dogs and dog owners had fewer cats during childhood. Of 40 subjects who expressed a dislike for a particular animal, only 2 owned that type during childhood. Kidd also linked distinct personality traits to pet ownership. For example, male dog owners scored high in aggression and dominance, female cat owners scored low in dominance and nurturance, and female pet people (who liked dogs and cats equally) scored high in nurturance. Interestingly, the males in the study scored significantly lower in aggression than males in the general population. It is not clear, says Kidd, how childhood pet ownership affects adult personality if it does so at all. Perhaps environments that favor certain traits, such as dominance or aggression, are favored in dog-owning homes.[13]

The work of Cambridge University psychologist James Serpell confirmed Kidd's work. Serpell sampled 120 adults and found a significant relationship between the person's childhood experiences and the tendency to keep pets, usually of the same species, as an adult.[14]

Learning theory applied to cultural manifestations also begins to explain the differing roles of animals within society and between societies. For example, most of us have learned to accept cows as food animals; in India, they have quite another role. In America dogs are loved and adored; in Muslim countries they are reviled as unclean. The European palate has a much greater affinity for horsemeat than the American one. How much of that difference can be explained by the mythic image of the wild horse as a symbol of the West?

Learning theory is surely necessary to explain at least some of our interest in and interaction with animals, but is it sufficient to interpret these multiple and complex interactions? If learning theory has much to say about why we like animals, it has less to say about why we don't. If animals are so valued by society, why doesn't everyone share an affinity for at least some of them? Negative learning experiences certainly could be a factor, but most individuals who recall a bad experience with an animal limit their dislike to a particular species or breed. Animal phobias cannot always be traced to an actual experience with an animal. Even so, learning theory tells us that the more powerful the conditioned response, the more difficult it is to extinguish. Certainly, it is reasonable to assume that most individuals have far more positive experiences with animals (including media examples and learning tools) than negative ones. Additionally, even persons who do not own pets seem to appreciate the many benefits of living with animals, such as love, companionship, and affection.[15] The reasons given for not owning pets is seldom strong dislike or aversion, but more a tendency not to want to be bothered. An animal, in spite of its benefits, is perceived as a bit of a nuisance requiring care and causing dirt and odor. Why does the conditioning "take" so easily for some and not for others?

Inherent in the learning model is the maintenance of the

bond through ongoing association with pets. The bond between an owner and a pet is reinforced and presumably strengthened many times a day. Why, then, are so many pets abandoned or surrendered to shelters, many for appallingly trivial reasons? How can this bond, cemented through continual reinforcement and daily association, be so casually broken?

Finally, the learning model has little to say about human bonding with wild animals, which we know can be awesome (Dian Fossey and the mountain gorillas, Greenpeace and the whales). Few of us have early, intimate exposure to wild animals, so we learn about these creatures through books and movies. But modeling seems inadequate to explain the initiation of bonds so intense that individuals defy their own species and even espouse a willingness to die for their chosen species. The operative mechanism here seems far more akin to inexplicable, passionate love than to prosaic learning.

Future research might compare members of activist humane or animal rights organizations to the casual pet owner or non-owner to see if childhood experiences with animals differed significantly among the groups. Such a study could support a childhood learning model, or it could suggest that additional theoretical concepts are needed.

PET THERAPY:
ANXIETY AND DISTRACTION

The ability of pets to relieve anxiety and provide emotional sustenance can be explained within an extinction model of learning, specifically that of competing-response theory, says Brickel.[16]

Recall that individuals learn by responding to stimuli within their environment. If a behavior is pleasant, it is positively reinforced; the individual will repeat that action and seek out the stimuli that produce it. Similarly, unpleasant experiences are negatively reinforced, and an individual learns to avoid them. Extinction is the unlearning of a response; a behavior can be eliminated (extinguished) when it is consistently not reinforced. The length of time it takes to extinguish a response generally depends on the strength of the learned response. Note that extinction can involve either an approach (positive) behavior or an avoidance (negative) behavior.

Explains Brickel:[17]

> In the clinical situation nonfunctional avoidance behavior is commonly encountered. The client perceives some stimulus or situation as anxiety-provoking, e.g., asking a person for a date, and the consequent avoidance behavior perpetuates itself by assuring minimal exposure to the stimulus in question. The strength of such avoidance behavior can be diminished or extinguished when its occurrence is prevented while the client is simultaneously exposed to the threatening stimulus. With no adverse consequences forthcoming, the frightening aspects of the stimulus are neutralized. Competing response patterns are then prime for development.
>
> This attentional shift aspect of competing response theory may explain how pets are of emotional benefit in pet-facilitated psychotherapy. Pets divert attention from an anxiety-generating stimulus which the client faces. This interference allows for self-monitored exposure to the stimulus instead of avoidance behaviors. Repeated exposure through the pet's diversional properties plus nonadversive consequences aids in the diminution or extinction of anxiety. The therapist then nurtures the appearance of functional alternative response patterns.

Because of their many appealing characteristics, pet animals are ideal distractors, says Brickel. He points out that the literature contains many examples of discomfort being relieved by far less positive diversions:[18]

> As distracting stimuli pets are complex, operating on tactile, auditory and cognitive levels, and most probably on an additional emotional level. When individuals experience a satisfying relationship with a pet, the owner develops an emotional bond. In effect, the pet becomes an emotionally-laden distractor, its attractive qualities generalizing to other pet animals.

Much of the "social lubricant" role of the animal (see Chapter 2) supports Brickel's model. A stranger, at least one we have no known reason to fear, is perhaps a mildly aversive stimulus, so it is relatively easy for an attractive pet to supersede our avoidance. But how potent a positive stimulus is a pet animal? Is it, for example, attractive enough to be used therapeutically to help an individual overcome a phobia? Would an agoraphobe, for example, be less anxious and more willing to venture outside his or her self-imposed safety zone if accompanied by a pet dog? Could a pet be used to help severely shy individuals overcome their reluctance to meet others? These are some questions that future research might address.

PET PSYCHOTHERAPY:
A GENERAL-EFFECT THEORY

Serpell does not think that the benefits attributed to pet therapy can be accounted for by a single, all-inclusive hypothesis. Nor does he think that ". . . we are observing the effects of some primordial psychophysiological response to "nature" and other life forms. The alternative, then, is that we are encountering not one phenomena, but several, all of which have the same general therapeutic outcome."

Serpell suggests three pathways in which animals could become a causal factor in initiating therapeutic change: instrumental, anthropomorphic, and passive. The pathways are not all-inclusive, but overlap to some extent.

The instrumental category includes horseback riding (hippotherapy) and the acquisition of guide, signal, and therapy dogs for the physically challenged. Serpell explains:[20]

We have here people with overt physical and mental disabilities who lack self-esteem and confidence because of this. The physical control of an animal lacking such disabilities and the use of it as an extension of the self, increases coordination, mobility and skill and, hence, improves confidence and self-esteem. The animal is primarily an object in this setting and need not be personified to affect improvement. Docile and highly trainable animals would tend to fit best into this context.

Passive interaction involves watching animals and includes such activities as watching birds or fish. Says Serpell:[21]

> The absorption in the animal's activities induces a relaxing state of meditation or reverie. The benefits are primarily short term and persist as long as the animal is observed. Animals are especially effective in this regard because their activities are relatively random and unpredictable and therefore sustain interest. They are always doing something new. As an ethologist I have often practiced this form of therapy on myself. Again the animal is essentially an object in this situation and one could probably derive similar, though inferior, benefits from watching a lump of kinetic sculpture. Small active and colorful animals such as tropical fish or cage-birds would probably be most suitable for this kind of therapy.

The third category, anthropomorphic, includes pet companion animals with bonding potential to the owner. According to Serpell:[22]

> The important thing about the anthropomorphic category is that the therapeutic outcome depends upon the person initially perceiving the animal as another person. Once this has happened, the behavioral signals transmitted by the animal are seen as expressing attachment, devotion and love for the person. It's becoming abundantly clear from research into human social behavior that people need to feel respected, needed and loved by others in order to maintain a state of psychological (and physical) well-being. Apparently, animals can supply this need, in some cases, when humans cannot. Therefore, animal therapy of this kind would be expected to have most benefit for individuals who, for whatever reason, feel unloved, rejected, socially alienated or friendless. It goes without saying that anthropomorphic species such as dogs, cats, and budgerigars would be expected to perform best in this category.
> The notion that all these different types of therapy could have the same general physical and psychological outcome is

not as unlikely as it might seem . . . A similar process is recognized as operating in the opposite direction in the case of the "general stress response." In this case we have a multiplicity of unpleasant stimuli, ranging from illness to divorce, affecting people's mental and physical health in similar detrimental ways. It therefore seems reasonable to postulate that a variety of pleasant stimuli could induce equally "general" effects of a restorative nature.

NOTES

1. Brickel, M. (1985). Initiation and maintenance of the human-animal bond: Familial roles from a learning perspective. In M. B. Sussman (Ed.), *Pets and the family* (pp. 31–48). New York: The Haworth Press.

2. Ibid.

3. Pavlov, I. P. (1927). *Conditioned reflexes*. London: Oxford University Press.

4. Brickel, C. M. (1985). op. cit.

5. Bandura, A., Grusec, J., & Menlove, F. (1967). Vicarious extinction of avoidance behavior. *Journal of Personality and Social Psychology*, *5*, 16–23.

6. Bandura, A. & Menlove, F. (1968). Facets determining vicarious extinction of avoidance behavior through symbolic modeling. *Journal of Personality and Social Psychology*, *8*, 99–108.

7. Bandura, A., Blanchard, E., & Ritter, B. (1969). The relative efficacy of desensitization and modeling approaches for inducing behavioral, affective, and attitudinal change. *Stanford University*, *13*: 173–199. Cited by Brickel, C. M. (1985), op. cit.

8. Hall, C. S. & Lindzey, G. (1957). *Theories of personality*. New York: John Wiley & Sons.

9. Brickel, C. M. (1985). op. cit.

10. Ibid.

11. Ibid.

12. Ibid.

13. Kidd, A. H. & Kidd, R. M. (1980). Personality characteristics and preferences in pet ownership. *Psychological Reports*, *46*, 939–949.

14. Serpell, J. A. (1981). Childhood pets and their influence on adults' attitudes. *Psychological Reports*, *49*, 651–654.

15. Vogel, L. E., Quigley, J. S., & Anderson, R. K. (1983). A study of perceptions and attitudes towards pet ownership. In A. H. Katcher & A. M. Beck (Eds.), *New perspectives on our lives with companion animals*. Philadelphia: University of Pennsylvania Press.

16. Brickel, C. M. (1982). Pet-facilitated psychotherapy: A theoretical explanation via attention shifts. *Psychological Reports*, *50*, 71–74.

17. Ibid.

18. Ibid.

19. Serpell, J. (1983, spring). Pet Psychotherapy. *People-Animals-Environment*, pp. 7–8.

20. Ibid.

21. Ibid.

22. Ibid.

CHAPTER 5

Depression

At some time in our lives, most of us have feelings of profound despondency, hopelessness, and futility. Our world seems dark and lonely, without optimism. Former pleasures lose their meaning, and we may experience unusual fatigue, insomnia, and a preoccupation with health concerns. It seems that nothing we do brings us out of our morass.

Transient depression is normal. It may follow the death of a loved one or the loss of a career opportunity; it may come as a feeling of letdown after a success, perhaps because we subconsciously feel we are unworthy of such good fortune. Sometimes it seems not to have been precipitated by any external events. When "the blues" are prolonged, unalleviated, and/or vastly out of proportion to external events, however, an individual may be clinically depressed and require treatment.

Depression has been recognized clinically since the times of Hippocrates, when it was called melancholia. Currently it is estimated to trouble almost 20% of the patients who seek psychiatric help. Women appear to be particularly vulnerable, and it is estimated that one in seven women will suffer from some form of depression at some time during late middle age. Symptoms include excessive fatigue, sleep disturbances, increased awareness of physical aches and pains, changes in appetite and energy, social withdrawal, and a negative mind set. Clinical depression is also recognized by a loss of activity, loss of ability to love, and a lowering of self-regard. Severely depressed patients are at high risk for suicide.

Once psychotherapists interpreted depression as anger turned inward. Current thinking, however, leans toward a predisposition scenario. Certain individuals, because of biochemical or genetic makeup, seem more vulnerable to depression, and certain life-style factors, such as stress management and social support system, contribute to the likelihood of a depressive episode. Both antidepressant medication and psychotherapy are used to combat severe depression; however, behavior therapy and/or psychotherapy may be recommended for the milder and longer-lasting forms of depression called dysthymia (traditionally known as neurotic depression).

Depression is particularly common in hospitals and geriatric institutions, and studies indicate that pet animals appear to play a significant role in alleviating the condition.

In his pioneer nursing home studies, Samuel Corson found that small, playful breeds of dogs such as wirehaired fox terriers and miniature and toy poodles were especially successful in bringing out depressed and withdrawn patients.[1] In an early British study, researchers Mugford and M'Comisky found that placing budgerigars with elderly pensioners markedly improved the patients' conception of their psychological well-being and alleviated their sense of loneliness. The birds were significantly more effective than either begonias or television.[2]

Gloria Francis and her colleagues at Virginia Commonwealth University studied the impact of visiting puppies and kittens on chronologically ill adult home residents. The depression rating and many other factors significantly improved in residents who had access to the pets. The control group, which saw only human visitors, showed no improvement.

David Lee, who implemented pet-facilitated therapy at the Lima State Hospital in Lima, Ohio (see Chapter 13, Prison Pets), found that patients involved in the program were, among other things, less depressed and less in need of medication. Psychiatrist Michael McCulloch noted that the presence of a pet can inspire humor and improve morale in otherwise depressed patients.[4]

Additional support for the value of pets in treating depression comes from anecdotal accounts of pet visitation programs. Although few of these efforts have been formally studied, the consensus of patients, staff, and the volunteers themselves is that animals improve morale; provide fun, entertainment, and diversion; and give the patients something to look forward to. Volunteers report withdrawn and uncommunicative patients opening up to dogs, and some residents who previously remained bedfast found the animal visitors an incentive to get up and participate in the facility's programs. Pet mascots are credited with making the institution seem more like home and providing patients with incentives to interact with and care for the pet. Animals also serve as a social lubricant, encouraging conversation between volunteers, patients, and staff. The pet is a common topic to which everyone can relate.[5]

Brickel says that depression is the most common disorder among the elderly, ranging from 4% to 6% in the healthy elderly and as high as 10% to 40% in those who have some physical ailment. He remarks:[6]

> Depression presents a special challenge to gerontological professionals. Behaviors symptomatic of depression require early detection. Efforts must be made to prevent vulnerable individuals from becoming depressed, and to keep persons already depressed from sinking deeper into their emotional abyss. In institutions depression also reverberates among staff, who experience frustration due to the condition's tenacious presence. This may have deleterious consequences on health care delivery.

Brickel designed a formal study to measure the impact of companion animals on depressed individuals. His subjects for this study were 50 white male volunteers, aged 45–84, from a hospital-based, nursing home unit. Patients selected were oriented as to person, place, and time; they were not bedfast, acutely ill, engaged in any immunosuppressive regimen, nor allergic to or fearful of animals.

Brickel administered numerous questionnaires including the Zung Self-Rating Depression Scale, which identified 21 of the 50 subjects as depressed. Six of the youngest were arbitrarily removed from the study, and the remaining 15 depressed patients were randomly assigned to one of three experimental conditions. Group I received conventional therapy, Group II received pet-facilitated psychotherapy with a dog, and Group III, the control group, received no treatment. Therapy consisted of two individually-held 45–90 minute sessions per week for 4 weeks conducted by Brickel.

The dog in the study was Fudge, a spayed female dachshund-terrier mix weighing 13 pounds that had been obtained at the age of 3 months from a local animal shelter. She was cleared by a veterinarian, socialized with Brickel's family, and obedience-trained.

Throughout the Group II sessions, Brickel was accompanied by the pet dog, which was available for the person to hold, stroke, or talk to. After each session, Brickel asked his subjects to "watch the dog" briefly. "Therefore participants were free to direct the conversation toward animals or to conventional material, but were always requested to briefly take responsibility for the animal," he says.

Additionally, on session days, behavioral observations of Group II subjects were taken, with and without the dog, to measure the impact of the pet on social responses. Results indicated that although no significant difference in depression was apparent before the therapy, both Group I and Group II showed significant reductions in depression after the treatment. The average rating for the conventional therapy group was a pretest rating of 56.2 and a posttest rating of 49.8, a decrease of 6.4 points. The pet-therapy group averaged a 67.6 score on the pretest and a 56.0 score on the posttest, a decrease of 11.6 points.

An analysis of the behavioral observations revealed that social interaction with the pet present were double those when the pet was not present. Fudge was instrumental in facilitating social interactions, and did act as the social lubricant so often reported in anecdotal accounts.

"The pet group displayed greater change than the conventional group, suggesting that the pet's presence contributed therapeutic impact," says Brickel.[8] Brickel also notes that the presence of the dog was a convenient conversation point with his patients. Often, as the subjects stroked the dog, they revealed information of a "highly personal nature." Two of the men actually admitted to ideas of suicide. Brickel also noticed that when his patients were stressed during the sessions, they used Fudge as a source of comfort.

Although no miraculous recoveries occurred, Brickel comments that discussion of animal-related topics was commonplace and enjoyable during the sessions. Much involved recollection of past pets and experiences with animals. "A good deal of this material was emotionally significant, indicated by tearfulness in discussing the

loss of past pets, or laughter regarding a former pet's idiosyncrasies," he says.

Finally, he adds:

> Dramatic reaction to pets suggests remarkable effectiveness
> with particular patients. One noncommunicative, withdrawn
> person displayed an almost immediate enchantment with the
> dog. By using the animal as a conversational lever other as-
> pects of the person's life could be gently probed. In other
> cases it has been continually impressive to observe animals
> draw out responses from otherwise nonresponsive patients.

That a cute, friendly dog should alleviate depressive feelings in
institutionalized patients probably comes as no surprise. Most institutions, by necessity, are antiseptic, sterile, and self-contained. Life
within them is predictable, orderly, mundane, and boring, factors
that, if they do not actually precipitate it, do little to discourage
depression. Animals are spontaneous and unpredictable. They are a
pleasant diversion from the rigors of institutional life. They offer a
means to give and receive affection and a comforting, undemanding
presence. Additionally, they prompt recollections of happier times
with former pets and are a link to the patient's life on the outside.
It's little wonder that nursing homes that have adopted mascot pets
report significant improvement, particularly in the patients who
help take responsibility for the animal's care.

Can a pet animal make a significant impact on a noninstitutiona-
lized patient suffering from depression? I believe that it can, particularly in individuals who, for whatever reason, have limited social
outlets. Psychologist James Lynch believes that isolation and lack
of companionship are the greatest unrecognized contributors to pre-
mature death is 2 to 10 times more common for individuals who live
alone.[10]

The lack of a social support system is recognized as an important
factor in the onset of depression. A pet animal is not meant to take
the place of another person; however, for an individual who is limited and lacking in social relationships, it can provide affection,
companionship, and a focal point—so vital for a healthy life.

Consider again three of the indicators of depression. The first is lack of activity — certainly caring for a pet is not an all-consuming occupation, but it does have to be done, day in and day out, for the pet's well-being. Even this small activity can provide some meaning and order to a patient's life, and often a person who is unwilling to care for himself or herself will make an effort to properly care for a companion animal. A young woman I knew suffered severe depression after a dissolved relationship. Her hobby was houseplants, and her apartment was filled with luscious, thriving flora. But in the throes of her illness, she told me how she watched them die one by one, deliberately refusing to water or care for them. I remarked that it was fortunate she didn't own a dog or cat or it would have starved to death. "Oh God, I would never have let that happen," she replied in horror.

The loss of ability to love is another symptom of depression. Loving an animal, however, is easier than loving a person, and unlike a person, the love a pet has for its owner is generally without condition or judgment. A dog or cat will accept the affection you give it and not criticize you for its lack of quantity or quality. The pet is also the one being with whom there is no loss of self-regard — a third indicator of depression — no matter how sloppy and ineffectual the rest of your life becomes. Depressed individuals withdraw from social contacts; they do not wish friends, family and coworkers to see them at their lowest ebb. With a pet, however, there is no such reservation.

Thus the pet can be an effective first step in therapy, a bridge to the rest of society. If the depressed individual feels comfortable with the pet, the next step may be animal-related activities. A walk around the neighborhood with the dog can result in pleasant social exchange.

SUICIDAL DEPRESSION

As in Brickel's example, suicide can be a serious problem with severely and clinically depressed individuals. The comforting role of the pet may be able to assuage some of the emotional pain, break through the isolation, and enable therapy to take place.

Most therapists can relate many cases of suicidal patients who insist their families and friends would be better off without them, despite the best arguments the clinician can give. A somewhat "better" argument could be given to a pet owner. Who would care for the pet if the owner died? It certainly cannot fend for itself, and with millions of unwanted animals destroyed yearly, its chances for another home are slim. I've known of sickly, elderly individuals who seemed to hang on to life solely for a pet and died within weeks of the animal's demise.

Several years ago the death of an elderly Florida woman made national headlines. The woman was forced to give up her pet dog because of housing regulations in her project. Although the dog found a home and was then taken to visit the elderly woman, her condition deteriorated rapidly. Within 2 months of giving up her beloved pet, she died, according to friends, of a broken heart.[11]

I'm not suggesting that therapists prescribe a pet for suicidal patients. For the other, darker side of the coin, I have only to recall an incident that happened in my childhood. The victim, a socially prominent doctor's wife, had a history of severe depression at a time when most in the medical community regarded the disorder as being "all in your head." The woman ended her troubled life in a locked car and took her devoted companion dog with her.

Intuitively, one might predict that suicide would be less frequent among pet owners; however, the only study available on this topic found this was not the case. Helsing and Monk compared dog and cat ownership between 48 individuals who committed suicide and 96 matched, nonsuicidal controls in the years 1975 to 1983. They found no association between pet ownership and suicide.[12]

But a pet may still forestall a would-be suicide. A particularly dramatic example was described in the Buffet Cat Club News, and the Siamese cat was runner-up for Hero Cat of 1984. The anonymous writer relates sinking into the holiday blues following a traumatic divorce. Although she worried about who would care for her cat, she still decided that suicide was the only answer. She prepared a glass of water and pills, and tried to explain to her sad-looking feline why this decision was the right one. But just as she raised the glass to her lips, the cat knocked it out of her hands and began to mew loudly. The astonished woman could no longer go through with the suicide. She weathered the crisis, but still relies on her "Siamese survival kit."[13]

At the very least, a pet can serve as a barometer of an individual's illness. Therapists should encourage patients to talk about their pets, and should inquire about them at each session. One of the warning signals in a potentially suicidal patient is an abrupt change in behavior or attitude. Giving away a previously cherished pet would certainly qualify as a danger sign, particularly if the patient's mood were unnaturally cheerful or euphoric. Patients who speak of finding others to care for a pet or those that seem to be emotionally distancing themselves from their animals should be monitored closely. All these signs could be indicators of a coming suicide attempt.

PET THERAPY
AND CANCER PATIENTS

Treatment of terminal cancer patients presents special problems, particularly the depression that inevitably accompanies a diagnosis of impending death. According to Kübler-Ross, dying patients work through five stages: denial, anger, bargaining, depression (reactive and preparatory), and acceptance. Working through these stages successfully reduces the anxiety and despair, and enriches the quality of remaining life for the patient. Essential to the individual's therapy are caring others who are sensitive and supportive of the patient's needs and who are available for physical and emotional closeness.[14]

In spite of the best of intentions, friends, relatives, and even health care professionals are not always able to relate empathetically to the dying patient. They may be impeded by their own fears about death or the coming separation and may deny the patient the opportunity to work out his or her pain and grief.

An important new study by Irene Muschel, a New York social worker, suggests that animals can effectively do what people often cannot. Muschel studied 15 individuals selected from a New York nursing facility for terminal cancer patients who interacted with kittens, puppies, dogs, and cats from the ASPCA.[15] Ambulatory patients had access to a large recreation room; bedbound individuals had access to the pet at their bedside with a volunteer providing assistance. Subjects had access to the animals for 1-1/2 hours each week for 10 weeks.

A preliminary evaluation revealed that 14 of the 15 patients studied were in a reactive depression, expressing regret about lost opportunities and sadness about missed loved ones. One patient had come to the acceptance stage and was beginning to separate from the world.

During the course of the study Muschel noticed a variety of positive interactions between the patients and the pets. Subjects sang to pets and played games with them; they reassured the pets, often about their own fears. Reminiscences of former pets were common. Additionally, the patients expressed genuine concern for the animals' welfare. The pets only provided comforting physical intimacy but emotional intimacy as well.

Unlike the findings about socialization in other studies, socialization among the patients, staff, and volunteers in Muschel's study did not increase, which the researcher says was probably due to the physical and emotional deliberation of the subjects. As noted before, interacting with animals is less stressful than interacting with other people.

Muschel's final evaluation revealed that the animal had a distinctly positive effect on the patients. Twelve patients credited the pets with easing their fears, despair, loneliness, and isolation. The patients were less negative, and said they would like animals at the facility on a permanent basis. Only three patients did not respond positively to the animals.

The positive effect of the pet interaction appeared independent of the health status of the individuals. Some experienced physical deterioration, but when these individuals were given a pet to hold, their despair lifted, and their mood continued to brighten as they petted and talked to the animal. Muschel observed that several of these individuals showed the beginnings of preparatory depression, the stage in which the individual leaves behind relationships and becomes aware of his own mortality. Accepting this stage, she says, shows a reduction of anxiety and increased ego strength. Most of the patients had had cancer for years and had made very little progress moving through the stages, yet even limited contact with a pet seemed to trigger this movement. This, she points out, is a further validation of the effectiveness of pet therapy.

Animals neither avoid nor intrude upon the patient, says Muschel. "The animal's quiet, accepting and nurturing presence strengthens and frees the patient to resolve his or her final experience successfully."[16] And mascot pets in homes for the terminally ill can help ease the stress of the caretakers.

In her suggestions for future research, Muschel wonders if pets can help newly diagnosed cancer patients deal with the stresses of the disease. There is every reason to think that they can. Darrell Sifford, popular *Philadelphia Inquirer* columnist, wrote about one woman's preliminary ordeal with breast cancer.[17] After her mastectomy, the woman, a former medical researcher, described herself as being "absolutely terrified, frozen with fear 24 hours a day."

The turning point came one day when a well-meaning friend let the woman's dog, Jacques, out alone while she was taking a shower. She was horrified. Jacques, a 12-year-old poodle, was partially deaf and did not understand about cars and big dogs. When they found him alive and well, she fell to the ground in tears.

"This is where my coping with cancer began," she said. "I realized, all over again, my many blessings. I had my dog back. I had a husband, a daughter, friends who loved me. I could say, 'Thank you God,' all over again."

REFERENCES

1. Corson, S. A. & Corson, E. O. (1979). Pet animals as nonverbal communication mediators in psychotherapy in institutional settings. In *Ethology and nonverbal communication in mental health*. Oxford: Pergamon Press.

2. Mugford, R. A. & M'Comisky, J. G. (1975). Some recent work on the psychotherapeutic value of caged birds with old people. In R. S. Anderson (Ed.), *Pet animals and society*. London: Balliere Tindall.

3. Francis, G. M., Turner, J. T., & Johnson, S. B. (1982). Domestic animal visitation as therapy with adult home residents. Unpublished report.

4. McCulloch, M. J. (1982, February). Talking with . . . *Redbook Magazine*, p. 12–14.

5. Cusack, O. & Smith, E. (1984). *Pets and the elderly: The therapeutic bond*. New York: The Haworth Press.

6. Brickel, C. M. (1984). Depression in the nursing room: A pilot study using pet-facilitated therapy. In R. K. Anderson, B. L. Hart, & L. A. Hart (Eds.),

The pet connection. (pp. 407–415). Minneapolis: The University of Minnesota Press.

7. Ibid.

8. Ibid.

9. Brickel, C. M. (1984). The clinical use of pets with the aged. *Clinical Gerontologist, 2* (4), 72–75.

10. Lynch, J. J. (1980, June 20). Warning: Living alone is dangerous to your health. *U.S. News and World Report,* p. 47.

11. Editorial. (1980, September 23). *Philadelphia Daily News.*

12. Helsing, K. & Monk, M. (1985). Dog and cat ownership among suicides and matched controls. *American Journal of Public Health, 75*(10): 1223–1224.

13. Anonymous. (1984). A Siamese survival kit. In *Buffet Cat Club News, 1*(7):5.

14. Kübler-Ross, E. (1969). *On death and dying.* New York: Macmillan.

15. Muschel, I. J. (1985, fall). Pet therapy with terminal cancer patients. *The Latham Letter,* pp. 8–11, 15.

16. Ibid.

17. Sifford, D. (1986, April 13). A sharing of cancer's pain. *The Philadelphia Inquirer.*

CHAPTER 6

Stress and Anxiety

Most of us are familiar with a certain amount of anxiety, that nagging feeling of apprehension or uneasiness that seems to surface in anticipation of an important event or even a desirous one. We may be nervous before a job interview, jittery before an important social engagement, worried about medical tests, or pacing the floor awaiting the birth of a child. Such anxiety is normal, even beneficial to us. Concern about a job interview, for example, will make us prepare for it so we are assured we are at our best. Anxiety about a symptom will prompt us to get an examination to allay our fears. Fear about walking on a deserted street will cause us to be more cautious and alert to danger. But if the anxiety is widely out of proportion to the event or appears without cause and interferes with your functioning in the world, it could be indicative of an anxiety disorder.

Anxiety can be defined as apprehension, tension, or uneasiness that stems from the anticipation of danger. The source is largely unknown or unrecognized. In addition to the feelings of fear and apprehension, physical symptoms of anxiety can include headaches, dizziness, heart palpitations, hyperventilation, shortness of breath, sweating, shaking, nausea, and vomiting. In some individuals, the physical symptoms manifest, and the patient is unaware of the underlying anxiety that causes them. Anxiety can also occur simultaneously with depression, further complicating diagnosis. Anxiety disorders afflict approximately 15% of the individuals seeking psychiatric counseling.

Stress is not the same as anxiety, although it can produce similar symptoms. Whereas anxiety is an inner state, stress results from external factors acting on the individual. It is among the body's natural survival mechanisms. When the organism is threatened, the body responds with a set of physiological indicators known as the "fight or flight syndrome." Stress is the pressure we feel when we approach a deadline or are actively involved in competition.

Just as anxiety is normal and healthy in certain situations, stress also can be productive and beneficial. It gears us toward increased output and activity, makes the pulse quicken and the blood rush. Stressful situations are challenges that enhance our self-esteem when we surmount them.

In today's world, however, we face a number of false alarms. The body acts as if threatened when, in fact, a threat does not exist. We've all watched individuals who pace anxiously in line or treat the smallest chore as a life-or-death situation. Physiologically although no emergency exists, the body is geared for one: the hormones pump and the heart pounds. This syndrome is now linked to a number of debilitating conditions including cardiovascular disease, digestive disorders, circulatory malfunction, even cancer. Unfortunately, treatment for stress management usually comes only after diagnosis of a severe physical illness.

EFFECT OF PETS ON ANXIETY

A number of studies suggest that the presence of a pet can reduce stress and anxiety and promote a feeling of safety, whether or not the threat an individual senses is real.

Randall Lockwood, of the State University of New York, asked two groups of subjects to interpret ambiguous line drawings of social interactions. One group included an animal; the other did not. His results indicated that the presence of the animal leads to the interpretation of social scenes as less threatening and improves the perceived character of the people associated with them. A person with a dog, thus, is considered more approachable and less dangerous than someone without one.[1]

Even when not potentially dangerous, most new encounters produce an element of anxiety. In an unfamiliar situation, we are less in control, less secure, and more vulnerable, but we feel safer in the presence of a friendly animal. Sebkova measured the anxiety levels of 20 individuals in two environments, one which included her dog and one which did not. She found that her subjects had much lower anxiety scores and fewer anxious mannerisms when the dog accompanied her to the psychology lab.[2]

Friedmann and colleagues measured the blood pressure and heart beats of 38 children over two 4-minute periods during which the child was asked to rest for 2 minutes and to read aloud for 2 minutes. A dog was present during either the rest or reading period. The researchers found that the presence of the dog resulted in lower blood pressures during both the rest and reading period. Additionally, if the dog was present at the beginning of the session, the children had lower blood pressures throughout the experiment.[3]

Judy Jenkins, of the San Francisco SPCA, went into pet owners' homes and measured blood pressure and heart rate of individuals while they petted their dog and while they read aloud. She found that both the diastolic and systolic pressure were lower while people petted their dog.[4]

According to Katcher, children entering a neighbor's home for the first time experience reduced blood pressure if the neighbor's dog is present. Persons interviewed in the waiting room of a veterinary clinic have lower blood pressure when touching or talking to their pet while questioned by the researcher than when interviewed alone. "There is no doubt," he says, "that companion animals make people feel safer in situations characterized by a high degree of novelty."[5]

EFFECT OF AQUARIUM ON ANXIETY

Previously, Katcher and colleagues demonstrated that contemplation of an aquarium would achieve blood pressure reductions in hypertense individuals equivalent to reductions realized by lengthy and extensive biofeedback training.[6]

More recently, Katcher along with Segal and Beck investigated the effect of contemplation of an aquarium on anxiety and discomfort prior to and during dental surgery.[7] Forty-two patients were assigned to five groups: (1) contemplation of a fish tank, (2) contemplation of a fish tank after hypnotic induction, (3) contemplation of a poster of a color photograph of a mountain waterfall, (4) contemplation of the poster after hypnotic induction, and (5) a control group that simply rested. The researchers measured blood pressure and heart rate; the subjects, the dentist, and an observer rated anxiety and comfort.

The researchers found that all the treatment groups were more comfortable and less anxious than the control group and that the aquarium conditions produced the greatest comfort and least physiological arousal. The primary benefit of the hypnosis appeared to be enabling the patient to focus concentration. Anxious subjects had difficulty paying attention, and hypnosis appeared to aid their concentration. Interestingly, although hypnosis enhanced the poster's effectiveness, it seemed to have no effect on the effectiveness of the aquarium.

The researchers further suggest that the maximum clinical benefits might be realized not merely by placing an aquarium in a waiting room, but by advising the patients about its beneficial role. "Patients in this experiment were explicitly instructed that the contemplation would produce relaxation and that they could continue the relaxation during surgery by closing their eyes and visualizing the aquarium," they explained.[8]

Although the researchers admit that a simple distraction mechanism, not necessarily animate, may be operative as anxiety inhibitors, they also suggest (as noted in Chapter 3) that observing calm living entities may historically have a calming effect on humans. This could be because (1) an innate neurological template discriminates between different patterns of movement in our environment and/or (2) our language and symbology use undisturbed nature as signs of safety, the most obvious example being the "Peaceable Kingdom," in which the predator and prey rest side by side. In fact, animals may be necessary for us to think, say the researchers, since touching or contemplating living things changes the character of our thoughts. We think with divided attention, in a revery. "This creative kind of thought play may well derive from our association with the living world about us."[9]

Said Nobel laureate Konrad Lorenz:[10]

A man can sit for hours before an aquarium and stare into it as into the flames of an open fire or the rushing waters of a torrent. All conscious thought is happily lost in this state of apparent vacancy, and yet, in these hours of idleness, one learns essential truths about the macrocosm and the microcosm.

BONDING INFLUENCES IN PETTING DOGS

Petting one's own canine companion can be more physiologically relaxing than petting a strange dog according to a University of Nebraska study.[11]

Previous research in the field suggested that people who talked to and petted their dogs experience lower blood pressure than when they read aloud. Katcher also points out that talking to other people tends to raise blood pressure.[12]

Gantt noted that petting results in a slower heartbeat and deeper respiration for the dogs themselves,[13] and the effect has also been noted in horses.[14]

Baun and colleagues[15] designed the study to determine, first, if tactile interaction with a pet would indeed reduce blood pressure, heart rate, and respiration and, second, how the pet-owner bond would affect these physiological factors.

The researchers measured blood pressure, heart rate, and respiratory rate in 24 subjects during three 9-minute sessions in which the volunteers petted an unknown dog, their own dog, or read quietly. The 24 subjects were 5 men and 19 women, none of whom were currently taking medication that affects heart rate or blood pressure and each of whom had formed a companion bond with a dog for at least 6 months. None of the subjects was allergic to or afraid of dogs in general. On degree of attachment, 8 subjects rated themselves as "very attached" and 16 subjects rated themselves as "extremely attached." The subjects had lived with their dogs from 1 to 11 years, and all subjects admitted the dog was important to them, that they enjoyed petting the dog, and that they often talked to the dog. Seven said they would be very upset if they lost the dog or the dog died, and 17 said they would be extremely upset if this happened.

The subjects were tested for blood pressure, heart rate, and respi-

ration during three 9-minute periods. The periods were (1) petting
one's own dog, (2) petting a strange dog, and (3) quiet reading.

Results indicated that all three experiences resulted in lowered
blood pressure. The greatest decrease occurred when the subjects
were petting their own dog. Both reading and petting one's own dog
resulted in a lower heartbeat. While petting the unknown dog, however, heart rate rose. Respiration rate fell slightly in all groups.

> Data from this study demonstrated that petting one's own
> dog with whom a companion bond has been established has a
> parallel relaxation effect to quiet reading.

The researchers conclude:[16]

> It is interesting that petting the unknown dog did not pro-
> duce the same relaxation effect, especially since the dog used
> for this protocol was very non-threatening, very relaxed him-
> self during the protocol, and usually ended up asleep, while
> the subjects' own dogs were more restless and less used to
> being in the laboratory. The effect of bonding, however,
> seems to have been stronger than that of any other variable.

The researchers also noticed a significant increase in the blood
pressure of the subjects when their own dog entered the room, and
called this the "greeting response." "Presumably the subjects experienced an initial excitement when their own dogs who had been
removed from them were brought into the room," they explained.[17]

This study contradicts previous research by Friedmann et al.,
who found that prior familiarity with the dog was not necessary to
produce the relaxation effect.[18] A 1984 Study at San Diego State
University confirmed Friedmann's original findings using college
students and unfamiliar, but friendly, dogs. Two very different
dogs produced consistent results in this population.[19]

Why did the Baun study contradict other work in the field? Perhaps the factor was not the bonding itself but the presence of the
owner's dog. During two of the three protocols, the owners' dogs
were removed from them and in the care of strangers, surely benign
individuals, but unfamiliar ones nonetheless. Perhaps the inability
to achieve the resting response with the strange dog was caused by

the owners' anxiety about their own absent pet. This would also explain the greeting response, which is a feeling of relief at seeing one's healthy, happy dog, a phenomenon I am sure occurs every day at the veterinarian's office when owners pick up their pets.

An interesting variation on this research might be to conduct the three protocols on three separate days so that no subjects would be required to be separated from their pet. Knowing that the pet is safely at home would very likely allow the owner to achieve relaxation with the unfamiliar dog.

An additional study by Oetting, Baun, and colleagues conducted in the subjects' homes with their dogs present, however, did not yield expected results.[20] Forty subjects were assigned randomly to one of four treatment groups: sitting quietly, listening to autogenic relaxation phrases, petting a companion dog, or petting a companion dog while listening to autogenic relaxation phrases. The researchers measured skin temperature, blood pressure, and heart rate at 3 minute intervals for a 9-minute baseline, 15 minutes of treatment, and 9 minutes post-treatment. No significant differences were found between the major treatments of listening to the relaxation phrases or petting a companion dog.

The researchers believe that the primary reason this study did not duplicate the results of previous research is that they did not use a within-subject design, in which all subjects received all treatments. They observed significant subject effects for each variable. Because of the long baseline used, they point out:[21]

> . . . treatment effects may have been negated by boredom. It is beginning to look like the relaxation effects of petting companion dogs are time-limited, i.e., the subjects relax for about ten minutes, after which they start to "unrelax." We have seen this trend in our first two studies of blood pressure but it is premature to draw any definite conclusions.

WAR AND THE HUMAN-ANIMAL BOND

Barbara Deeb, a veterinarian based in Beirut, Lebanon, during the strife-ridden summer of 1982, surveyed pet owners in the city to determine the impact of the stresses of war on the human-animal bond.[22]

Deeb used two questionnaires: "Human/Animal Bonds during Wartime," and "Pet Stress during Wartime," which were completed by 47 owners with 21 dogs, 36 cats, and 2 pet birds. Thirteen respondents had more than 2 pets, and 20 either adopted or cared for animals other than their own during the war. Deeb says:[23]

> . . . on more than one occasion a minor medical problem for the pet seemed nearly to be the "straw that broke the camel's back" for an owner losing his or her ability to cope with stress. On several occasions, the animal's problem seemed directly related to its own stress and fear.

Deeb's survey revealed several noteworthy points. Of those surveyed, 56% replied that they had remained in Beirut at least partly because of their pets; 75% of these people replied that they kept their animals primarily for companionship. During bombing and shelling raids 53% took their companion animal with them, and the 41% who could not do that worried about their pets. During bombing, shelling, and shooting episodes, 32% of the respondents felt comforted by their pet(s), and 66% felt a "mutual comforting." During the bombings, 72% reported that they handled or caressed the animal more than usual; none reported that they paid less attention to the animal.

Seventy-eight percent of the sample reported that they took at least minor risks to provide for their pets. During times of food shortage, 71% of the respondents shared supplies with their pets, and 27% actually were more deprived than their pets.

Says Deeb:[24]

> The responses indicate that companion animals played a significant role in their owner's daily lives and mental health during the war. The animals gave the people comfort when they needed it most. These people devoted considerable effort to the well-being of their pets, providing proper diets, drinking water and attention at times when preserving their own lives presumably would have been uppermost in their minds. Aside

from war injuries, the animals did not seem to have any extended health problems related to the stresses of war.

HOW PETS REDUCE STRESS AND ANXIETY

Why are pet animals such effective stress reducers? Two key ingredients in stress management are exercise and relaxation, and a pet lends itself beautifully to such therapies. Briskly walking a dog or playing with a pet offers two benefits: the actual physical output involved in the activity and the feeling of security that accompanies association with an animal. Petting and stroking a companion animal triggers physiological relaxation in the owner. Pets calm and soothe their human companions. Quality time spent with a pet is thus beneficial to persons suffering from stress or anxiety. They are literally forced to calm down and relax.

A recent study by Gage and Anderson[25] has confirmed the effectiveness of pets as stress reducers. The researchers sampled 5,003 adults and found that individuals who were attached to their pets coped significantly better with their stress. In fact, these pet owners actively sought out their pets during times of high stress. Petting and playing with their animals was an important stress management technique. "We cannot always change stress levels in our lives," says Gage, "but we can learn to cope with it better. These results show how important pets can be in this effort." Currently Gage is conducting research to determine if association with pets plays a socializing role in approaching parenthood. Her preliminary results strongly suggest that individuals with experiences with pets have a more favorable attitude toward parenthood than those who do not.[26]

Pets are also valuable as a focal point of interest diverting the patient from self-absorption (see Brickel's discussion of how pets reduce anxiety by distraction in Chapter 4). Many who suffer from anxiety, for example, are anxiety-ridden about their anxiety. They fear the onset of an attack, and can become apprehensive of even the simplest task. It might be helpful if these persons could keep their pets with them at stressful times. The animal is not only a soothing presence but a point of interest, something to take the person's mind off his or her fear.

None of us can rid ourselves entirely of stress and anxiety, nor would we want to. However, if the tension becomes unbearable and the pressure continues to mount, it seems clear that taking a few minutes to walk the dog or pet the cat may be just what the doctor ordered.

REFERENCES

1. Lockwood, R. (1983). The influence of animals on social perception. In A. H. Katcher & A. M. Beck (Eds.), *New perspectives on our lives with companion animals*. Philadelphia: University of Pennsylvania Press.

2. Sebkova, J. (1977). Anxiety levels as affected by the presence of a dog. Cited in E. Friedmann (1985). Health benefits of pets for families. In M. B. Sussman (Ed.), *Pets and the family* (191–203). New York: The Haworth Press.

3. Friedmann, E., Katcher, A. H., Thomas, S. A., Lynch, J. J., & Messent, P. R. (1983). Social interactions and blood pressure: Influence of animal companions. *Journal of Nervous and Mental Disease, 171*, 461–465.

4. Jenkins, J. (1985, October). Physiological effects of petting a companion animal. Paper presented at the Annual Delta Society Conference, Denver, CO.

5. Katcher, A. H. (1981, October). Health and the living environment. Paper presented at the International Conference on the Human/Companion Animal Bond, Philadelphia, PA.

6. Katcher, A. H., Friedmann, E., Beck, A. M., & Lynch, J. (1981, October). Talking, looking, and blood pressure: Physiological consequences of interaction with the living environment. Paper presented at the International Conference on the Human/Companion Animal Bond, Philadelphia, PA.

7. Katcher, A. H., Segal, H., & Beck, A. M. (1984). Contemplation of an aquarium for the reduction of anxiety. In R. K. Anderson, B. L. Hart, L. A. Hart (Eds.), *The pet connection* (pp. 171–178). Minneapolis: University of Minnesota Press.

8. Ibid.

9. Katcher, A. H., & Beck, A. M. Safety and intimacy: Physiological and behavioral responses to interaction with companion animals. (1983). In *The Human-Pet Relationship* (pp. 122–128). International Symposium on the Occasion of the 80th Birthday of Nobel Prize Winner Prof. Dr. Konrad Lorenz. Vienna: IEMT.

10. Lorenz, K. Cited in Katcher, A. H. & Beck, A. M. (1983). op. cit. p. 126.

11. Baun, M. M., Bergstrom, N., Langston, N. F., & Thoma, L. Physiological effects of petting dogs: Influences of attachment. (1984). In R. K. Anderson, B. L. Hart, & L. A. Hart (Eds.), *The pet connection* (pp. 162–170). Minneapolis: University of Minnesota Press.

12. Katcher, A. H. (1981). Interrelations between people and their pets: Form and function. In B. Fogle (Ed.), *Interrelations between people and pets*. Springfield, IL: Charles C. Thomas.

13. Gantt, W. H. (1972). Analysis of the effect of person. *Conditional Reflex*, 7(2), 67–73.

14. Lynch, J. J., Fregin, G. F., Mackie, J. B., & Monroe, R. R., Jr. (1974). Heart rate changes in the horse to human contact. *Psychophysiology*, *11*(4), 472–478.

15. Baun, M. M., Bergstrom, N., Langston, N. F., & Thoma, L. (1984). op. cit.

16. Ibid.

17. Ibid.

18. Friedmann, E., Katcher, A. H., Meislich, D., & Goodman, M. (1979). Physiological response of people to petting their pets. *American Zoologist*, *19*, 327.

19. Grossberger, S. San Diego State University. (1984, February). Personal communication with Friedmann, E. Cited in E. Friedmann (1985). Health benefits of pets for families. In M. B. Sussman (Ed.), *Pets and the family* (pp. 191–203). New York: The Haworth Press.

20. Oetting, K. S., Baun, M. M., Bergstrom, N., & Langston, N. F. (1985, October). Petting a companion dog and autogenic relaxation effects on systolic and diastolic blood pressure, heart rate, and peripheral skin temperature. Paper presented at the Annual Delta Society Conference, Denver CO.

21. Baun, M. (1986, June). Personal communication.

22. Deeb, B. (1984, spring). War's impact on the people-pet bond. *People-Animals-Environment*, pp. 17–18. Also in *Pure-Bred Dogs American Kennel Gazette*. (1985, August). pp. 60–63.

23. Ibid.

24. Ibid.

25. Gage, M. G. & Anderson, R. K. (1985, October). Pet ownership, social support and stress. Paper presented at the Annual Delta Society Conference, Denver, CO.

26. Gage, M. G. (1986, June). Personal communication.

CHAPTER 7

Psychiatric Patients

EFFECT OF DOGS
ON PSYCHIATRIC PATIENTS

The use of animals as adjuncts in the therapy of institutionalized psychiatric patients began with the Corsons, who, while researching canine behavior at Ohio State University, discovered that, upon hearing the dogs bark, previously unresponsive individuals broke their self-imposed silence to ask to play with the dogs. The Corsons selected the most withdrawn and uncommunicative of the subjects and allowed them to interact with the dogs. Forty-seven of 50 participants showed improvement; many eventually left the hospital.[1]

EFFECT OF A PUPPY
ON ELDERLY VETERANS

More recently, Suzanne Robb and her colleagues[2] conducted a study at the Veterans Administration Medical Center in Pittsburgh, Pennsylvania, to determine the effectiveness of certain objects as catalysts for social behavior on a population of elderly male alcoholic patients. The researchers found that a puppy was far more effective than either a plant or wine bottle in stimulating appropriate conversation, smiling, and animated behavior, Additionally, Robb noted a decrease in hostility in the presence of the animal. "Invasion of personal space had frequently triggered verbal arguments and physical violence between clients," she explains. "When the puppy was present, invasion of personal space increased as clients moved to get closer to the puppy, but no hostility resulted."

EFFECT OF CAGED BIRDS
ON PSYCHIATRIC PATIENTS

According to Alan Beck, of the Center for the Interaction of Animals and Society at the University of Pennsylvania's School of Veterinary Medicine:[3]

> The therapist who conducts therapy along with the pet becomes less threatening, and the patient can reveal more of himself. Just as the therapist becomes less forbidding and more human, the patient with the pet is perceived by others as more human and hence less "sick" and more treatable. These expectations create a positive cycle with the patient being treated in ways that encourage recovery.

Pets are particularly effective as a bridge between therapist and withdrawn, uncommunicative, and uncooperative patients. This aspect, say Beck and his associates, inspires optimism among staff members and encourages conversation beyond the patient-caretaker role.

However, a major problem with pet-facilitated therapy studies to date, he points out, is that a therapeutic effect is presumed to take place simply because the animal is present. Unless therapeutic goals have been previously defined, a favorable response to an animal (which may be little more than a reaction to the usual diversion and pleasure normally associated with human-animal interactions) may be erroneously interpreted as a breakthrough.

To address this criticism, Beck and his colleagues Louisa Seraydarian and G. Frederick Hunter designed a controlled study with a preplanned hypothesis and preplanned measures of effectiveness, the first, they say of its kind in pet-facilitated therapy research. The researchers hypothesized that the presence of pets, in this case caged birds, would make the environment less threatening. Thus, patients who attended therapy in a room containing birds would attend more frequently, participate more, and benefit more overall from the therapy.

Seventeen patients whose average age was 41 years, whose average hospital stay was 3-5 years, and whose primary diagnosis was schizophrenia were chosen from patients in an extended treatment building in Haverford State Hospital. They were randomly assigned to two treatment groups: The bird-facilitated therapy group consisted of 6 males and 2 females, and the non-bird group consisted of 6 males and 3 females. The groups were matched for age, sex, length of stay in the hospital, or diagnosis, and were treated with daily sessions of group and activity therapy with the same therapists for 12 weeks. Treatment rooms for the sessions were similarly furnished; however, the bird-facilitated therapy group's room contained four society finches in two large flight cages, whereas the other group's room did not. The birds, however, were not a focal point of discussion and were mentioned only if brought up in the general course of discussion.

The patients had volunteered for the study and had previously indicated that they had no allergies to animals and enjoyed their company. The subjects received a schedule of the therapy sessions and were encouraged to attend, but attendance was voluntary.

Several measures were used to evaluate the study. Patient attendance was monitored, and the frequency of verbal participation at each session was recorded by an independent observer. The Brief Psychiatric Rating Scale (BPRS), developed by Overall and Gorham to assess symptom severity, was administered prior to the onset of the study and after its completion, as was the Nurses' Observation Scale for Inpatient Evaluation (NOSIE), which measures six subscales: social competence, social interest, personal neatness, irritability, manifest psychosis, and retardation.

Interestingly, the project, which had been scheduled for 12 weeks, was terminated after 10 weeks because 4 of the 8 patients in the bird-facilitated therapy group were no longer at the hospital. Three had been discharged, and 1 patient was given an authorized absence with good probability of discharge. All of the patients assigned to the non-bird group were still at the hospital.

The results indicated that attendance was significantly greater for patients assigned to the bird-facilitated therapy group (76%) than for the non-bird group (67%). The bird-facilitated therapy group also had more contributions to the sessions: 5.22 per person, compared with 4.41 for the non-bird group. Analysis of the post-treatment BPRS scores did not reveal a significant difference overall, but comparison of the subscales revealed that on two of the subscales, hostility and suspiciousness, the bird-facilitated therapy group scored lower. "At the conclusion of the project, the patients in the bird group were significantly less hostile and less suspicious than the patients in the non-bird group," said the researchers. They explain:[4]

> For the group therapeutic process to have any value, the patient must attend and participate in the group. As the presence of animals has been shown to make the perception of settings safer and also to encourage conversation, their inclusion within the group setting seems to be associated with better attendance and more frequent interactions with the group. The reduction in hostility scores identified by the BPRS may be the general effect that animals are perceived as less hostile and therefore patients are more trusting and less hostile in an environment containing animals.

The researchers also suggest that the benefits of the animal contact may have provided the final impetus in the discharge of the patients. "The presence of animals in a mental hospital setting appears to serve some subtle but important value purposes. It appears to have facilitated the group therapy process without undue risk or cost," they conclude.[5]

EFFECT OF PETS ON
MENTALLY ILL YOUNG ADULTS

A second institutional study involved the placement of various pet animals with chronically mentally ill young adults. Researcher Joanne Holland[6] selected 6 patients who had not responded well to other therapies, who had volunteered for the program, and who were assessed as likely to benefit from a pet. Her subject population was complex, she notes, diagnosed with chronic multiple disabilities and emotional disturbances, including schizophrenia, physical or metabolic disorders, and traumatic histories.

Holland assessed her subjects using before and after Global Assessment Scales and daily staff evaluations scoring depression, agitation, goal-oriented behavior, and disruptive behavior. Additionally, she measured staff attitudes regarding pets and unit residents' attitudes regarding pets prior to the animals' placement and 6 months after the study had started.

Holland found that staff attitudes toward the pet placements were initially positive and increased slightly (though not significantly) during the study. Residents' attitudes, on the other hand, were initially extremely positive and decreased slightly (but not significantly with one exception) during the study.

Holland found there was a significant decrease in the desire to keep a rabbit in the institution, which she says could have reflected the practical difficulties in keeping the animal there. This finding supports an earlier study by Marina Doyle,[7] who found that the placement of a rabbit on a ward of psychiatric male inpatients prompted noticeable improvement at the onset, but eventually the patients began to resent caring for the rabbit and voted to have it removed from the ward. Possibly, a rabbit is a poor choice for an institutional setting. However, Santostefano[8] had excellent results using rabbits with a group of institutionalized adolescents (see Chapter 9, "Pets and Adolescents"). Also, Bubba, a floppy-eared rabbit in residence at the San Francisco Recreation Center, a facility for severely retarded adults and youngsters, appears to be an unending source of delight to the residents, who not only take turns caring and interacting with the rabbit but also helped construct its hutch.[9]

Two of Holland's initial subjects left the ward before the study was completed. One of them exhibited psychotic behavior after a medication change, and was removed from the ward. The second improved to such a degree that she was discharged, and took her pet bird home with her. After 8 months, a follow-up report indicated she was still functioning well.

Of the remaining 4 patients, each showed significant increased functioning as measured by the Global Assessment Scales. However, staff evaluations judged that 1 patient had greatly improved, 2 showed moderate improvement, and 1 in fact had reacted adversely.

Of the four indicators measured, goal-oriented behavior appeared to be the most affected by the presence of the animals, with 1 patient showing a highly significant increase and 2 patients showing moderate but significant increases. One young man showed a highly significant decrease in goal-oriented behavior as well as increased agitation and disruptive behaviors. "He cared well for his rabbit," notes Holland, "but the effort cost him in other areas."[10] In contrast to Brickel's study, which showed a definite decrease in depression among a therapy group having access to a pet dog (see Chapter 5), Holland found no changes in depression ratings.

This study does suggest, as Holland points out, that careful placement of pets may prove beneficial to certain patients; however, the determination of these patients is hardly precise. It may be that in spite of the best intentions and most ardent desire, some individuals are simply overwhelmed by the responsibility of caring for another living thing. This factor may not be readily ascertainable in a pre-study assessment.

A second area of consideration is the choice of pet for such a setting. Why should a rabbit, for instance, become less desirable during the course of ownership? Perhaps because the practical aspects of owning a rabbit do not live up to expectations. A rabbit is conceptualized as a warm, furry creature, soft and gentle, not unlike a cat or dog. Yet, in terms of interaction and companionship, rabbit ownership is considerably more limited than either cat or dog ownership, but not necessarily less demanding. Thus, a rabbit is maintained at a cost (physical care, emotional energy) perhaps deemed too high for the benefits received.

This could also help explain why birds as a group do extremely well as therapeutic choices. We generally don't expect much of birds: pretty plumage, a flurry of activity, maybe a pleasant vocalization. But their care is minimal, so we don't mind. Yet, some birds learn to talk (parrot species and mynahs), become hand tame, or learn to do tricks (parrots, parakeets, cockatiels, lovebirds). And those that don't (notably finches) may sing beautiful songs and interact with one another in constant, fascinating activity. Birds, thus, not only meet our expectations, but usually exceed them. The cost is minimal, the benefit high, and the animal is a therapeutic success.

EFFECT OF A DOG ON
HALFWAY HOUSE RESIDENTS

According to researchers Lisa D. Allen, director of operations of the Massachusetts County Mounted Patrol, and Richard D. Budson, associate professor of psychiatry at Harvard Medical School:[11]

Pet dogs can make a positive contribution to the therapeutic experiences of residents in a psychiatric halfway house. The pet is considered to be a natural member of the halfway house community, which itself is viewed as a family-modeled milieu. These pets can have a profound effect upon the psychology of the individual resident, help build social bridges between residents, and be significant companions in facilitating outer community relationships.

Unlike a hospital setting, which is not naturally conductive to the presence of an animal, a halfway house is a family-modeled social system, a natural environment for the family pet, say the researchers. And the presence of the pet facilitates growth not only through its impact on the individual but through the group and the outer community as well.

A pet dog offers special qualities that facilitate its relationship with residents including its capacity for affection, play, intelligence, and acceptance. Dogs are particularly effective with individuals who have difficulty establishing trusting relationships with other people. Numerous risks are involved in establishing communication with others including evaluation, correction, punishment, inattention, contradiction, and unsolicited advice and instruction. None of these risks is present in a relationship with an animal.

Many residents have deep-rooted needs for closeness which have gone unexpressed, note Allen and Budson. In addition to providing an opportunity for the needed closeness, a relationship with an animal also reaffirms the resident's capacity to give and accept affection. The researchers also note the positive and empathetic non-verbal communication expressed by the animal. Corson has previously observed that, good intentions aside, emotionally and physically healthy persons, including health care professionals, often radiate unconscious, negative, non-verbal signals to patients.[12]

Equally important is the tactile interaction with the dog. Levinson notes:[13]

> . . . many disturbed children who are afraid of human contact because they have been hurt so much and so often have a strong need for physical contact. Since the hurt is not associated with the dog, this conflict resolves itself. They will permit

a dog to approach them, they will pet a pet dog, and tell him all about their difficulties.

Allen and Budson identify two important elements of the attachment mechanism:[14]

> . . . the dogs' ability to offer love and tactile reassurance without criticism and their perpetual, infantile, innocent dependence [neoteny] that may stimulate humans' natural tendency to offer support and protection. For example, in a halfway house, a collie would regularly upon sighting a depressed and weeping woman resident, follow her to her room and push her arms away from her face and lick away her tears, The dog began to be known as "the little nurse."

Allen and Budson point out that no matter how long-suffering a pet may appear to be, the relationship between animal and master is not one-sided. The dog will respond to kind treatment, thus teaching the resident that caring for an animal goes hand in hand with responsibility, As the patient takes on increased responsibility for the pet, its feeding, walking, and grooming, he or she experiences a needed ego boost.

Furthermore, a resident, in caring for a pet, they say:[15]

> is in the unique position of being the caretaker instead of the receiver of care — the depended upon instead of the dependent. The resident is, thus, in a position to acquire an enhanced sense of inner strength, independence and self-worth. Performing chores for a dog is also unique in that the dog emanates such joy in expectation of being fed or being taken for a walk that the performance of the task is experienced by the resident as natural instead of a burden dictated by a higher authority. This may, in some cases, be the first such joyful performance experience.

Pets also provide a bridge between residents and other residents and between residents and the community. The social-lubricant effect of the pet, noted in so many other environments, is not absent from a group home. Allen and Budson point out that otherwise shy residents are encouraged to communicate because of shared experiences with the pet, thus enhancing the individual's social skills.

Through walking the dog, the resident becomes part of the larger community. He or she is able to walk around the neighborhood and communicate with other pet owners and will be better received because of the friendly canine at the end of the leash. Through play, the resident is also able to release tension and energy in an enjoyable and socially acceptable manner.

"In conclusion," say Allen and Budson:[16]

> pet dogs in a psychiatric community residential setting provide a wide spectrum of helpful benefits to patients — uncritical affection, comfort, tactile reassurance, the joys of energy release, the opportunity for responsibility, the bridge to relationships with fellow residents as well as outside neighbors. The dogs exert a stabilizing influence upon the residents' lives. The animals serve as an "icon of constancy" in an unpredictable world. The capacity to give and accept love helps the psychiatric patient feel equal with his pet at a deep emotional level. Since egalitarian socialization is an integral element in the development and formation of friendships, the relationship with a pet is a rich opportunity to bring new capabilities and a feeling of increased confidence in human relationships.

EFFECT OF PETS ON PREVIOUSLY INSTITUTIONALIZED PATIENTS

British social worker Dorothy Atkinson[17] has also found pets to be of immense importance to former patients who had become reintegrated into their communities, so much so that she talks about social workers "attempting a new and little researched form of intervention: a pet counseling service."

Atkinson's survey of pets was part of a larger survey studying the lives of 50 mentally handicapped persons who were discharged from hospitals. Sixteen of the 18 households she surveyed had at least one pet, and in one of the two remaining non-pet households, the woman had recently lost her cat and was thinking about getting a dog. Only one man, who admitted to feeling lonely and isolated, refused to consider getting a pet.

Atkinson divides pets into three categories: background pets, foreground pets, and contact pets. Background pets are primarily fish and birds, mostly parakeets. These are minimal-care, stay-at-home pets, much the favorite of social workers because they tend to be harmless and cause no trouble.

The foreground pets, predominantly cats, are described by Atkinson as those ". . . that feature in case notes and star in interviews, who stalk through the pages of client diaries, and determine the shape of people's days."[18] Atkinson reports cats that are featured in paintings, that are invited to neighbor's house (along with its owners) for a drink after a house fire, overindulged spoiled fat cats that have a favorite chair and favorite tea-time snack, and a cat whose human owner makes special cycling trips to buy him fresh fish. Most importantly, these cats occupy a central position in their owners' lives.

Atkinson considers dogs contact pets because they draw the owner into the outside world. Caring for a dog and tending to its physical needs provides a rhythm to its owners' lives, she says, and is also frequently a conversation starter. Atkinson counsels certain clients against dog ownership, persuading them to adopt cats or parakeets instead. When clients already have a dog or have taken in a stray or neighborhood vagrant, Atkinson works with them, often smoothing relations if, for example, neighbors consider the dog a nuisance.

Atkinson's pet counseling includes health advice, both for the client and for the animal, grief counseling when the beloved animal dies, selection and training of a new or replacement pet, and as noted above, neighborhood diplomacy in cases where one person's pet is another's poison. She concludes by advocating that pet counseling become a formal part of social work courses.

After reading Dorothy Atkinson's study, I could not help but recall the many times I have read or heard of individuals pressured or coerced into giving up a pet because the animal is considered a nuisance or a bother. Marginal populations — the elderly, the mentally impaired, outpatients — are particularly subject to these pressures because, with all good intentions, we presume these individuals have enough trouble caring for themselves let alone caring for an animal. Perhaps instead of complaints and criticisms, we should offer a helping hand and guidance. So often the pet is the impetus to improved mental health, the focal point of a life, the bridge between the individual and the community as a whole. For those who are on the fringes of normalcy or reentering the world of sound mental health there may be, as the title of Atkinson's article so aptly says it, "nothing more precious."

EFFECT OF DOLPHINS
ON AN AUTISTIC YOUTH

Finally, no discussion of pet therapy with severely mentally impaired subjects is complete without mention of the unusual and sometimes extraordinary work of Betsy Smith, of Florida International University. Smith is developing dolphin therapy, which although necessarily limited in application, has had remarkable results with at least one autistic individual.

The initial phase of Smith's work, Project Inreach,[19] was designed with the aid of Henry Truby, president of the World Dolphin Foundation. The researchers had observed neurologically impaired children responding enthusiastically to free-swimming dolphins who, in turn, reacted with uncharacteristic patience and gentleness. They wondered if the dolphins could prompt communication responses, previously unrealized, in youngsters diagnosed as autistic, language impaired, and retarded.

Truby and Smith selected 8 children and their families from the Southford Society for Autistic Children and 3 dolphin entertainers from the Wometco Seaquarium. During the initial session the youngsters and families were familiarized with the dolphins and the setting. During the second and third sessions, the researcher introduced play behavior such as ball tossing between parent, child, and dolphin and splashing water on the dolphins. Several children initiated play with no prompting, and some mimicked the clicking vocalizations of the dolphins.

Truby and Smith initially planned eight encounter sessions, but abandoned the project after six sessions since the risk of injury was too great in that environment. By that final session, however, 2 of the children were in the pool with the dolphins, splashing, "clicking," spitting out water, in general demonstrating behavior similar to that of their playful water mammals. The families were disappointed when the sessions ended because the times with the dolphins were among the happiest they had known as families. They reported joy and relaxation immediately after each session and an ease of tension that lasted for weeks.

One youth in particular, Michael Williams, aged 18, who had been labeled nonverbal autistic since the age of 6, reacted dramatically to the sessions. His reproduction of the dolphin clicks was virtually indistinguishable from that of the animals, and he engaged in this vocalization whenever he saw a billboard, photograph, or video presentation of a dolphin. One year after the project ended, Michael's class went to Seaquarium on a field trip. The boy broke away from his classmates and ran to the project area, now locked, where he clicked furiously, hoping to reach the dolphins. In the fall of 1981, a year and a half after the boy had previously encountered the dolphins, the NBC television series "Those Amazing Animals" filmed the interaction for a future segment of the series. Williams happily engaged in water play for more than 3 hours for the film crew's takes and retakes. Says Smith:[20]

> The full implication of Michael's behavior cannot be appreciated unless one is familiar with or has worked with autistic children. Autism, which has no known cause or cure, is defined as the profound inability to establish affectionate and meaningful relationships and language.

Smith was able to continue observing Williams' remarkable human-dolphin bond at Dolphin Plus, a coral cove in Key Largo, Florida.[21] The cove was populated by 6 free-swimming dolphins destined to become performers. To interact with them, Michael, who has a fear of motion and does not like to ride elevators, had to maneuver down to a floating platform. To the surprise of both his parents and his therapist, Williams' acted without hesitation and began, at Smith's instruction, to feed fish to the dolphins. With minimal instruction the boy let the dolphin take the fish from his hand.

During the second session Williams, for the first time ever, initiated play behavior with the dolphins with a ball placed on the platform. Only 3 dolphins were available for play that session, and after the encounter was complete, the boy, alone, strolled down the long dock until he found the other 3 dolphins on the opposite side. "Throughout his entire life, Michael had had a fear of motion and open spaces; without hesitation, he had spontaneously strolled out onto a shaky dock, with several missing slats, to satisfy his curiosity about the missing dolphins," said Smith.[22]

During a later session Michael made his first human vocalization. His father asked him if he wanted to go down to the platform, and he answered "Yep." Previously, he would only shake his head. The boy continued to use the word correctly, but not consistently, in the coming months. Perhaps most importantly, the smiles and affection first reserved exclusively for the dolphins are now shared with his parents, his therapist, and even the family dog, which he previously ignored. Says Smith:[23]

> Much time is spent teaching autistic children to hug, to kiss, to be warm and to smile. Youngsters may be tickled, for example, and than taught to tickle themselves. The dolphins have enabled Michael to find within his own symbolic universe the meaning for his pats and smiles. By reaching out to them, he has been able to reach out to other beings as well.

Smith's sessions with the boy ended abruptly because of a serious illness in the family. Several months after that the cove was sold, and the dolphins were transported to their new home at Marine World in Pensacola. But dolphin therapy may be just beginning. Smith hopes ultimately to develop a camp for autistic children and their families that will include therapeutic sessions with the marine mammals as well as other treatment modalities. Certainly, it would be the most unique program yet in a unique field for, as Smith points out, in dolphin therapy, unlike other pet-facilitated treatments, the dolphins themselves are the therapists.

REFERENCES

1. Corson, S. A., Corson, W. L., Gwynne, P. H., & Arnold, E. L. (1977). Pet dogs as nonverbal communication links in hospital psychiatry. *Comprehensive Psychiatry, 18*, 1.

2. Robb, S. S., Boyd, M., & Pristash, C. L. (1980). A wine bottle, plant and puppy: Catalysts for social behavior. *Journal of Gerontological Nursing, 6*(12), 722–728.

3. Beck, A. H., Seraydarian, L., & Hunter, G. F. (1984). The use of animals in the rehabilitation of psychiatric inpatients. Unpublished manuscript.

4. Ibid.

5. Ibid.

6. Holland, J. (1984). A preliminary report on a pilot project using animals in therapy with chronically mentally ill young adults. Paper presented at the October 1984 annual meeting of the Delta Society, Texas A & M University, College Station, TX.

7. Doyle, M. C. (1975). Rabbit—Therapeutic prescription. *Perspectives in Psychiatric Care, 13*:79–82.

8. Santostefano, P. G. (1984). The effect of a pet therapy program on the aggressive behavior of institutionalized adolescents. Unpublished manuscript.

9. Cusack, O. & Smith, E. (1984). *Pets and the elderly*. New York: The Haworth Press.

10. Holland, J. (1984). op. cit.

11. Allen, L. D. & Burdon, R. D. (1982). The clinical significance of pets in a psychiatric community residence. *American Journal of Social Psychiatry, 2*(4), 41-43.

12. Corson, S.A. & E. O. (1979). Pet animals as nonverbal communication mediators in psychotherapy in institutional settings. In Corson & Corson (Eds.), *Ethology and nonverbal communication in mental health*. Oxford: Pergamon Press.

13. Levinson, B. M. (1962). The dog as co-therapist. *Mental Hygiene, 46*, 59–65.

14. Allen, L. D. & Burdon, R. D. (1982). op. cit.

15. Ibid.

16. Ibid.

17. Atkinson, D. (1985). Nothing more precious. *Social Work Today, 16* (46), 13–14.

18. Ibid.

19. Smith, B. (1983). Project inreach: A program to explore the ability of atlantic bottlenose dolphins to elicit communication responses from autistic children. In A. H. Katcher & A. M. Beck (Eds.), *New perspectives on our lives with companion animals*. Philadelphia: University of Pennsylvania Press.

20. Ibid.

21. Smith, B. (1984). Using dolphins to elicit communication from an autistic

child, In R. K. Anderson, B. L. Hart, & L. A. Hart (Eds.), *The pet connection* (pp. 154–161). Minneapolis: University of Minnesota.
   22. Ibid.
   23. Smith, B. (1984, February). Personal communication.

CHAPTER 8

Pets and Children

EFFECT OF DEVELOPMENT ON CHILDREN'S ATTITUDES TOWARD ANIMALS

"The two times that people need animals most in their lives are when they are very young and when they are very old," says Bustad.[1]

Certainly the bond between children and animals often seems intensely deep, spontaneous, exclusive, even magical. And part of the pleasure of adult pet ownership is that our animal friends, by their exuberant joy and acceptance, inspire us to let down our guard and become children again.

No one has determined at exactly what age attachment occurs between a pet and a child, but a study by Kidd[2] suggests it may begin within the first year of life. Kidd observed 5 infants between the ages of 6 and 12 months react to the family pet. All of the infants smiled when the animal entered the room, and the 8-12-month-olds tried to follow the pet.

From this early attraction grows a strong and deepening attachment. Virtually all the studies to date show an overwhelming interest in and affection for animals, although attitudes differ along age and sex lines. An early study by Brucke[3] reviewed 2,804 essays about pets by youngsters between the ages of 7 and 16, and found that pets were considered companions, confidants, and playmates who were responsive to their human masters and dependent upon them for their needs. The favored pets for boys were dogs, horses and rabbits, whereas the favored pets for girls were cats, parrots, and canaries. Dogs were the overall favorite animals and were regarded by the children as intelligent members of the family. Brucke also found that interest in dogs increased steadily between the ages of 7 and 16. In reviewing Brucke's findings, Hall and Browne[4] found that 28% of the sample preferred cats to dogs and believed their cats experienced the same thoughts and feelings they did. Cats were rarely abused or neglected, and the researchers decided that cat ownership fostered responsibility.

A 1927 study by Lehman[5] placed dogs as the favored play companion of both boys and girls between the ages of 8 and 16. In a survey of 382 fourth-grade students, Amatora[6] found that pets ranked third after money and success as the most important interest for both boys and girls. Dogs, again were the favorite animals, followed by horses and cats.

In a 1982 study, Bryant[7] found that 83% of a group of 7-10-year-olds considered the family pet a special friend. She also noted that children who reported regular intimate talks with their pets had lower competitive attitudes than those who did not. MacDonald,[8] in a survey of 31 10-year-olds, found that talking to the dog, along with playing and exercising, was the most common child-pet interaction. Most of the sample felt the dog understood them.

In a survey of 216 5-13-year-olds, Salomon[9] found that, regardless of current ownership, 98% of the youngsters wanted a pet: The younger children wanted a playmate, whereas the older children wanted a companion. Dogs were the favored pet, followed by cats and horses. Kidd and Kidd[10] surveyed 300 boys and girls between the ages of 3 and 13 years, and found that 99.3% wanted a pet. Only 2 13-year-old boys neither had nor wanted pets.

Animals are common in the dreams of children. In the Salomon study,[11] 29% of the sample reported dreaming about animals. In examining the dreams of 457 children, Van de Castle[12] found that 60% of the dreams of 4-year-olds involved animals, but by the ages of 15 and 16, animals were involved in only 4% of dreams. Spungeon[13] noted that 85% of a sample of 53 5-6-year-olds daydreamed about their pets during school. Pines has noted that the imaginary playmates of gifted verbal children are very often animals.

Because children and animals — particularly pet animals — mesh so well, popular perception assumes children are innately caring and protective of animals. However, a study by Stephen Kellert[15] of

Yale University suggests that this viewpoint might be too idealistic. Kellert measured the attitudes of a total of 267 children distributed among the 2nd, 5th, 8th, and 11th grades. Although the most prevalent attitude among all the children was the humanitarian one (primary interest and strong affection for individual animals, particularly pets), he found distinct developmental stages based on the children's ages. Younger children consistently placed the needs of people over the needs of animals, and had little concern for the rights and protection of animals. They were as a whole also far less interested in animals in general, and wildlife in particular.

Kellert found that fifth graders were characterized by a dramatic increase in emotional concern and affection for animals. Eighth graders were characterized by their factual knowledge and intellectual understanding of animals. By the 11th grade, ethical concern for animals and the environment and awareness of ecological considerations were manifested.

In their 1985 study examining the attitudes of children towards pets, Kidd and Kidd[16] also found attitudinal differences based upon developmental stages. They interviewed 300 boys and girls between the ages of 3 and 13 years; 90% of the sample were current pet owners.

Very young children (3-5-year-olds) demonstrated numerous misconceptions about animals, attributing human speech and actions such as kissing and hugging to their pets. They also reported playing video games and board games with their animals. Three-year-olds, report the researchers, showed no awareness that pets feel pain, and several of the youngsters suggested physical punishment for ill pets because pets are not supposed to get sick.

By the age of 7, children no longer confused human and animal behaviors. They understood that pets could show affection and communication in body language and actions different than those of children. Seven-year-olds also showed awareness of pets' feelings, and were concerned about their animals' pain, a finding that suggests an earlier development of empathy than is suggested in the Kellert study.

Bonding appeared to peak at the age of 11, when children exhibited both an understanding of the animal and empathy to its needs and feelings. The age of 13 appeared to be a break point; significantly fewer of these children reported either loving their pet or being loved by their pet than did younger children. The researchers suggest that many of these adolescents were becoming autonomous and breaking away from prior attachments, which included the family, the home, and even the family pet.

Overall the research supports the concept of a strong, positive child-pet bond. Regardless of ownership status, 99.3% of the sample wanted a pet; only two 13-year-old boys had no interest in pets. Ninety-four percent of the children said they loved their pets; 95% of the sample believed their pets loved them. Reported benefits of pet ownership included happiness, comfort, remedy for loneliness, learning experience, playmate, unconditional love, and in the case of dog owners, protection of child and house. Interestingly, 10% of the children reported no benefits from pet ownership, although several of these children believed a different pet from the one they owned would be more desirable.

The Kidds' research, however, yielded two disturbing findings. One, the generally negative perception of veterinarians, is discussed in Chapter 14. The second is a finding that children of all ages believed in physical punishment for pets. Thirty-five percent of the sample in all age groups reported using such punishment to correct dog and cat misbehavior. Slapping and hitting were perceived as effective means of altering undesirable behavior. Only 3% of the sample, and these were the 13-year-olds, were using positive reinforcement.

This finding, which would have been expected 20 years ago, is particularly unsettling because in recent years positive reinforcement has virtually dominated the training arena. Obedience classes, how-to books, even video cassettes are available to help an owner raise an obedient, well-behaved pet, and I can't think of one that suggests anything more threatening than a forceful verbal "no." Obviously what is taken for granted in pet aficionado circles has not yet filtered down to the more casual pet owner. The researchers suggest that the children's perception of the effectiveness of physical punishment may reflect the possibility that physical punishment has been used on them. I suggest it may also be an indicator of the strong symbols of violence in our times. Physical punishment or the threat of it is a dominant behavior modifier, particularly in cartoons and in children's adventure series. And animals are certainly not exempt. The children may be expressing what they believe to be a perfectly appropriate method to deal with undesirable behavior. Certainly, a distinction can be made between a mild slap, for example, and abuse; however, since these children obviously love and care for their animals, it might be interesting to ask the children how they feel after they punish their pets.

BORIS LEVINSON AND JINGLES

As all these studies demonstrate, the family pet occupies an important place in the life of the normal, healthy youngster. But for an emotionally troubled youngster, the animal's role can be paramount, offering solace, comfort, security, and a listening post in a way that no human can.

"A child who finds it most difficult to tell us how he feels about his dreams and relationships finds his tongue when he has to discuss his problems with a dog," says Levinson.[17]

Levinson's pioneering work with pets and children began with a shaggy dog named Jingles. Levinson introduced his young patients to the dog and encouraged them to shake hands and dance with the canine companion. Often Jingles received cookies as an incentive.

Of one case, Levinson said:[18]

> One child said to me, "I am also Jingles. I also want to dance." This child got down on his knees, started to bark like a dog, and asked me to give him a cookie. In great joy and glee, he then picked up the waste basket, scattered its contents, put it on his head and started howling like a wolf.
>
> This apparently relieved him and he went on with his play as usual. He then said to me, "Why can't you have two dogs and why can't you take me as one of them?"
>
> Interspersed with his request were questions about myself — whether I had a wife; how many children I had; how big they were.
>
> It was clear that the child wanted to become part of my family. If the human complement was full, the dog comple-

ment was not, and he would like to be considered, if a vacancy existed.

EFFECT OF PETS
ON EMOTIONALLY DISTURBED
CHILDREN

In another case history, Levinson described the case of John, an adopted child 7 years old, who felt he was abandoned by his birth mother because he was "bad." His disturbance was so severe, he had threatened to kill his sister, also adopted.

The turning point came when John noticed Levinson's cat. The late psychologist wrote:[18]

> Although my cat slept in her basket on the table, a few sessions passed before John noticed her. Eventually he began to fondle her and later he wanted to feed her. He asked many questions about the cat. Finally he wanted to know where the cat came from. I explained that we had picked her up at the SPCA from an abandoned litter of kittens, emphasizing that we love the cat very much. . . .

Although John was initially reluctant to accept that a cat abandoned by both her mother and a former owner could be loved and accepted by someone else, eventually he was willing to consider that perhaps he was really loved by his adoptive parents.

Levinson found that pet-facilitated psychotherapy worked best with children who are nonverbal, inhibited, autistic, schizophrenic, withdrawn, obsessive-compulsive, or culturally disadvantaged. Autistic children are especially helped because the animal strengthens their contact with reality.[20]

The animal's presence promotes a natural situation, one in which the child is more relaxed and less aware of being observed. The therapist can gather valuable diagnostic clues by the child's reaction to, behavior toward, and conversation with and about the animal. The pet may also be used as a projective procedure in which the child completes a story about the animal begun by the therapist.[21]

The animal is more effective than traditional toy or game objects because the pet can provoke a wider range of responses from children. Because the pet is alive and itself reacts, it becomes easier for the child to transfer his interest to humans, and eventually he will be able to communicate directly with the therapist.[22] Levinson even suggested that for some disturbed children the animal cotherapist is a must because it provides unconditional positive regard to the child, which enables the youngster to develop a rapport with the therapist.[23]

Since Levinson and Jingles made animal therapy acceptable, many accounts have surfaced illustrating the value of animals for disturbed or displaced children.

Kerlikowski[24] describes an early effort to introduce animals on a children's ward. The assortment included birds, rabbits, and deodorized skunks. The children not only loved the animals, but learned to take care of them as well, and became less withdrawn and depressed in the process.

After 20 years' experience with pets in an institution caring for foster children, Duane Christy[25] reported that dogs provide the greatest benefits. They function as companions, and also foster a sense of responsibility. Molly Douglas[26] tells the story of a 7-year-old boy, previously verbal, who had become withdrawn and mute. Billy was given a puppy, and immediately began to talk to it. Through his relationship with the puppy, Billy learned to trust, notes Douglas, and eventually this trust generalized to other people in his environment. A stray dog was adopted by a group of mentally retarded youngsters, and not only gave the children love and security, but shared in their triumphs and disappointments as will.[27] Certainly, one of the most celebrated animal therapists is Skeezer, the mixed-breed dog that became a valuable member of the therapy team at the University of Michigan's Children's Psychiatric Hospital. Skeezer's story has been told in a poignant book by Elizabeth Yates[28] and a well-received television movie starring Karen Valentine.

Hannah Hayman,[29] a teacher of prekindergarten children, made a practice of bringing her own dog, a magnificent black Newfoundland named Ebunyzar, with her to accustom the children to animals. Hayman found the dog an excellent learning aid. ''Dogs add an emotional element to learning and teaching, the value of which is impossible to deny but often hard to come by. A wide range of emotions are elicited, all of which make learning easier and more meaningful," she says.

Even an animal-induced phobia can be overcome with some patience and ingenuity, she explains:[30]

> Terry panicked when any dog was anywhere in sight. After some investigation his teachers discovered that the child had been disciplined as a toddler by having a mean dog turned on him. For this reason he had been placed in a foster home before his enrollment at our school. A program of desensitization was started through pictures of dogs, dog books, dog puzzles and dog puppets. Before any dog came to the classroom, the child was told ahead of time what was going to occur. The child was told that he could stay on the carpeted area of the room while Eb would have to stay on the tiled area. Great care was taken to keep this promise. The child was unable to watch the dog while other children petted and groomed him. One day, Eb carried a basket filled with cookies to each child. After some time, Terry sent another child over to get a cookie out of Eb's basket. From that day on, Terry's self-concept improved. Though he was still self-conscious with dogs, he no longer panicked. Also his trust in the adults around him grew so that he was able to function better in every way.

"There is no doubt that children and many adults learn more readily when animal subjects are involved," says Judith Star,[31] director of the American Humane Education Society (AHES) in Framingham Center, Massachusetts.

AHES conducted 12 weekly classes for 30 special-needs students including an elementary school, Hispanic, emotionally disturbed class; a middle school mentally retarded class; and a high school mentally retarded class. The classes were taught by an AHES instructor along with regular classroom teacher and a teacher's aid.

Farm animals were used as the model through which teachers and pupils investigated basic animal needs. Then, through observation and experience, the students realized that people and animals have many needs in common. Teachers were thus able to instruct the students in health, nutrition, and grooming, along with the needs of association, communication, and appropriate behavior.

Star explains:[32]

> For example, in order to introduce the idea of basic needs, students were asked to cut out pictures of various animal activities. These pictures were brought to the AHES classroom where each activity was discussed and categorized according to the need it illustrated. Later each class made a collage illustrating all the concepts discussed in the classroom. . . .
>
> The final and most exciting portion of the lesson was a visit to the farm. In the barns students discussed the activities and needs of each animal. They were allowed to provide for these needs by feeding, grooming, and giving drinking water to specific animals. To emphasize the need for health care, each student was given a pictorial health check chart and a stethoscope. It was fascinating to watch the children carefully observing eyes, ears, and noses for signs of mucous discharge and listening intently to heart beats.

The regular classroom teachers evaluated the program. No teachers reported that their students were completely unaffected by the program. Star reports:[33]

> A minimum of forty percent of one class to a maximum of 100 percent of another class were judged by their teachers to have learned and retained specific information which corresponded to the AHES unit goal: the students learned the basic needs common to people and other animals. A minimum of one-half of one class to 100 percent of the other two classes were judged to have gained general understandings and developed new attitudes. Teachers cited sensitivity to animals, understanding animal needs, ability to relate to an unfamiliar instructor and sensitivity to people among the understandings and attitudes accrued during the course.

Green Chimneys, a 150-acre farm near Brewster, N.Y., was founded in 1947 and currently is a home for 88 emotionally and mentally disabled children and adolescents. An integral part of the therapeutic milieu at Green Chimneys is association with and caring for farm animals. Youngsters are instructed in horseback riding, animal husbandry, gardening, and farming. Some are taught to become farm guides, and host school groups that visit the farm. Staff monitor the children carefully, watching for improved relationships with the animals and subsequent improved academic performance and social behavior.

"Many of the children referred to Green Chimneys have experienced problems in their relationships with adults and peers," says Samuel B. Ross, Jr., executive director of the facility, "but readily relate to docile and friendly farm animals. This new-found relationship is used as a means of enhancing adult and child interaction, where the staff members work with the child using the animal as the point of mutual involvement."[34]

Successful completion of farm chores and animal husbandry care can be utilized to promote the child's self-esteem, says Ross. Additionally, they can eventually offer an opportunity for life-long occupational and leisure interest.

According to Ross:[35]

> The ownership and care of a pet may aid in the development of such personality traits. Nurturance and companionship heighten the capacity to be loved and to give love. In many cases, animals have helped children at Green Chimneys work through feelings of rivalry, possessiveness and jealousy. This experience, in turn, helps provide the basis for wholesome feelings toward siblings and adults.

Through providing for and protecting a pet, says Ross, children can learn what their own parents are experiencing. The pet, in addition to supplying love and companionship, can give a child purpose and make him feel wanted. Also, it can provide the impetus for the child to develop relationships with other people. A pet can bring the family together, Ross, points out, because it is something the whole family can share.

Some of the activities at Green Chimneys include construction, landscaping, animal husbandry, gardening, indoor plant care, tillage, harvesting, vegetable stand management, and other farm chores.

Ross explains:[36]

> The competence displayed by a youngster in these activities can gain him acceptance where even minimal recognition has not been possible before. The opportunities to belong and to participate, and the personal interaction that occurs as part of the involvement with a pet may be enough to change a child's entire outlook on life. Activity relevance can have an immediate effect and may awaken interest in an otherwise uninterested youngster.

Ross and colleagues[37] designed a study to determine the impact of farm involvement on emotionally disturbed, multiply handicapped youngsters. They selected 22 subjects from a group of 88 early adolescent urban youths, many with no previous farm experience. The study explored how the youngsters became involved with animals and people and how their levels of involvement were related to age, sex, diagnosis and other critical variables.

Prior to the study the researchers postulated several hypothesis:

1. that emotionally disturbed children would become more involved with animals than with either people or tasks
2. that the level of involvement would be unrelated to such demographic factors as age, sex, IQ, length of placement, or psychiatric diagnosis
3. that a high level of involvement with animals, people, and tasks would produce the best overall adjustment.

The researchers found that emotionally disturbed children become involved more strongly and readily with animals than with either people or tasks, and that animal involvement is much less affected by clinical factors than with either people or tasks, and that animal involvement is much less affected by clinical factors than are interpersonal involvement or work. They identified three main groups among their subjects: those children who are well involved with animals, people, and tasks; those who are well involved only with animals (a significantly larger percentage of the children); and those not involved with any group. Not surprisingly, the children with the strong multiple attachments were found to be the best adjusted in all areas of residential treatment. Children involved only with animals or not involved anywhere were least adjusted.

According to the researchers "There seems to be little question that animals employed in therapeutic and educational intervention have a strong involving influence and can be an agent for the development of rapport and therapeutic change."[38]

EFFECT OF PETS
ON LEARNING DISABLED
YOUNGSTERS

A Shetland sheepdog named Charmin provided the impetus for two preschool youngsters to overcome severe speech problems, says speech pathologist Larry Hill.[39] Charmin, who holds a Companion Dog obedience title and is a member of Therapy Dogs International, is so well-trained that she was featured in a local commercial. Since her specialty is retrieval, Hill developed short stories about Charmin's talent to help the youngsters with the use of pronouns and verbs. Hill says Charmin's effect was dramatic. One of the children — who previously refrained from using the word "I" — no longer has this problem, and both children doubled their task attention span. Hill was so pleased with this pilot study that he hopes to initiate the same sort of treatment for adult stroke victims.

Finally, although the programs involving the therapeutic use of animals with children are increasing daily, many gaps exist. One of these, says Jamia Jasper Jacobsen, is programs for handicapped children.

Jacobsen, who is director of the Family Support Center in Indianapolis, Indiana, and a past program director to the Association for Children with Learning Disabilities — Research and Demonstration Project, says:[40]

> Although it has been widely believed that many handicapped children have social and personal adjustment problems, the strategies that have been implemented to cope with these problems have been limited in variety and effectiveness.

Although children generally are thought to gain satisfaction from interaction with pets, few attempts have been initiated systematically to use pets in planning and programming for handicapped children.

Jacobsen has identified seven main functions animals can fulfill in the educational and therapeutic arena.

1. Provide emotional support for:
   a. youths who are physically isolated
   b. youths who are depressed, withdrawn, emotionally disturbed, insecure, or anxious or who have communication problems
   c. youths who are severely mentally ill or severely mentally retarded
2. Provide control for:
   a. youths who exhibit aggressive behavior
   b. youths who have phobias of animals and lose control upon sight of an animal.
   c. youths who have had difficulty revealing their personality for therapeutic diagnosis.
   d. youths who exhibit poor behavioral control
3. Provide socialization skills for:
   a. youths to improve relations with peers and others
   b. youths to have an intermediate-level relationship
   c. youths who are mentally retarded
4. Provide assistance with physical competency for:
   a. youths who are hard of hearing or visually impaired
   b. youths who have a muscle disorder and need to use their muscles
   c. youths who are deaf and need to learn language
5. Provide assistance with mobility problems for:
   a. youths who are bedridden
   b. youths who have degenerative diseases
   c. youths who have short-term illnesses
6. Provide responsibility training for:
   a. youths who are hospitalized for mental illness or emotional disturbance

b. youths who are not responsible
7. Provide motivation and content for education in academic skills for handicapped youth for:
   a. youths who are hospitalized
   b. youths who are in residential treatment centers for the emotionally disturbed, the mentally retarded, or juvenile delinquents
   c. youths who are in special classes

REFERENCES

1. Bustad, L. K. (1981, October). Companion animals and the aged. Paper presented at the International Conference on the Human/Companion Animal Bond, Philadelphia, PA.
2. Kidd, A. H. (1983). Infants' behaviors towards pets. Unpublished paper. Cited in A. H. Kidd & R. M. Kidd (1985). Children's attitudes towards their pets. *Psychological Reports, 57,* 15–31.
3. Brucke, W. F. (1903). Cyno-psychoses: Children's thoughts, reactions, and feelings towards pet dogs. *Journal of Genetic Psychology; 10,* 459–513.
4. Hall, G. S. & Browne, C. E. (1904). The cat and the child. *Journal of Genetic Psychology, 11,* 3–29.
5. Lehman, H. C. (1927). The child's attitudes towards the dog versus the cat. *Journal of Genetic Psychology, 34,* 62–72.
6. Amatora, Sr., M. (1960). Expressed interests in later childhood. *Journal of Genetic Psychology, 96,* 327–342.
7. Bryant, B. K. (1982). Sibling relationships in middle childhood. In Lamb & Sutton-Smith (Eds.), *Sibling relationships: Their nature and significance across the lifespan* (pp. 87–122). Hillsdale, NJ: Lawrence Erlbaum.
8. MacDonald, A. J. (1981). The pet dog in the home: A study of interactions. In B. Fogle (Ed.), *Interrelationships between people and pets* (pp. 101–123). Springfield, IL: Charles C. Thomas.
9. Salomon, A. (1982). Montreal children in the light of the test of animal infinities. *Annales Medico-Psychologiques, 140,* 207–224.
10. Kidd, A. H. & Kidd R. M. (1985). Children's attitudes toward their pets. *Psychological Reports, 57,* 15–31.
11. Salomon A. (1982). op. cit.
12. Van de Castle, R. L. (1983). Animal figures in dreams: Age, sex, and cultural differences. In A. H. Katcher & A. M. Beck (Eds.), *New perspectives on our lives with companion animals.* Philadelphia: University of Pennsylvania Press.
13. Spungeon, A. (1982). Kindergarten children's attitudes toward school and separation from home. Unpublished paper. Cited in A. H. Kidd & R. M. Kidd (1985). Children's attitudes toward their pets. *Psychological Report, 57,* 15–31.
14. Pines, M. (1978). Invisible playmates. *Psychology Today, 12*(4), 38–42.

15. Kellert, S. R. (1984). Attitudes toward animals: Age-related development among children. In R. K. Anderson, B. L. Hart, & L. A. Hart (Eds.), *The pet connection* (pp. 76–88). Minneapolis: The University of Minnesota Press.

16. Kidd, A. H. and Kidd, R. M. (1985). op. cit.

17. Editorial. (1979, November 8). Dogs, other pets, used to treat emotionally ailing. *The Times Herald,* Plymouth Meeting, PA.

18. Ibid.

19. Ibid.

20. Levinson, B. M. (1964). Pets: A special technique in child psychotherapy. *Mental Hygiene, 48,* 243–248.

21. Levinson, B. M. (1966, April). Some observations of the use of pets in psychodiagnosis. *Pediatrics Digest,* pp. 81–85.

22. Levinson, B. M. (1965). Pet psychotherapy: Use of household pets in the treatment of behavior disorders in childhood. *Psychological Reports, 17,* 695–698.

23. Levinson, B. M. (1968, September). Pets – A new way to help disturbed children. *Parents Magazine*.

24. Kerlikowski, A. C. (1958). Animals help them get well. *Modern Hospital, 91,* 105–106.

25. Christy, D. W. (1974, April). The impact of pets on children in placement. *The National Humane Review*.

26. Douglas, M. (1977, November). Getting Billy to talk. *American Humane Magazine*.

27. Gaunt, J. (1975, December). A snowball's chance. *The National Humane Review*.

28. Yates, E. (1973). *Skeezer: Dog with a mission*. New York: Harvey House.

29. Hayman, H. L. (1975, December). Dogs serving the community. *Off-Lead,* pp. 9–13.

30. Ibid.

31. Editorial (1983, summer). In Massachusetts – A unique PFT program for special need youngsters. *The Latham Letter,* p. 18.

32. Ibid.

33. Ibid.

34. King, K. (1983, fall). Green Chimneys. *People-Animals-Environment,* pp. 10-11.

35. Ibid.

36. Ibid.

37. Ross, S. B., Jr., Vigdor, M. G., Kohnstamm, M., DiPaoli, M., Manley, B., & Ross L. (1984). The effects of farm programming with emotionally handicapped children. In R. K. Anderson, B. L. Hart, & L. A. Hart (Eds.), *The pet connection* (pp. 120–130). Minneapolis: University of Minnesota Press.

38. Ibid.

39. Editorial. (1985, spring). Sheepdog helps children speak. *People-Animals-Environment*, p. 24.

40. Jacobsen, J. J. (1984, May). Personal communication.

CHAPTER 9

Pets and Adolescents

THE ADOLESCENT-PET BOND

The adolescent years are a time of turmoil, self-doubt, bewilderment, and a growing awareness of one's changing role. Neither child nor adult, the boy-man and girl-woman is at the center of biological, social, and emotional conflict. The adolescent is pressured by peers, family, hormones, and society at large. Dreams of the future must be reconciled with lost illusions, personal limitations, and realistic objectives. Adolescence is a time of decisions—demanding, unending decisions—and none are insignificant or minor to the young person who has to make them. And it is a time of extreme loneliness, when the overwhelming feeling is: "No one has ever felt like this before. No one understands."

Young people have more choices today than at any time in our history. But this glittering opportunity is also a two-edged sword since decisions must be made. To choose a career that reconciles one's own aspirations and abilities with the hope and resources of one's parents; to follow the steps of one's peers or listen to one's own inner voice. Perhaps the strongest indicator about the turmoil of adolescence is the rising incidence of suicide, which claims 5,000 young lives annually and is the third leading cause of death among teenagers.

Michael Robin and Robert ten Bensel[1] suggest that, for adolescents, a pet functions as a transitional object much as a teddy bear does for an infant. The pet makes the youngster feel safe without the presence of parents and is a far more acceptable "security blanket" for an older child than a stuffed toy. The relationship between the pet and adolescent, they note, is simpler and less riddled with conflict than relationships with humans. As Fogle[2] has noted, at this time the pet can be a confidant, a love object, a protector, a social facilitator, or even a status symbol.

However, adolescent-pet bonds are also fragile. Often in striving for autonomy, breaking away from the home and family means breaking away from the family pet as well. In their sample of 300 children, Kidd and Kidd[3] found that 13-year-olds were, more than any other age group, significantly less likely to say they loved their pet or that their pet loved them. However, the researchers point out, 20 boys and 17 girls of that age group continued to love and be loved by their pets.

The presence of a friendly dog can have a positive impact on emotionally disturbed youngsters undergoing counseling. Carol Peacock[4] conducted an exploratory study to determine the effect of her dog's presence on 12 17-year-old boys held at a detention center awaiting court trial. She chose a sample of 24 subjects, and randomly assigned them to an experimental group in which the youngsters were interviewed with the dog present and a control group that saw only the interviewer. Peacock examined both a post-interview questionnaire given to the subjects and a content analysis of the sessions themselves.

Peacock found that subjects who had access to the dog cotherapist were more relaxed, demonstrated a higher level of enjoyment when talking about themselves, and exhibited less resistance than the controls. Analysis also revealed that the experimental group made more statements expressing love and more comments regarding loss and loss experience than the control group. These findings, says Peacock, suggest that the presence of the dog permitted the adolescents to enjoy self-disclosure and to cooperate in the psychotherapy process.

"For many abused and disturbed children, a pet becomes their sole love object and a substitute for family love," say Robin and ten Bensel.[5] They, along with Joseph Quigley and Robert Anderson,[6] compared the attitudes of 238 institutionalized delinquents to those of 269 high school students. They found that 47% of the disturbed children said that pets were valuable for growing youngsters because they provided someone to love. The control group of regular high school students believed pets were important for children growing up because they taught responsibility. They also found that the abused children were more likely to discuss their problems with their pets and that the pet was often the child's only comfort during times of stress, loneliness, or boredom.

DELINQUENT BEHAVIOR AND PETS

That delinquent children should value and love their pets may at first seem surprising, since we associate antisocial behavior with animal abuse. Research, however indicates that the relationship is not a simple one.

Although the suggestion that cruelty to animals leads to criminal action toward people dates back to St. Thomas Aquinas, not until 1966 did a study provide statistical fuel for the theory. In reviewing the cases of 31 violent criminals, Hellman and Blackman[7] found that three fourths (23) of the group had a childhood history of cruelty to animals, enuresis (bed-wetting), and fire setting. They theorized that the aggressive behaviors of the subjects were a backlash against parental neglect and abuse, and postulated that the presence of the triad in childhood was an effective predictor of later criminal behavior.

Tapia[8] studied 18 young boys with a history of animal abuse and found that a third of the group were also involved in setting fires. Parental abuse was common in the group. Justice, Justice, and Kraft,[9] however, found that four factors—fighting, temper tantrums, school problems, and truancy—seemed to appear more frequently in violent offenders than the triad. But Felthous,[10] in a 1980 study, found the triad to be of predictive value, but suggested that parental neglect rather than parental abuse might be the causative factor for animal abuse.

In a subsequent study, however, Kellert and Felthous[11] found an unusually high incidence of cruelty to animals among the most violent criminals, and three-fourths of this group reported excessive and repeated abuse as children. In contrast, 31% of nonaggressive criminals and 10% of noncriminals reported parental abuse. However, 75% of noncriminals who reported animal cruelty also reported parental abuse.

As Robin and ten Bensel point out, these studies appear to identify extreme parental cruelty as the most common denominator
among those who mistreat animals. However, the researchers believe that there has been a focus on those abused children who are
cruel to pets and that this has given a narrow and one-sided impression of the nature of the relationship. Almost all (99%) of the institutionalized children surveyed expressed very positive feelings
about their pets. Ninety-one percent identified a very special pet;
72% of these children said they loved the pet very much, and 27%
said they liked the pet, which mirrors the feelings of regular school
children.

Even though both groups of adolescents had overwhelmingly
positive attitudes towards pets, the researchers found important differences between the groups. Far fewer delinquent youths viewed
their pet as part of the family, for example. Whereas regular students considered the pet a means to enhance family enjoyment and
togetherness, the institutionalized children saw the pets as their sole
love object.

Responsibility for the pet also evoked differing responses. Forty-
four percent of the regular school students believed that caring for a
pet teaches responsibility, but only 22% of these students had sole
responsibility for their animal. The majority (56%) shared it with
another family member. In contrast, only 25% of the delinquents
believed that owning a pet promoted responsibility, yet 49% of
these students were solely responsible for their pet. Perhaps the
delinquent students already perceived themselves as more responsible for their lives than the regular school students because of the
previous lack of controls in their lives.

> Forty-seven percent of abused children said a pet provided
> someone to love, as opposed to 29% of regular school stu-
> dents. As one child said, "A pet is important as it gives the
> child something to hold and love when his parents or one par-
> ent doesn't love him."

The special pets of abused children were owned for a shorter
period of time and were more likely to meet a violent death. The
delinquents also had far less support than regular school students
regarding the death of their pets. The lack of support coupled with

the greater incidence of violent pet deaths contributed to a situation in which the abused children could not adequately resolve the death of their pets, the researchers point out.

The pets of institutionalized children were more likely to be abused than the pets of the regular school children, but the abuser was usually someone other than the youth. Subjects who did acknowledge abusing their pets, however, appeared remorseful about doing so. The adolescents reacted with a mixture of anger and sadness when other individuals mistreated their pets and several of the youngsters tried to intervene on behalf of the animal.

The researchers conclude:[13]

> Pets clearly play a prominent part in the lives of abused children. That relationship is characterized by deep feelings of love, care and empathy. What seems to divide those youths who are sadistic to animals from those who are not is the extreme degree of parental abuse. Thus, if we are to prevent child cruelty to animals, we must also prevent cruelty to children.

EFFECT OF RABBITS
ON INSTITUTIONALIZED DELINQUENTS

Since even aggressive youngsters love and value their pets, can caring for a pet reduce or alter aggressive behavior?

Peter G. Santostefano, of the University of Rhode Island, designed a study to determine the impact of pet ownership on aggression in institutionalized adolescents. Following the view of Abraham Maslow, Santostefano describes the pet-owner bond as an actualizing relationship in which the pet is a "significant other," appreciated for itself rather than as a means of status, utility, or emotional support.

Santostefano explains:[14]

> It is easier for many people to establish such an actualizing relationship with an animal, rather than with a person, since

the latter's insecurities, ego defenses and attitudes can be additional barriers to the subject's own barriers. These barriers are absent in a pet facilitating the establishment of a natural unconditional openness and receptivity by the pet.

Thus, youngsters who could develop a close relationship with an animal would be less aggressive because of the emotional support provided by the pet or by the "actualizing relationship" developed with the pet.

Santostefano used 3 groups for his study. The subjects selected were 9 males and 6 females, ranging in age from 12 to 18. They were long-term, institutionalized patients at the Chamberline Unit at the Altobello Youth Center in Meriden, Connecticut. The subjects were assigned to 3 treatment groups: Group A was the pet therapy group; Group B was the baking group, and Group C was the control. During the 6 weeks of the study, staff members monitored all subjects and tallied every aggressive behavior exhibited. Passive-aggressive acts such as not eating and not relating to staff members were also included. Tallying began a week prior to the study to establish a baseline and continued for 7 days after the treatments.

Group A received a pet rabbit that they were instructed to fondle, play with, and care for. The subjects were encouraged to name their pet to foster the close bond between owner and pet, and all of the adolescents did. The subjects had two 45-minute sessions each day with their pets, which were housed off-unit in a building basement. They could play with the rabbits either inside or outside in a fenced-in yard, which resulted in games such as rabbit races and high jumping contests with both rabbits and subjects hopping. At the end of the sessions, staff members supervised the children in feeding and clean-up chores for their pets.

Group B was taken to an off-unit building with a full kitchen where the members could choose an item to bake. Subjects were permitted to eat baked goods to control for the reward and immediate gratification of the pet-subject interaction.

The control group was permitted, during the times the other two groups were in the pet or baking therapy, to go off-ward to the unit store to control for the intrinsic reward of being off-ward. Thus, says Santostefano, behavior changes could be attributed to the particular therapy used, not to its location.

Results of the study indicated a significant decrease in the total number of aggressive actions for the pet therapy group. Statistical analysis also revealed a significant difference in aggressive acts as a condition of treatment: The pet therapy group was significantly less aggressive than the baking group, which was significantly less aggressive than the control group. Further analysis determined that only the pet therapy group showed a tendency to become less aggressive over the 6-week treatment period. Group B exhibited no change, and Group C increased significantly during the course of the study.

A slight increase in aggressive behavior was noted in all groups at the beginning of the study, which Santostefano explains as increased staff vigilance and awareness of aggressive behaviors:[15]

> This heightened staff awareness can also be used to further illustrate the effectiveness of the pet therapy program. Even while the staff reported an increase in the number of aggressive behaviors in Groups 2 and 3 over the four weeks of therapy due to their "heightened awareness" Group 1 showed a marked decrease in its aggressive behaviors. Thus, the therapy seems to have a profound effect in decreasing the aggression of its subjects, even when the staff is diligently looking for any aggressive acts to tally.

Although this study offers some striking support for pet-facilitated therapy, the researcher admits to some problems that could have influenced the results. The staff, he notes, could have learned which subjects were in which group and inadvertently given the pet therapy group fewer tallies. Or they could have overlooked certain aggressive behaviors in that group because they perceived the members as improving.

Santostefano also admits that the youngsters who did not receive pets may have felt unfavored or rejected. These feelings could have resulted in hostility and anger and attributed for the increase in aggressive acts in groups B and C.

Additionally, says the researcher, although the frequency of aggressive acts was tallied, the intensity was not. Thus, a mildly aggressive act such as not eating was given the same weight as for example, hitting someone. Although the frequency of aggression may decrease, the intensity of aggression may not decrease as a result of therapy, he points out.

PERCEPTIONS OF ANIMALS
BY EMOTIONALLY DISTURBED ADOLESCENTS

Lisa Okoniewski, a clinical psychologist specializing in the treatment of adolescents in Philadelphia, analyzed the perceptions of human-animal and human-human relationships by an emotionally disturbed adolescent population.

Following the thinking of Searles[16] and Sullivan,[17] who postulated that adolescence is the developmental period when the focus of affection becomes a person rather than animate nature, Okoniewski[18] suggests that emotionally disturbed youngsters, being developmentally arrested, may not yet have altered their focus. Thus, they may still prefer relationships with animals to relationships with humans.

She chose 35 adolescents (21 males and 14 females) between the ages of 15 and 20 years from the population of a residential treatment center in a rural area outside Philadelphia, Pennsylvania. In addition to interviews and rating scales, the research asked the subjects to complete two drawings, one that included a person and an animal and one that included two people. The subjects were also asked to write two stories related to their drawings.

Assuming that the figure drawn reflects in some degree the individual's concept of self, the drawings can be analyzed by equating physical proximity with emotional distance, explains Okoniewski. For example, figures far apart can indicate fear, alienation, or rejection. The story length reflects verbal fluency, which is related to the individual's cooperation or resistance to the task. Thus, a lengthy story would suggest a positive attitude, and a brief response a negative or depressive one.

Okoniewski's results indicated that the subjects used significantly more words in their stories about people and animals than in those about people alone. Additionally, 57% placed the animal-human pairing closer than the human-human pairing. Fifty-seven percent rated the animal-human relationship as more positive than the human-human relationship, and 49% indicated that the animal-human pairing was more active.

Analyzing the interview data reveals similar trends, says Okoniewski. All of the subjects reported that they liked animals.

Several of the students anthropomorphized animals and attributed to them human feelings and emotions. Others enjoyed play and recreation with animals and had fun caring for their needs. Still others saw animals as part of a grander view.

Benefits attributed to human-animal interaction were numerous. Seventy-seven percent cited communication and understanding; 47% believed that a relationship with an animal increases responsibility and affords an outlet for affection. Several subjects thought that relationships with animals facilitate relationships with humans.

Okoniewski explains:[19]

> In general, relations between humans and animals were perceived more positively and more actively than relationships with other people. . . . Based on these results, additional support appears to be given for the growing awareness and recognition that animals are significant beings in the overall schema of humans' relatedness to the world around them. This appears to be especially true for emotionally disturbed adolescents, who may not yet have developed the capacity to relate meaningfully to human beings. Thus, animals may serve to help these individuals within a therapeutic milieu to become more related to the world beyond themselves.

Based on the results of this study, Okoniewski postulated that emotionally disturbed adolescents would perceive human-animal relationships and human-human relationships differently than normal youngsters.

With Zivan,[22] she compared 50 adolescents from a residential treatment program who demonstrated severe emotional or behavioral problems with 50 "normal" adolescents living at home or in the community.

Evaluation methods included projective stories and drawings, semantic differential rating scales, and objective and subjective interview questions. The researchers found the following results:

— Emotional distance is determined by the distance between figures in the drawings. They found no significant differences in the two groups between the human-human figures and human-animal figures.
— Degree of resistance or fear was measured by the number of words in the stories, i.e., the more words, the less fear. Surprisingly, the emotionally disturbed youngsters, in general, gave longer stories than the normal group. Both groups, however, approached human-animal relationships with less fear than human-human relationships.
— Human-animal relationships were rated significantly higher than interpersonal relationships for both groups. Human-animal relationships were evaluated more positively than human-human relationships, and human-animal interactions were regarded overall as more active than interpersonal relationships.
— The emotionally disturbed adolescents did perceive human-animal relationships even more positively than the normal group, but as the researchers point out; "Perhaps the most significant finding of this study is the undeniable importance of animals to both groups of adolescents regardless of their degree of normality/pathology."

The animals functioned at least in part as surrogate friends, parents, and siblings, and Okoniewski and Zivan noted that for some youngsters the pet supplemented family love, while for others, it replaced it:[21]

Especially for the emotionally disturbed group, animals become transitional objects which had the potential to enhance relationships with human beings. In other words, the bond operates as a kind of practice ground which eventually enables them to become more emotionally involved with others. This attachment provides a sense of kinship and intimacy rather than promoting feelings of isolation and withdrawal. Both groups of adolescents also claimed that interaction with animals could have a positive effect on their reaction to themselves. Thus, the bond had the capacity to alleviate depression, decrease feelings of loneliness, and heighten self-esteem by creating a feeling of being needed, accepted, and loved.

REFERENCES

1. Robin, M. & ten Bensel, R. (1985). Pets and the socialization of children. In M. B. Sussman (Ed.), *Pets and the family* (pp. 63–78). New York: The Haworth Press.
2. Fogle, B. (1983). *Pets and their people*. New York: The Viking Press.
3. Kidd, A. H. & Kidd, R. M. (1985). Children's attitudes toward their pets. *Psychological Reports, 57*, 15–31.
4. Peacock, C. A. (1984, October). The role of the therapist's pet in initial psychotherapy sessions with adolescent males. Paper presented at the annual meeting of the Delta Society, Texas A & M University, College Station, TX.
5. Robin, M. et al. (1985). op. cit. p. 69.
6. Robin, M., ten Bensel, R. W., Quigley, J., & Anderson, R. K. (1983). Childhood pets and the psychosocial development of adolescents. In A. H. Katcher and A. M. Beck (Eds.), *New perspectives on our lives with companion animals*. Philadelphia: University of Pennsylvania Press.
7. Hellman, D. & Blackman, N. (1966). Enuresis, firesetting, and cruelty to animals: A triad predictive of adult crime. *American Journal of Psychiatry, 122*, 1431–1435.
8. Tapia, F. (1971). Children who are cruel to animals. *Child Psychiatry and Human Development, 2*, 70–77.
9. Justice, B., Justice, R., & Kraft, I. A. (1974). Early warning signs of violence: Is a triad enough? *American Journal of Psychiatry, 131*(4), 457–459.
10. Felthous, A. (1980). Aggression against cats, dogs and people. *Child Psychiatry and Human Development, 10*, 169–177.
11. Kellert, S. & Felthous, A. (1983). Childhood cruelty toward animals among criminals and non-criminals. Unpublished manuscript. Cited in Robin, M. et al. (1985).
12. Robin, M., ten Bensel, R. W., Quigley, J., & Anderson, K. (1984). Abused children and their pets. In R. K. Anderson, B. L. Hart, & L. A. Hart (Eds.), *The pet connection* (pp. 111–118). Minneapolis: University of Minnesota Press.
13. Ibid.
14. Santostefano, P. G. (1984). The effect of a pet therapy program on the aggressive behavior of institutionalized adolescents. Unpublished manuscript.
15. Ibid.
16. Searles, H. (1960). *The nonhuman environment*. New York: International Universities Press.
17. Sullivan, H. (1953). *The interpersonal theory of psychiatry*. New York: Norton.

18. Okoniewski, L. (1984). A comparison of human-human and human-animal relationships. In R. K. Anderson, B. L. Hart, & L. A. Hart (Eds.), *The pet connection* (pp. 251–259). Minneapolis: University of Minnesota Press.

19. Ibid.

20. Okoniewski, L. & Zivan, M. (1985, October). Adolescents' perceptions of human-animal relationships. Paper presented at the Annual meeting of the Delta Society, Denver, CO.

21. Ibid.

CHAPTER 10

Pets in the Family

We have reviewed the impact of a pet on the physiology, psychology, and social behavior of individuals of various age groups and of differing mental and physical health statuses. But what is the impact of a pet on the family system? Does it occupy a similar or unique role in the family environment? Are there characteristics that define pet-owning families, and if so, do these factors have anything to say about the families' general well-being?

These are just a few of the questions posed by human-animal bond investigators, and the research to date suggests that the pet's place in the family is as rich and complex as its place in the life of the individual.

PETS IN NORMAL FAMILIES

Pets are immensely popular in the United States, residing in approximately 60% of American homes.[1] And the majority of pet owners consider their animal companions to be an important and valuable member of the family.

In a study of 500 pet owners, veterinarian Victoria Voith[2] found that 99% of the sample considered their dog a member of the family. This resulted in such behaviors as allowing the dog to sleep with a family member (56%), sharing tidbits from the meal (64%), sharing their snacks with the dog (86%), and celebrating the dog's birthday (54%). The substantial bonding exhibited by these families may at least in part be attributed to the fact that they were all clients from a major veterinary referral service.

In her study of the characteristics of pet relationships in 60 families, Ann Ottney Cain[3] found that 87% considered their pet a family member, and 36% thought of the pet as a person. Eighty-one percent of the sample believed their pets were sensitive to the moods of other family members and some noted that the pet displayed such physical symptoms as diarrhea and loss of appetite when the family was stressed or in conflict.

In a sample of 896 military families, Thomas Catanzaro[4] discovered that even in this highly mobile unit, in which a pet may be a transitory member, 98% of the sample considered their pet a family member or close friend. Seventy-two percent of the sample said the pet usually to always had people status, and 39% said it always did. Seventy-five percent said the pet was of great importance to the family at all times; other significant times noted were during the temporary absence of a spouse (73%), during free time (71%), during childhood (70%), during lonely or depressed times (68%), when children were absent (53%) or if the marriage was childless (59%), during illness or death of other family members (52%), during crises, separation or divorce (50%), during relocation (48%), during adolescence (45%), and during unemployment (36%).

Companionship is the number one benefit of pet ownership as cited by pet owners and nonowners alike.[5] Australian researchers Salmon and Salmon[6] found in a survey of 308 Melbourne households containing 1,063 people that divorced, separated, widowed, and childless people — those who do not have access to a normal family network — have more of their needs satisfied by pet dogs than do dog owners with families. For example, childless dog owners described their dogs more positively than did dog owners with children, who seemed more aware of the problems of dog ownership. However, according to Schneider and Vaida,[7] pet ownership is most prevalent among married couples with children, the very population that has the most visible human companionship.

Acquisition of a family pet may be viewed as a means to enhance the family unit. Cantanzaro[8] found that 70% of the military families said there was an increase in family happiness and fun after getting a pet, 60% reported increased affection around the pet, and 52% said the family spent more time together after getting a pet. Bridger[9] noted that a pet can enable a family to widen its social network and that an animal can make a family setting a safer place to test out love, hate, preferences, rivalries, independence, cooperation, and destructive and creative feelings. Levinson[10,11] said that the pet's role in the family was a function of the family structure dependent upon the emotional strengths and weaknesses of the family members, the emotional undercurrents in the family, and the social climate of the family itself. A pet can function as surrogate child, spouse, sibling, significant other, friend, confidant—even, as Veevers[12] points out, a surrogate enemy.

In spite of the pet's varied and unique role in the family, however, its place there is not necessarily assured, as indicated by the 15 million plus euthanasias annually.[13] There are simply not enough caring homes to absorb the number of dogs and cats born and subsequently surrendered or abandoned. One study by Arkow and Dow[14] surveyed 13 shelters to ascertain characteristics of the "broken bond" in 918 owner-surrendered dogs. The typical unwanted dog cost nothing, was kept about 17 months, and was acquired for emotional reasons (to give it a home, for the children) rather than utilitarian reasons (hunting, for example). Life-style changes, such as moving and divorce, and behavioral problems were the most frequently cited reasons for abandoning the pet. A study by Bedell[15] of widowers and their children found that pets tended to be disposed of as a luxury a motherless family could not afford.

Life-style changes, even positive ones, are stressful, and these findings indicate that pets may be discarded at the very time when psychologically their owners need them most. Cantanzaro's[16] military families believed pets to be extremely important during relocation because the pet served as a support stabilizer during the move. Seventy-two percent of his sample said they would personally take or have their pet shipped to a new home within the country, and almost 50% said they would take or ship their pet to a new overseas home.

Cantanzaro's families were asked a hypothetical question, but a 1985 study by Lynn Anderson[17] asked 184 military families recently transferred to Hawaii what they had actually done with their pet and what impact it had on the family. It should be pointed out that although Hawaii is not a foreign transfer, the practical aspects of this state's quarantine (120 days at a total cost of about $500) cause inconvenience far beyond that of a usual stateside move.

Anderson found that although 98.8% of pet-owning families considered their pet a member of the family, 65.5% of these families had left their pet behind. Reasons most often cited were expense and length of quarantine. When asked what effect leaving the pet had had on the family, 96.4% reported long-term or temporary sadness. For those families who brought their pets with them, however, 97% reported greater family happiness because of the decision. Anderson stratified his sample into junior enlisted personnel, senior enlisted personnel, and officers. Not surprisingly, fewer officers than enlisted personnel left their pets behind. Senior enlisted personnel who left their pets behind cited quarantine as the major reason, whereas junior enlisted personnel cited expense as the most important consideration.

PETS IN ABUSIVE FAMILIES

The role of pets in the abusive family is not clear. Lenoski[18] observed that only 3.7% of abusive parents had a significant pet as a child, compared with 96.1% of the controls. Disbrow[19] compared abusing and nonabusing families and not only found fewer pets in the abusive families, but also noted that abusive parents were more likely to have had a bad attachment to a pet as a child. However, in a study of 100 violent offenders and a control group of 75 noncriminal males, ten Bensel and colleagues[20] found no difference in special pets between the groups. Violent offenders were more likely to have a dog and to have an "atypical" pet (see Chapter 13, "Prison Pets"). This finding is supported by the Robin et al.[21] study, in which 99% of institutionalized adolescents reported very positive feelings about their pets (see Chapter 9).

Recently Sheldon, Levy, and Shott[22] examined the distribution of pets in a sample of children suffering from child abuse or neglect. They obtained their sample of 917 from children admitted to the Emergency Department of Mount Sinai Hospital Medical Center during a 6-month period. Upon evaluation they divided their sample into three groups: acute or chronic illness (552, or 60%); accidental, unintentional injury (303, or 33%); and victims of child abuse or neglect (62, or 7%). Twenty-nine percent (267) of families owned pets, with cats (59%) being the most frequently owned pet followed by dogs (45%).

The researchers found no significant differences in pet ownership among the three groups, although abusive families were less likely to own pets (23% owned pets, compared with 30% in groups 1 and 2). They found, however, a significant difference in pattern of attachment exhibited by sleeping with the pet. None of the abused children slept with the pet, but 6% of Group 1 and 9% of Group 2 did. The pet in abusive families was most likely to sleep outside or in the basement and not with the family. Interestingly, only 7% of the children from all the pet-owning families slept with the pet, a much lower figure than has been found in other studies.

The researchers found no significant group differences in families in which the child was the primary caretaker of the pet. They did find some significant differences in type of pet owned. No abusive families owned birds, while 7% of Group 1 and 6% of Group 2 owned them. Families in Group 1 were significantly more likely to own cats than families in Group 2.

Say the researchers:[23]

> It appears, that the mere presence of a pet in the home (or access to a pet) does not by itself prevent child abuse or neglect. Attachment to a pet may indicate the level of empathy present in a family and the capacity of the family members for emotional bonding.

The finding that no abused children sleep with pets appears again to indicate that what is important is not so much the presence of an animal, per se, but the person's relationship to it. Certainly, families that allow the pet to sleep with the child would be more likely to consider the pet a family member rather than a thing or an object. Most children who are attached to their pets express a desire to sleep with them, and a family that allows this may be more oriented to the child's needs and less likely to be abusive.

There are several possible reasons for the small percentage of children who slept with pets. Perhaps children in Group 1 who were acutely or chronically ill were not considered well enough to sleep with a pet. This may also explain why the families in this group were more likely to own a cat, which is a less demanding pet than a dog. Overall, one must consider that the parents were being interviewed after seeking emergency hospital treatment for their children. In some circles it is considered unhygienic or unsanitary to sleep with an animal. The parent who were already concerned about the perception of themselves as proper parents might simply not have admitted that the pet slept with the child.

The absence of pet birds among abusive families is an intriguing finding. Kidd, Kelley, and Kidd[24] characterize bird owners as social, altruistic, contented, courteous, and nurturant. Certainly, we would hardly associate these traits with an abusive parent, and it may be that the psychological mechanisms that result in bird ownership are not compatible with abusive actions. Or it may be that caged birds, which are fragile and easily succumb to chills and poor diets, simply do not last long in abusive households.

PETS IN
DYSFUNCTIONAL FAMILIES

Cecelia Soares[25] points out that the role of the companion animal varies according to the function or dysfunction of the family unit. I know of no study similar to the Sheldon et al. research that investigates the pet distribution and attachment patterns of disturbed families; however, the research clearly indicates that the pet occupies a significant role in family pathology.

Both the Cain and Catanzaro studies of normal families point out that members believe their pets are sensitive to the family environment, sometimes to the point of "acting out" feelings displayed in the family. In the dysfunctional family, this empathetic relationship between pet and human owners is emphasized. Soares cites a case in which the abnormal behavior of the family dog was the presenting sign of the family's dysfunction.[26] In observing schizophrenic families, Jungreis and Speck[27] and Speck[28] report that the pet's behavior was a reflection of the "feeling-tone" of the family, even to the point that if the family was angry at the therapist, the pet appeared to be also. Speck[29] also notes that the pet can exhibit illness either with or instead of another family member, and may even die as a result.

Sometimes the pet is a tragic victim of the family pathology. Levinson[30] describes a young woman who shot herself after her parents ordered her to kill her dog as punishment for a sexual transgression. Rynearson[31] describes a young woman who had a phobia of her parents and siblings, and turned to her cat as confidant. The girl's mother beat the animal to death with a shovel because it had scratched the sister, and then told the young woman it was really her fault because she had not watched her pet closely enough. Both researchers have noted that disturbed children often become abnormally attached to their pets. Summit[32] has observed that child abusers commonly threaten a child's pet as a means to keep the child quiet, and Robin and ten Bensel[33] suggest that mental health practitioners should routinely ask young people if anyone has threatened to harm their pets.

TRIANGLED PETS: THE BOWEN MODEL

The Bowen family systems theory perceives emotional disorder as dysfunction in the family emotional system. The basic building block of any social system is the triangle, a three-person system (or a system of two persons and a thing or issue that takes on emotional significance). According to Murray Bowen,[34] a two-person system is innately unstable and immediately begins to form a series of interlocking triangles, which in the family system include not only the nuclear family but the extended families of both the husband and wife. Essentially, the triangle forms when the tension in the two-person system exceeds a certain level; when this occurs, one or the other of the parties will attempt to ease the tension by bringing in a third party (triangling).

The triangle model, thus, describes how family members relate to one another, and reflects distinct patterns. For example, during calm periods there is closeness between two people and a third, more distant, less secure person outside. The preferred position is to be inside. However, in times of stress the role changes, and the preferred position is to be outside the sphere of tension.

Pets, of course, can be triangled just like humans. Cain[35] observes that pet triangles usually provide a display of affection, anger, or distancing. In her own study, for example, she found that some family members would talk to the pet within hearing distance of other family members, thus conveying information indirectly, at a distance. Other examples of triangling include family members yelling at or even hitting the pet instead of another family member, or using the pet as a diversion during a crisis. In several instances the pet was viewed as actively intervening to dissolve the tension. Respondents remarked that the pet would act silly or cute, and people would laugh or forget they were angry; or the pet would actively seek love and affection during these periods and thus defuse the tension. Still other families said that they would deliberately remove the animal from the scene of the conflict because the pet got upset or would try to intervene.

Family therapist Alan Entin [36] says that triangles can be observed in family photographs by studying the physical closeness of the individuals to measure the emotional closeness. For example, he says:

> one snapshot showed a lawyer hugging his two children tightly, at a distance from his wife. The dog was in an affectionate embrace with her. A few months later, to everyone's shock, the "happy couple" split up. He won a legal battle for joint custody of the youngsters: the dog stayed with the wife.

Entin describes an example of a pet inhibiting a couple's sexual activity: [37]

> The pet's role in the family is to help the couple connect with each other, that is, they relate to each other through and about the animal, yet do not relate to each other in a person to person manner and so maintain their distance from each other. For example, when the dog slept in the bed between the couple, their lovemaking was limited by the presence of the dog. And, when the dog died suddenly, their distance and emptiness, previously dealt with through focusing on the dog, rose to the foreground and the couple separated shortly thereafter.

This particular role of the pet may be more prevalent than common sense might dictate; Ruby [38] reports that 65% of animals sleep in their owner's bedroom, 45% in the owner's bed.

PETS IN FAMILY THERAPY

Because the pet-owner relationship is nonverbal and entirely at the discretion of the human partner, the owner has much more freedom to express his or her unconscious aspects than he or she does in a person-person relationship, says psychoanalyst Leonard Simon.[39] According to Simon:

> Pets give people a chance to feel certain things that they cannot allow themselves consciously to feel. Pets give people a chance to keep themselves from experiencing new wounds. Our spouses will eventually complain if we persist in treating them like some person out of our past. Our pets will not only not complain, they may even thrive on a relationship that would be impossible for a sensible person. . . .
>
> Much of human behavior is inherently self-regulating. Whatever our foibles happen to be we have reasonable means — when we play them out with other people — of correcting them. Unfortunately, because pets are unable to provide people with this kind of feedback, circular and self-fulfilling maladaptive processes are too often set in motion.

An example, says Simon, is the pet's proclivity to bring out the child in the adult, which is fine, he says, as long as it is temporary. "The trouble comes when a childlike way of dealing with the world becomes a stable feature of a person's style. In my experience there is always a significant risk of this when an individual adopts a pet."[40]

A 1984 survey, Horn and Meer[41] examined the psychological aspects of pet ownership. Generally, the results indicated that pet owners thought better of themselves and felt less depressed and less isolated than nonowners. However, the report also compared owners who mildly humanized their pets with those who excessively humanized their pets, and found that less humanization was a more positive indicator. Owners who highly humanized their pets felt less positive about themselves, were more likely to be lonely, to be depressed, to lack a sense of accomplishment, to have less fun, and to enjoy life less. Additionally, these owners were more likely to deal with their depression by withdrawing from others and turning toward their pets.

Wessells[42] sees the pet's role in the family as one of many possibilities in a continuum:

> On the one hand the pet owner comes from a balanced family system in which the pet is incorporated. This end of the continuum humanizes the pet to some degree. Members of their family are able to relate well to each other. They are successful, have a strong sense of self-esteem, and have pets as an additive element that helps enhance their lives. The other end of the pet-owning continuum is characterized by an out-of-balance family system in which functioning is marginal. An unhealthy focus on the pet animal may serve to compensate a failing relationship system. Here, humanization of the pet can be extreme. Usually the family member most emotionally involved with the pet acts out most of the humanizing of the pet. This family member is often the one who experiences the most difficulty relating to other family members. The pet may come to serve a focal point in family life to band the family together or serve as the focus of conflict. The well-being of pets in these families may take on exaggerated significance since the pet has become highly significant in maintaining emotional stability in the family.
>
> Wessells illustrates how the human/pet relationship can be used as a diagnostic tool. He recounts the case of a suicidally depressed mother who could focus on her husband's abusiveness to her children only after she described how abusive he had been to their pet dogs.[43]

The pet can also serve as an intermediary between the patient and the therapist, says Wessells. He cites the case of a depressed woman whose therapist helped her to understand that the warmth and happiness she experienced with her pet dog could be evoked in her relationship with her husband.[44]

A pet can be used as a metaphor, says Wessells.[45] Whether the pet is infantilized, made a sibling, friend, or parent, the interactive patterns involving the pet often mirror those of human relationships. Using the pet relationship as a means of understanding family dynamics often provides an avenue into guarded relationship issues that patients find easier to discuss around the pet than each other.

Wessells cites an example of the pet used as metaphor. A tough, uncommunicative, runaway young teenager began to discuss with her therapist the issues of affection and tenderness only after describing the meaning of the caption on her embroidery, which read: When no one else loves you, your dog will.[46]
Wessells concludes:[47]

A final consideration for clinical uses of pets in therapy, is through prescribing of pet animals to aid patients in coping with specific situations. It is of paramount importance in these circumstances that patients are interested in pet animals and can responsibly care for them if they follow through on the therapist's suggestion. Pets are frequently suggested to aid in coping with losses. Examples of specific situations include: death of a spouse or parent, divorce, "empty nest" issues, latch key children, the elderly or persons coping with loss of function. It is important in these circumstances that the relationship with the newly acquired pet be processed in therapy to help the patient address the emotional issues associated with the loss.

REFERENCES

1. Cain, A. O. (1985). Pets as family member. In M. B. Sussman (Ed.), *Pets and the family* (pp. 5–10). New York: The Haworth Press.
2. Voith, V. L. (1983, June). Behavior, attitudes and interactions of families with their dogs. Paper presented at the Conferences on the Human-Animal Bond, Irvine, CA, and Minneapolis, MN. Cited in C. J. Soares (1985). The companion animal in the context of the family system. In M. B. Sussman (Ed.), *Pets and the family* (pp. 49–62). New York: The Haworth Press.
3. Cain, A. O. (1983). A study of pets in the family system. In A. H. Katcher & A. M. Beck (Eds.), *New perspectives on our lives with companion animals*. Philadelphia: University of Pennsylvania Press.
4. Catanzaro, T. E. (1984). The human-animal bond in military communities. In R. K. Anderson, B. L. Hart, & L. A. Hart (Eds.), *The pet connection* (pp. 341–347). Minneapolis: University of Minnesota.
5. Vogel, L. E., Quigley, J. S., & Anderson, R. K. (1983). A study of perceptions and attitudes towards pet ownership. In A. H. Katcher & A. M. Beck

(Eds.) *New perspectives on our lives with companion animals*. Philadelphia: University of Pennsylvania Press.

6. Salmon, P. W. & Salmon, I. M. (1983). Who owns who? Psychological research into the human-pet bond in Australia. In A. H. Katcher & A. M. Beck (Eds.) *New perspectives on our lives with companion animals*. Philadelphia: University of Pennsylvania Press.

7. Schneider, R. & Vaida, M. L. (1975). Survey of canine and feline populations: Alameda and Contra Costa Counties, California. *Journal of the American Veterinary Medical Association, 166*, 481–486.

8. Catanzaro, T. E. (1984). op. cit.

9. Bridger, H. (1976). The changing role of pets in society. *Journal of Small Animal Practice, 17*, 1–8.

10. Levinson, B. M. (1964). Pets: A special technique in child therapy. *Mental Hygiene, 48*, 243–248.

11. Levinson, B. M. (1969). *Pet-oriented child psychotherapy*. Springfield, IL: Charles C. Thomas.

12. Veevers, J. E. (1985). The social meaning of pets: Alternate roles for companion animals. In M. B. Sussman (Ed.), *Pets and the family* (pp. 11–30). New York: The Haworth Press.

13. Knight, S. T. & Knight, J. A. (1984, October). Ethical and value issues in the human-companion animal bond. Paper presented at the annual meeting of the Delta Society, Texas A & M University, College Station, TX.

14. Arkow, P. S. & Dow, S. (1984). The ties that do not bind: A study of the human-animal bonds that fail. In R. K. Anderson, B. L. Hart, & L.A. Hart (Eds.), *The pet connection* (pp. 348–354). Minneapolis: University of Minnesota.

15. Bedell, J. W. (1971–1972). Role reorganization in the one-parent family: Mother absent due to death. *Sociological Focus, 5*(2), 84–100.

16. Catanzaro, T. E. (1984). op. cit.

17. Anderson, L. J. (1985). The pet in the military family at transfer time: It is no small matter. In M. B. Sussman (Ed.), *Pets and the family* (pp. 205–222). New York: The Haworth Press.

18. Lenoski, E. F. (1984). Personal communication. Cited in ten Bensel et al.

19. Disbrow, M. (1984). Personal communication. Cited in ten Bensel et al.

20. ten Bensel, R. W., Ward, D. A., Kruttschnitt, C., Quigley, J., & Anderson, R. K. (1984). Attitudes of violent criminals toward animals. In R. K. Anderson, B. L. Hart, & L. A. Hart (Eds.), *The pet connection* (pp. 309–318). Minneapolis: University of Minnesota.

21. Robin, M., ten Bensel, R. W., Quigley, J., & Anderson, R. K. (1984). Abused children and their pets. In R. K. Anderson, B. L. Hart, & L. A. Hart (Eds.), *The pet connection* (pp. 111–118). Minneapolis: University of Minnesota.

22. Sheldon, S. H., Levy, H. B., & Shott, S. (1984, October). The distribution of pets and the pet attachment patterns in a sample of victims of child abuse and neglect. Paper presented at the annual meeting of the Delta Society, Texas A & M University, College Station, TX.

23. Ibid.

24. Kidd, A. H., Kelley, H. T., & Kidd, R. M. (1983). Personality character-istics of horse, turtle, snake and bird owners. *Psychological Reports, 52,* 719–729. Also in R. K. Anderson, B. L. Hart, & L. A. Hart (Eds.). (1984). *The pet connection* (p. 200–206). Minneapolis: University of Minnesota.

25. Soares, C. J. (1985). The companion animal in the context of the family system. In M. B. Sussman (Ed.), *Pets and the family* (pp. 49–62). New York: The Haworth Press.

26. Holland, J. M. & Perlmutter, M. (1983, June). A case study of a dysfunc-tional family system with the family dog behavior abnormality as the presenting sign. Paper presented at the Conferences on the Human–Animal Bond, Irvine; CA and Minneapolis, MN. Cited in Soares, C. J. (1985). op. cit.

27. Jungreis, J. E. & Speck, R. V. (1965). The island family. In A. S. Fried-man (Ed.), *Psychotherapy for the whole family in home and clinic.* New York: Springer.

28. Speck, R. V. (1965). The transfer of illness phenomena in schizophrenic families. In A. S. Friedman (Ed.), *Psychotherapy for the whole family in home and clinic.* New York: Springer.

29. Ibid.

30. Levinson, B. M. (1969). op. cit.

31. Rynearson, E. K. (1978). Humans and pets and attachment. *British Jour-nal of Psychiatry, 133,* 550-555.

32. Summit, R. (1983). The child sexual abuse accommodation syndrome. *Child Abuse and Neglect, 7,* 181.

33. Robin, M. & ten Bensel, R. (1985). Pets and the socialization of children. In M. B. Sussman (Ed.), *Pets and the family* (pp. 63–78). New York: The Ha-worth Press.

34. Bowen, M. (1971). Family and family group therapy. In H. Kaplan & B. Sadock (Eds.), *Comprehensive Group Psychotherapy.* Baltimore: Williams & Wilkins.

35. Cain, A. O. (1983). op. cit.

36. Entin, A. D. (1983, August). Pets, photos and family theory: Triangles in the family. Paper presented at the Division 42 Symposium: The Extended Family Pet: Psychology of the Human/Companion Animal Bond at the Annual Conven-tion of the American Psychological Association, Anaheim, CA.

37. Entin, A. D. (1984, August). The pet focused family: A systems theory perspective. Paper presented at the Annual Convention of the American Psycho-logical Association, Toronto, Ontario, Canada.

38. Ruby, J. (1982, summer). Images of the family: The symbolic implica-tions of animal photography. *Phototherapy, 3*(2G), 2–7.

39. Simon, L. J. (1984). The pet trap: Negative effects of pet ownership on families and individuals. In R. K. Anderson, B. L. Hart, & L. A. Hart (Eds.), *The pet connection* (pp. 226–240). Minneapolis: University of Minnesota Press.

40. Ibid.

41. Horn, J. & Meer, J. (1984, August). The pleasure of their company. *Psychology Today*, (pp. 52–57).

42. Wessells, D. T., Jr. (1984, August). The psychology of pet ownership. Paper presented at the 92nd Annual Convention of the American Psychological Association, Toronto, Ontario, Canada.

43. Ibid.

44. Ibid.

45. Ibid.

46. Ibid.

47. Ibid.

CHAPTER 11

Pets and the Elderly

Animals are as important to the elderly as they are to youngsters and adolescents. Says Bustad:[1]

> Many older people have discovered that animal companions satisfy some of their greatest needs. Pets restore order to their lives; provide a more secure grasp of reality; and link their owners to a community of caring, concern, sacrifice and intense emotional relationships. When older people withdraw from active participation in daily human affairs, the nonhuman environment in general, and animals in particular, can become increasingly important. Animals have boundless capacity for acceptance, adoration, attention, forgiveness and unconditional love. Although the potential for significant benefits to a variety of people exists through association with companion animals, the potential seems greatest in the elderly, for whom the bond with animal companions is perhaps stronger and more profound than at any other age.

Considerable evidence for the therapeutic value of companion animals has come from the anecdotal accounts of nursing home volunteers and staff who noticed the tremendous positive effect of animals on their elderly residents. When friendly, trained dogs mingle with the patients, the results are often astonishing. Both staff and volunteers report numerous instances in which usually uninterested patients seem to gain a new interest in life after visiting with the dogs. Some nonverbal patients who have maintained their silence for months begin to speak after interacting with the animals, and patients who were unwilling to get out of bed and participate in activities become mobile and alert when the dogs come.[2]

Visiting pet programs are novel only in the tremendous upsurge and wholehearted endorsement they have received in recent years. Rebecca Tansil, a poodle breeder and herself an octogenarian, is a volunteer with both Therapy Dogs International and the Baltimore-based Pets on Wheels. She says she has been visiting institutions with her friendly powder puffs for over 50 years. Still, as recently as 1970, Levinson,[3] speaking of the tremendous need of the elderly to give and receive affection and companionship wrote: "Shocking as it may sound, what I am about to recommend is the introduction of pets into the nursing home as part of a carefully planned and structured method of therapy for the aged."

Fortunately, the idea is not nearly so shocking today as the concept of visiting pets, institution mascots, even personal pets for patients becomes more and more acceptable. In 1982, almost 1.5 million[4] persons were housed in geriatric institutions, and the number is expected to be 2.4 million by the end of the century.[5] Yet patient/staff ratios have been reported as high as 30 to 1.[6]

According to Robert Andrysco, originator of Companion Animal Services in Columbus, Ohio:[7]

> In order to cope with these increasing figures, nursing and retirement homes have begun to develop new means of care and new therapies, aimed at lessening the burden of the staff while maintaining a high quality of care for the residents. Traditional care is seen as detrimental in that residents are expected to be sick and fulfill a passive role. The lack of demands on the residents has been demonstrated to lead to physical and psychological deterioration and does not provide for the learning of new skills and activities. It has become apparent that the elements of the physical environment must be changed and utilized as therapeutic agents. Many geriatric facilities have reported changing their physical environments to encourage socialization between residents and self-management within residents.

> Companion animals can be utilized in nursing-retirement communities to relieve residents' feelings of loneliness, depression and boredom. Individuals have also exhibited dramatic improvement in their ability to interact and communi-

cate with other residents and staff. These beneficial effects
have resulted in a decreased staff work-load as well as an improved cost-benefit ratio.

The dramatic impact a companion animal can make on an elderly
disabled person is described by Brickel:[8]

> Mr. J. was an average patient on the long-term, total care
> unit where I worked. This 75-year-old male, a victim of Or-
> ganic Brain Syndrome, stared vacantly into space, hour after
> hour, wherever he was placed by the nursing staff. He pre-
> sented no behavioral problems, but the rudimentary self-care
> behaviors we acquire early in life had been lost by Mr. J., a
> consequence of gradual brain deterioration. Dressing, eating,
> bathing, all were duties which could be carried out only with
> the aid of dedicated nursing staff.
>
> Communication with this man seemed out of the question.
> In the footsteps of other staff I had carried out lengthy mono-
> logues with Mr. J., hoping to establish some degree of verbal
> contact. To no avail. I was consistently greeted with silence
> and two soft almond eyes which seemed to look through me.
>
> Yet there were specific behaviors which I could not recon-
> cile with Mr. J's overall behavior pattern. What prompted this
> otherwise low functioning patient to save scraps from his
> meals for two cats kept on the ward? And when I later stood by
> this man with a small pet dog, what neurological activity
> sparked him to tug at the leash of the animal and activate his
> neglected vocal cords in a strained request for "Dog?" Why
> would this patient respond to animals when most other stimuli
> were ignored?
>
> From a clinical standpoint such isolated behaviors appear
> remarkable. And encouraging. If some behaviors consistent
> with the "real world" can be engendered with the presence of
> animals, other behaviors can be generated. But the underlying
> questions are why a person will respond to animals when other
> entreaties at communication fail; when most synaptic passage-
> ways appear to have been erased, why will persons who suffer

the ravages of debilitating functional or organic disorders still respond — and respond appropriately — to animals?

Mr. J. is not an isolated story; in fact, probably more accounts of animal-facilitated therapeutic benefit have been reported about the elderly than any other clinical group. A comprehensive overview of the therapeutic value of animals for older persons is available in Cusack and Smith's *Pets and the Elderly: The Therapeutic Bond.*[9] For the purpose of this volume, what follows is a brief summary of the research.

OUTPATIENT STUDIES

Effect of Caged Birds on Elderly Pensioners

Although organizations such as the San Francisco SPCA and Bustad's People-Pet-Partnership-Program place pets in the private homes of elderly individuals, there are few studies to date that have measured the impact of such placements. One of the earliest and most frequently cited was conducted in 1975 by British researchers Mugford and M'Comisky,[10] who selected 30 elderly outpatient pensioners ranging in age from 75 to 81. They divided their subjects into five groups: two groups received parakeets, two groups received begonias, and a control group received neither. At the onset of the study, a 30-item questionnaire that measured attitudes towards self and others as well as the physical and psychological environment was administered to all participants. The researchers also factored in the presence of a television, theorizing that a pet might be less important to television owners since television does provide interaction with society and could affect the patient's evaluation of his or her loneliness.

Mugford and M'Comisky found that pet ownership had a positive effect on the pensioners' lives, much more so than flowers or television. The subjects reported improved psychological health and more social relations with their neighbors. One subject built an elaborate playpen for the pet, and another taught her bird to talk. As a consequence, she enjoyed frequent visits from neighborhood children.

Effect of Goldfish on Elderly Outpatients

Even a minimal-care pet appears to benefit elderly patients. Clover Gowing[11] assessed the impact of goldfish on clients from home health care agencies by assigning 20 clients to a treatment group that received goldfish and supplies and 13 clients to a control group that received no fish.

Results indicated that although keeping a goldfish had no significant effect on the health and social interaction of the subjects, the patients did develop a degree of attachment to the goldfish. Says Gowing:[12]

> It confirmed that goldfish could serve as pets which provided cognitive stimulation and that interest and responsibility could be sustained over time for frail elderly people. Caregivers perceived the fish-keeping as a diversion which promoted conversation, and for 50% of them, relation with their clients improved.

Effect of an Aquarium on Elderly Individuals

Carol Riddick selected 22 elderly persons living in a low-income housing project in Maryland to participate in a study evaluating the effects of aquarium placement.

Although those who received the aquarium understood that eventually they would take full responsibility for its upkeep, during the first few months of the study tank maintenance was provided. To control for the social effect of the maintenance, Riddick also assigned individuals to a visitor group. A third group received neither visitors nor an aquarium. After 6 months the three groups were analyzed for blood pressure, happiness, anxiety, loneliness, and leisure satisfaction. Results indicated that the aquarium group experienced a significant decrease in diastolic blood pressure and a significant increase in leisure satisfaction, particularly in the aspect of relaxation. The visitor group, however, experienced a significant decrease in overall loneliness. No significant changes for happiness, systolic blood pressure or anxiety were noted for any group.

Perhaps the most unexpected finding is that whereas members of the visitor group experienced much less loneliness, members of the aquarium group, who had the fish at all times and also had the benefit of visitors (via the tank maintenance service) did not. One possible explanation, suggests Riddick, is that when members of the aquarium group had visits, the visits focused on the fish, whereas in the visitor group, the visits focused on the subject. Fish, also, may simply not provide the companionship that a dog or cat does.

Attachment to Pets Among the Elderly

John New[14] interviewed 21 elderly pet owners to measure their level of attachment to their pet and their perceived benefits. He also interviewed 88 nonowners to determine the reasons for not owning a pet. His results found that 95% of the pet owners reported being attached to their pets, and up to 81% of them reported receiving some benefits from the ownership. All the owners mentioned companionship as a major benefit of pet ownership, but 19% admitted their pet was sometimes a burden, and 28% worried about the pet's future.

Thirty percent of the elderly nonowners were bothered that they did not own a pet, and 39% of this group mentioned current housing restrictions as the reason for not owning a pet. Most of these individuals cited companionship as the major reason for wanting a pet. New concludes that elderly owners can be extremely attached to their pets and that denying such individuals the companion of a pet animal can have serious consequences.

INSTITUTIONAL STUDIES

Cat Mascots and the Institutionalized Elderly

There are considerably more studies that measure the impact of resident institutional animals. In 1979 Brickel[15] reviewed the effect of 2 mascot cats who had been on the particular hospital ward for 2 years. He found that most patients enjoyed the cats and a few had a strong interest in them. Even for those patients who were not particularly fond of the cats, no problem resulted.

From his interviews with the staff, Brickel found many benefits attributed to the presence of the cats, with patient responsiveness the one most frequently cited. The cats were the subject of numerous conversations between patients and between patients and staff, and were a point of interest in common. Other benefits included the physical pleasure of stroking the animals, the enhancement of the ward's atmosphere (it was "more like home"), and the incorporation of the animals into the patients' daily reality. This latter effect was expressed by patients' concern and awareness of the cats' health and by the patients' saving of food scraps for the cats.

A Dog in Residence — The JACOPIS Study

In 1981, the research team of Salmon, Salmon, Hogarth-Scott, and Lavelle,[16] with the Caulfield Geriatric Hospital in Melbourne, Australia, and the guidance of JACOPIS (the Joint Advisory Committee on Pets in Society) began the first formal patient-pet interaction program in that country.

Honey, a golden retriever and former guide dog was introduced to the hospital to interact with 60 patients in 2 long-term care wards. The researchers selected patients who were frail, uncommunicative, and nonambulatory, and who had an average age of 80. Preliminary questionnaires were administered to both the staff and patients to measure benefits and problems anticipated. During the 6-month study, the patients were closely monitored both in responses to the dog and in general social, psychological, and physical behaviors. The researchers also administered a questionnaire that measured actual benefits and problems experienced because of the dog at the completion of the study.

Results indicated that Honey's presence promoted a greater joy in living among the patients. Honey inspired increased laughter, happiness, a sense of humor, alertness, responsiveness, an easygoing attitude, enjoyment of life, and an increased incentive to live. Additionally, the presence of the dog resulted in improved relationships between patients and patients and between patients and staff. Honey's presence was something everyone could share, relate to and talk about. The researchers also noted that, on the whole, the positive expectations about the dog (e.g. companionship, love/affection) were not only realized but exceeded, whereas the negative expectations (e.g., barking, smell, mess) were not realized. The researchers also measured the impact of hospital living on Honey and found that, except for a weight gain, no doubt the result of patients feeding her tidbits, her lengthy stint as a hospital dog had no ill effects on her.

Pet-Facilitated Therapy in an Ohio Nursing Home

Robert Andrysco[17] conducted a study at the Westminster Thurber Retirement Community with his therapy dog, Obee. Of 23 residents who interacted with the dog, 15 improved significantly in the areas of activity involvement, verbal communication, conversations about animals, socialization with nonnursing personnel, socialization with other residents, and socialization at mealtime.

Andrysco also reported an extremely dramatic turnaround for an elderly woman who had been delusional and physically and verbally abusive with the staff, whom she had been convinced were trying to hurt her. Eventually she reached out and petted the dog, and this contact provided the impetus for her recovery. After 6–8 months, she became so well-integrated that she helped newcomers to the home adjust to the environment.

"She trusted the dog," explained Andrysco, "then she transferred that trust to me, and eventually to the staff of the home. She was our miracle."[18]

Effect of Wild Bird Feeders on Nursing Home Residents

In a 1983 study of 40 nursing home residents, Banzinger and Roush[19] found that individuals who received a wild bird feeder outside their window experienced greater happiness, life satisfaction, and control and higher activity levels than those who did not. This study, along with the Gowing and Riddick research, suggests that the investment of a small amount of money and minimal upkeep can considerably enrich the lives of elderly individuals.

VISITING PET STUDIES

An enormous amount of anecdotal information, most of it positively glowing, supports the notion that visiting pet programs are valuable. These accounts, however, are often dismissed or at least devalued by many researchers because they did not take place in a controlled and scientifically verifiable milieu. And, to date, the studies attempting to measure the impact of visiting pets, although verifying their value, have not demonstrated the dramatic effects often noted by the volunteers. Nonetheless, *Pets and the Elderly* contains numerous accounts, and even if caution demands that one take them with a grain of salt, there are simply too many from too many different sources to be ignored. At the very least they should provide suggestions for future research and contribute to the credibility of a treatment that is benign, non-invasive, and relatively inexpensive, as the following studies verify.

Effect of Visiting Pets on Group Home Residents

Gloria M. Francis and colleagues[20] at Virginia Commonwealth University conducted a study to determine the value of domestic animal visitation to semi-institutionalized elderly living in group homes. The researchers used two group homes: One was visited once weekly by kittens and puppies and their handlers from a nearby humane shelter; the second home was visited only by humans. Each group was pre- and posttested for eight variables: health self-concept, life satisfaction, psychological well-being, social competence and interest, personal neatness, psychosocial and mental function, and depression.

The residents who interacted with the animals improved in six of the eight areas tested. Only personal neatness and health self-concept were unaffected. Nothing happened to the other group, whose human visitors appeared to stimulate little interest. One resident remarked matter-of-factly: "People come and go."

Effect of Pet Presentations on Nursing Home Residents

Hendy studied the effects of different pet presentations (no pets, stuffed pets, videotaped pets, live pets) on the sociability and health activities of nursing home residents (proximity to others, talking, smiling, being ambulatory, alertness to the surroundings, and eating a variety of foods offered at lunch). Thirteen subjects (9 men, 4 women) whose average age was 73 years participated in the study. Hendy found that live pets were far more effective in eliciting smiles and alert behavior than other pet presentations. The effects lasted over a 4-week period, and female residents seemed more affected by the live pet presentation than were male residents.

Unlike the Francis study, which found human visitors to be of little value, Hendy's study found a positive relationship between the number of people present and such behaviors as smiling and alertness. People, she says, may be an even more effective stimulator than pets. "Perhaps the pet and people effects are additive, with the pets providing a 'conversation piece,' a common experience, or a pleasant reminiscence to discuss with the visitor," she concludes.[22]

Effect of Visiting Pets on Elderly Veterans

Susanne Robb and her colleagues[23] found a puppy to be more effective than either a wine bottle or a plant to stimulate social behavior in a population of elderly male alcoholics institutionalized at a Veterans Administration Hospital. Robb found that the puppy induced appropriate verbalization and a decrease in hostile behaviors. "Invasion of personal space had frequently triggered verbal arguments and physical violence between clients. When the puppy was present, invasion of personal space increased as clients moved to get closer to the puppy, but no hostility resulted."

In a later study, however, Robb[24] found no significant differences in such areas as loneliness, depression, morale, and activity among a group with access to a dog and handler, a group with access to just a human visitor, and a control group. Robb suggests that since all her subjects (male veterans in a long-term care facility) had relatively favorable initial scores, there was little opportunity for the program to effect change.

Effect of Visiting Pets on Severely Impaired Veterans

But severe impairment may also limit the effect of dog therapy. Jendro and Watson[25] studied the effect of interaction with puppies on male veterans in an extended care ward of a Veterans Administration Medical Center. The researchers selected 22 unit-confined men ranging in age from 43 to 85 years. Length of hospitalization ranged in age from 1 to 56 years. Diagnoses consisted of chronic alcoholism (12 subjects), chronic schizophrenia (7 subjects), and Alzheimer's disease (3 subjects).

The patients selected were cognitively impaired; some did not respond to their names, and most were unable to participate in recreational or occupational activities because of their impairment. Socialization and communication were largely absent, and behavior often consisted of ritualistic, nonpurposeful behaviors such as vacant staring and rocking back and forth.

The evaluation measures used were the Nurses Observation Scale for Inpatient Evaluation (NOSIE-80, which measures seven factors: social competence, social interest, personal neatness, cooperation, irritability, manifest psychosis, and psychotic depression) and the Stockton Geriatric Rating Scale (SGRS) which measures severity of impairment, specifically physical disability, apathy, communication failure, and socially irritating behavior.

A third scale, the Behavioral Characteristics Instrument developed by Hunter, Schooler, and Spohn, adapted to suit the needs of the ward, measured purposeful behaviors (such as responding to name or watching TV) versus nonpurposeful behavior (such as sleeping all day or staring vacantly).

The researchers postulated that pet therapy would have the greatest impact on sociability, and rated this separately. Sociability was defined by the researchers as physical contact, gestures, and verbal expressions toward others that are not annoying, disruptive, or harmful.

The researchers designed their study so that each of the 22 subjects served as his own control. They were divided into a pet group, which had contact with 3 or 4 puppies for an hour per week for 5 weeks, and a control group, which did not have access to the puppies. After the 5th week, the groups reversed, the control group becoming the pet group and vice versa.

During the pet group meetings the subjects were placed in a circle surrounding 3 or 4 puppies. The subjects were then allowed to interact with the puppies as they wished. A veterinary technician supervised the puppies and introduced such subjects as to grooming, feeding, and looking at dog books. Some of the patients were so impaired that they had to be instructed how to pet the puppies.

The researchers found that the subjects showed significantly more purposeful behavior during the puppy session than in comparison periods the day before of the day after treatments. However, they found no significant differences in the NOSIE and SGRS interaction effects, which they attribute to the severe mental impairment of the subjects and the small amount of time spent with the puppies. They also note:[26]

> The applicability of standard behavior rating scales when evaluating pet therapy is questionable since companion animals apparently offer enjoyment and possibly improve the quality of life — conditions that were not specifically measured by the instruments used in this study. Perhaps a more continuous environmental stimulation, such as a resident pet, would be of more benefit than periodic contacts when dealing with the chronically ill, confused, geriatric patient.

Effect of Visiting Pets on Wheelchair-Bound Nursing Home Residents

However, a 60–90 minute visit once a week with a friendly dog or cat resulted in significant improvement for the residents of a nursing home in Westchester County, New York. Daniel and Burke[27] studied the effect of pet and volunteer visits on 36 elderly wheelchair-bound residents; they measured selected behaviors before the study, 5 weeks and 10 weeks into the study, and 1 month after the study concluded. Patients improved in areas of socialization, cooperation, responsiveness, activity, and smiling. Several behaviors such as cooperation and responsiveness persisted for a month after the visits ended. The patients initiated more activity on their own, showed an increased alertness and awareness of their surroundings and actively sought the company of other residents. The program was so successful that after its conclusion the nursing home adopted a mascot cat.

Effect of a Visiting Dog on Nursing Home Socialization

Buelt and colleagues[28] from the University of Nebraska selected 17 elderly residents to act as self-controls in a study designed to measure the impact of a friendly canine on socialization among institutionalized elderly. The subjects participated in both a nonpet session and a pet session using an elderly former show champion beagle who was especially appealing and on her own would wander from resident to resident placing her paws in their laps. Many residents would comment on her noticeably grey face, saying: "You are old and grey like me."

The researchers found that although the subjects focused more on the dog than on each other, the total number of interactive behaviors (smile, lean forward, verbalization) increased, and response time to questions shortened.[29]

> It seems that the dog stimulated the residents. One interesting finding was that residents who had been in the treatment session first responded to each other more during the control session than those not previously exposed to the pet. Since groups were randomized, the same persons were not in each group.

The Cornell Companion Animal Project

The Cornell Companion Animals Program (CCAP), which began in 1982, promotes pet visitation and educational programs to nursing homes, day-care centers, Headstart centers, adolescent halfway houses, and institutions for the developmentally disabled and educationally handicapped. It is sponsored by the college's Department of Preventive Medicine, yet is staffed almost entirely by volunteers from Cornell, nearby Ithaca College, and the surrounding community.

To assess the impact of the work, anthropologist Joel Savishinsky[30] and students conducted an anthropological study of the program's effect in 3 nursing homes. The homes were treated as small societies and the researchers involved themselves as participant-observers. The researchers worked alongside CCAP volunteers with their own or borrowed pets, and also studied the institutions when pet visits were not in session.

Savishinsky's findings support Hendy's conjecture; namely, that human contact is at least as important as the animal companionship. He notes, for example, that people who initially might ignore the animals readily interact with the people who bring them, that volunteers and residents develop close ties over a period of time, and that initially reticent patients eventually open up on a wide variety of issues.

Savishinsky describes his main findings in the study:[31]

1. Pets evoke memories from childhood and other life stages that contribute to the integrative process of reminiscing for the elderly.

2. People draw conclusions between human loss and pet loss through which they confront issues of mortality and morality.

3. Animal visits help to counteract the decline of domesticity inherent in institutional life: pets are symbolic and literal embodiments of the more complete domestic experiences that residents once had, and companion animal volunteers help contribute to a family definition of the situation.

4. Visiting pets are associated with animals that residents have had to give up, as well as with the family members currently caring for them. Sessions thus provide opportunities for people to praise, criticize and explore these other domestic ties.

5. When residents' kin visit during the pet sessions, animals help to ease the process of interaction between them and their institutionalized relatives.

Health Risks of Visiting Pet Programs

Finally, although the studies evaluating pets in nursing homes have not conclusively demonstrated that they are the tremendous asset supporters say they are, there is much evidence that they do significantly benefit some patients and probably cause no harm at all.

Stryler-Gordon, Beall, and Anderson[32] conducted a 12-month study of both visiting and live-in pets in 284 Minnesota nursing homes, and found that pets are safer than people in terms of infection and accident risk to residents. None of the homes reported a pet-related allergy or a pet-related infection. Only 18 of the 284 homes reported a total of 19 untoward incidents during the study period, of which only 2 were regarded as serious. Both involved falls with live-in dogs, and both were the result of a violation of the nursing home policy that an attendant be present when a resident walks the dog.

The researchers broke down the data as follows: For every 1,000,000 person-hours of exposure, there are one pet-related untoward incident and 506 untoward incidents unrelated to pets. For every 1,000 nursing home untoward incidents, 4.5 are pet related and 995.5 are not pet related.

Assuming these data are valid for other states, the researchers conclude that the fears concerning pets in nursing homes have no basis in fact.

SURVEY STUDIES

These studies compare elderly pet owners to nonowners and attempt to measure the impact of a companion animal on such conditions as loneliness and happiness.

Differences Between Pet Owners and Nonowners

In 1981 Kidd and Feldman[33] surveyed 104 adults between the ages of 65 and 87 years. The participants — 52 men and 52 women, of whom 51 were pet owners and 53 were not — were asked to complete the Gough and Heilbrun Adjective Check List, which measures such traits as self-confidence, personal adjustment, abasement, deference, and need for succorance.

The researchers found that pet owners checked significantly more favorable adjectives than nonowners. They scored higher on the nurturance scale and lower on both the need for succorance and need for abasement scales. The favorable adjectives checked showed that pet owners were more responsible, more dependable, less egotistical, and less self-centered than nonowners. Their higher nurturance scores indicated that they were more helpful and benevolent. Lower need for succorance scores indicated that the pet owners were more self-sufficient and independent. Lower abasement scores showed that pet people were more optimistic, poised, and productive. There was also a nonsignificant trend for pet owners to score higher on the self-confidence scale.

Although the results of this study suggest significant differences in the psychological health of pet owners and nonowners, the researchers point out that it is not clear whether pet ownership produces the benefits or if psychologically healthier individuals chose pets.

Impact of Pets on Health and Happiness

Connell and Lago[34] interviewed 80 elderly pet owners residing in a rural county in Pennsylvania to ascertain the impact of pets on health and happiness. A favorable attitude toward a pet was, they found, an indicator of happiness, and more important than either social satisfaction or daily activity. The most important factors, however, turned out to be physical health, social behavior, and income. Interestingly, although a favorable attitude toward a pet was a strong indicator of happiness for unmarried people (3rd, after physical health and income), it had a negative impact on married people. That is, married people who had favorable attitudes toward their pets reported more unhappiness. The researchers suggest that the social aspect of pet owning is more important for the unmarried and that the presence of a pet may interfere with marital closeness. A pet's care or upkeep, for example, may be a source of friction between a couple.

Impact of Pets on Health and Happiness of Rural Elderly Women

A somewhat different finding comes from Ory and Goldberg,[35] who, as part of a 5-year study investigating the social factors affecting the health of older women, studied the role of pets in the lives of this group. They interviewed 1,073 married women between the ages of 65 and 75; about 1/3 of the sample had pets.

Pet ownership alone, they found, was not an indicator of happiness. Attachment to the pet, however, was a powerful factor, with women of a high socioeconomic background who were attached to their pets reporting the greatest happiness. Women who were least attached to their pets were the most likely to be unhappy. Geography was also a significant indicator. Pet ownership was associated with greater happiness among urban women, and the researchers suggest that pet ownership has a different meaning for urban and rural populations. They also found that though the elderly were less likely than the general population to be pet owners, they were, on the whole (75%), very attached to them.

Psychological Health of Pet-Owning and Nonowning Veterans

Robb and Stegman[36] surveyed 56 elderly veterans receiving home health services from a Veterans Administration home care program. Her sample, which was predominately male, included 26 pet owners and 30 nonowners. Factors assessed included morale (measured by the Philadelphia Geriatric Center Morale Scale), control of one's life (measured by Rotter's Locus of Control Scale), and variables such as social interaction, mental status, psychological symptoms, physical and instrumental functional ability, diseases, and medications (measured by the Duke University Older Americans Resources and Services Multidimensional Functional Assessment Questionnaire).

Robb found no significant differences between the pet and nonpet groups. Robb assigned clients to a high-bond or low-bond subgroup, depending upon how they answered the question: "Do you prefer pets or people?" Nonowners were asked: "Do you wish you owned a pet?" A subsequent analysis revealed no significant differences between the high-bond and low-bond subjects.

Says Robb:[37]

> Perhaps in living with companion animals on a day-to-day basis, in the absence of crises, no measurable impact exists. When events threaten or result in loss of contact between people and their animals or serve to restore contact after a period of separation or loss, however, this may be the time when measurable impacts occur.

Pet Owners and Loneliness

We intuitively believe pets to be an effective deterrent to loneliness. Francis[38] found that after people, pets are the frequently missed "thing" when the owner is away. However, in a study comparing the levels of loneliness of pet owners and nonowners living in a private residential treatment community, Wille[39] found no significant differences in perception of loneliness based on the UCLA Loneliness Scale. Her findings were based on a sample of 100, including 47 pet owners and 53 nonowners.

Wille suggests that one reason for her findings is that her study community offered ample opportunities for socialization for all residents. Residents who did not own pets gave pain and grief on losing the pet as the primary reason. Lack of transportation to the veterinarian was also an important consideration. Interestingly, 92% of the sample of pet owners and nonowners alike believed that pets did contribute to the health of people.

Health of Pet Owners versus Nonowners

Finally a demographic survey of pet ownership in rural California[40] yielded these intriguing findings among elderly (65 and older) adults:

1. 3.9% of nonowners surveyed reported they had cancer, compared with 1.8% of pet owners
2. 28% of pet owners reported being hypertensive, compared with 20% of nonowners
3. 14% of nonowners reported having a heart condition, but only 5% of pet owners reported that they did
4. frequent headaches were reported by 25% of pet owners and 14% of those without pets

The third finding is consistent with the Friedmann and Katcher research with coronary care patients (see Chapter 2), but appears to be inconsistent with the second finding. The researchers suggest that the pet owners may simply have been more aware of their hypertension than the nonowners. Certainly, these are findings worthy of further research.

REFERENCES

1. Bustad, L. K. & Hines, L. M. (1983, March). Placements of animals with the elderly: benefits and strategies. In R. L. Lee, M. E. Zegler, T. Ryan & L. M Hines (Eds.), *Guidelines: Animals in nursing homes. California Veterinarian Supplement* (pp. 32a–38a).

2. Cusack, O. & Smith, E. (1984). *Pets and the elderly* (p. 31). New York: The Haworth Press.

3. Ibid. p. 75.

4. *Statistical abstract of the United States, 1986.* Table 169: Hospitals and nursing homes — summary characteristics: 1971 to 1983. Washington, DC.

5. Cusack, O. & Smith, E. (1984). op. cit.

6. Andrysco, R. (1982, December). "Companion Animal Service, Inc." Proposal prepared for the Columbus Foundation.

7. Ibid.

8. Brickel, C. M. (1985). Initiation and maintenance of the human-animal bond: Familial roles from a learning perspective. In M. B. Sussman (Ed.), *Pets. and the family* (pp. 32–33). New York: The Haworth Press.

9. Cusack, O. & Smith, E. (1984). op. cit.

10. Mugford, R. A. & M'Comisky, J. G. (1975). Some recent work on the psychotherapeutic value of caged birds with old people. In R. S. Anderson (Ed.), *Pet animals and society.* London: Bailliere Tindall.

11. Gowing, C. B. (1984). The effects of minimal care pets on homebound elderly and their professional caregivers. Ph.D. dissertation abstracted in *People-Pets-Environment* 3(1), 25–26, 1985.

12. Ibid.

13. Riddick, C. C. (1985). Health, aquariums and the non-institutionalized elderly. In M. B. Sussman (Ed.), *Pets and the family* (pp. 163–174). New York: The Haworth Press.

14. New, J. C., Jr. (1985). Pets and community-based elderly. Paper presented at the annual meeting of the Delta Society, Denver, CO.

15. Brickel, C. (1979). Therapeutic roles of cat mascots with a hospital-based geriatric population: A staff survey. *The Gerontologist, 19,* 368–372.

16. Salmon, I. M., Salmon, P. W., Hogarth-Scott, R. S., & Lavelle, R. B. (1983, February). A dog in residence. A Companion-Animal Study commissioned by JACOPIS [the Joint Advisory Committee on Pets in Society] Melbourne, Australia. A summary of the study appears in *The Latham Letter* (1982, spring), 4, 6, 10, 13.

17. Andrysco, R. M. (1982, spring). "PFT in an Ohio retirement-nursing community. *The Latham Letter.*

18. Andrysco, R. M. (1983, February). Personal communication.

19. Banzinger, G. & Roush, S. (1983). Nursing homes for the birds: A control-relevant intervention with bird feeders. *The Gerontologist, 23,* 527–531.

20. Francis, G. M., Turner, J. T., & Johnson, S. B. (1982). Domestic animal visitation as therapy with adult home residents. Unpublished manuscript.

21. Hendy, H. M. (1984). Effects of pets on the sociability and health activities of nursing home residents. In R. K. Anderson, B. L. Hart, L. A. Hart (Eds.), *The pet connection* (pp. 430–437). Minneapolis: University of Minnesota Press.

22. Ibid.

23. Robb, S. S., Boyd, M., & Pristash, C. L. (1980). A wine bottle, plant and

puppy: Catalysts for social behavior. *Journal of Gerontological Nursing*, 6(12), 722–728.

24. Robb, S. S. (1981). Pilot study of pet dog therapy for elderly people in long-term care. Unpublished manuscript.

25. Jendro, C. & Watson, C. (1984). The effects of pets on the chronically-ill elderly. In R. K. Anderson, B. L. Hart & L. A. Hart (Eds.), *The pet connection* (pp. 416–422). Minneapolis: University of Minnesota Press.

26. Ibid.

27. Daniel, S. A. & Burke, J. (1985, October). The psychological effects of a pet visitation program on nursing home residents. Paper presented at the annual meeting of the Delta Society, Denver, CO.

28. Buelt, M. C., Bergstrom, N., Baun, M. M., & Langston, N. (1985, October). Facilitating social interaction among institutionalized elderly through use of a companion dog. Paper presented at the annual meeting of the Delta Society, Denver, CO.

29. Ibid.

30. Savishinsky, J. (1985). Pets and family relationships among nursing home residents. In M. B. Sussman (Ed.), *Pets and the family* (pp. 109–134). New York: The Haworth Press.

31. Ibid.

32. Stryler-Gordon, R., Beall, N., & Anderson, R. K. (1985, October). Facts and fiction: Health risks associated with pets in nursing homes. Paper presented at the annual meeting of the Delta Society, Denver, CO.

33. Kidd, A. H. & Feldman, B. M. (1981). Pet ownership and self-perception of older people. *Psychological Reports*, *48*, 867–875.

34. Connell, C. M. & Lago, D. J. (1984). Favorable attitudes toward pets and happiness among the elderly. In R. K. Anderson, B. L. Hart, & L. A. Hart (Eds.), *The pet connection* (pp. 241–250). Minneapolis: University of Minnesota Press.

35. Ory, M. G. & Goldberg, E. L. (1982). Pet possession and well-being in elderly women. In A. H. Katcher & A. M. Beck (Eds.), *New perspectives on our life with companion animals*. Philadelphia: University of Pennsylvania Press.

36. Robb, S. & Stegman, C. (1983). Companion animals and elderly people: A challenge for evaluators of social support. *The Gerontologist*, *23*, 277–282.

37. Ibid.

38. Francis, G. (1981, March). Animals and nursing: A neglected affair. *Nursing Outlook*.

39. Wille, R. (1985, spring). A comparative study of the relationship between loneliness and pet companionship in a retirement community. *The Latham Letter*, p. 16.

40. Franti, C. E., Kraus, J. F., Borhani, N. O., Johnson, S. L., & Tucker, S. D. (1980). Pet ownership in rural Northern California (El Dorado County). *Journal of the American Veterinary Medical Association*, *176*, 143–149.

CHAPTER 12

Tiffany:
Portrait of a
Canine Cotherapist

While researching material for *Pets and Mental Health*, I had
the good fortune to find Carroll Meek, an innovative psychologist who shared her experiences with her cotherapist, Tiffany,
with me. By focusing on a single therapist and her canine
companion, I hope to give the reader a personal glimpse into
the world of pet-facilitated therapy.

Tiffany, a regal Maltese dog, has been a working cotherapist
since 1976. That was when her owner, psychologist Carroll L.
Meek, first brought her to Washington State University. Meek, then
a counseling psychologist at the facility, found it impractical to
housebreak the 4-month-old puppy with no one at home all day.
She discovered, however, that Tiffany's presence contributed far
more than simply convenience.[1,2,3]
Says Meek:

The change in the nature of the waiting room, alone, was evident in the first minute she was introduced. Students who seek
counseling are reluctant, they are frightened by the prospect —
they do not know what is going to happen to them, they are
fearful of being seen by someone they know or don't know,
they imagine that others are imagining bad things about them,
they wonder what others are there for, they worry about being
found wanting/crazy, etc. They may be lonely or isolated.
They may have few human friends. They have probably had to

153

leave their own animals at home unless they live in an apartment which permits pets. They may be homesick. Check with counseling services across the nation. The waiting rooms are noticeably void of conversation (like any doctor's office); everyone sits staring straight ahead, hoping no one will see them, hoping the counseling hour will never come.

At the beginning of Tiffany's arrival, it was apparent that students forgot their feelings of self-consciousness. They began talking to each other. They speculated about this funny little Maltese dog and about the type of agency that would be crazy enough to allow something "from home" into the institutionalized atmosphere of Counseling Services at Washington State University. They probably thought that someone who would bring this bit of humor into their lives must be every bit as nutty as they. They talked to each other about whether they were hallucinating this experience. . . . Some would bring her a morsel on the next visit, some would try to coax her attention. The result was the same, the students in the waiting room lost a little of their self-consciousness and began talking to one another. One student came in asking to see the counselor who had the little dog.

As Tiffany matured, her role in Meek's practice expanded. She began to "greet" the patients formally, lie at their feet, and at the appropriate time, escort each to the office. Most patients are surprised and delighted with the unexpected visitor and try to garner her friendship, which Meek thinks is akin to wanting to garner the friendship and caring of the therapist. But Tiffany is not especially social. Meek describes her 5-pound companion as aloof, explaining:

She does not want to be the center of attention; she dreads it. She doesn't want to be held or petted very much. She wants to be with me — she is content with that.

She does not relate to everyone. She has, however, related very closely to schizophrenics, borderline personalities and some who were severely depressed. She seems to pick her favorites and no one can ascertain why or who she will greet with enthusiasm. It is clear, however, that she relates more to the severely withdrawn person—she seems able to pick out those who are isolated and more lonely than others—perhaps because such people respond less aggressively to her, she seems more free to respond to them without being over-whelmed.

One of the few patients whom Tiffany seemed particularly fond of was a woman I'll call Meg . . .

Whenever she came to our appointments, Tiffany would give one of her rare fanfares . . . she would race and race around and around in circles in the waiting room—much to the delight of all of us, including Meg. I don't have any idea why Tiffany held such an affinity toward Meg, but we would all exclaim, "Meg is here! Meg is here!" and Tiffany would do her wonderful little display until exhausted and the three of us settled down in my office to do our work. Meg later suffered from a major depression. It was difficult for all of us. One of the strangest things about it was that Tiffany began to ignore her after that. It was as though Tiffany withdrew from her the more she withdrew into herself. We all commented on the fact that one of the things that people who are depressed have to deal with is that others withdraw from them. I don't know if Tiffany's withdrawal stimulated Meg's desire to re-reach out, or not, but it was clear to all of us that depression affects others around us—and that, too, needs to be given attention.

In 1982, Meek, along with her special helpmate, left Washington State University for private practice in Pullman, Washington. Their office in the Pullman Professional Building is sandwiched between the Social Security Office and a pharmacy. Tiffany is now known as the "Professional Mall Dog," and greets not only Meek's patients, but visitors to the Social Security Office and the pharmacy as well.

Meek's office decor includes Persian rugs, original art, a chiming clock, plants, an hourglass, even a crystal ball.

The paintings, the plants, the dog—all of these elements are potential pathways of establishing a relationship without which people cannot (or would rather not) delve into the areas of their lives which cause them anger and anxiety and fear. People have walked into my office red in the face from anger or frustration that caused them to look 20 years older than their chronological ages—I have seen them come to me anxious that I will find them lacking, that I will not like them, or that I will see them as bizarre—all of the aspects in my office produce profound indications of almost immediate relaxation. It is a joy to me to see them nestle into this little world of wonder that I have created and to hear their comments of how peaceful they feel.

Meek points out that none of her unusual accoutrements, including Tiffany, have ever interfered with the process of psychotherapy:

I believe they set the required stage for the successful resolution of difficulties which seem profound enough to have been either referred to me by someone else or compelled them to come to confer with me.

Meek, who describes herself as a directive nondirective therapist, admits that some of her colleagues have been less than enthusiastic about Tiffany. Once, when her husband, psychiatrist Saul Spiro, was consulting at a mental hospital in Idaho, she and Tiffany went along as volunteers. The adolescent ward was particularly enthusiastic, and Meek sat with a group of the youngsters on the floor. She recalls:

One young boy had trouble talking. He had been [discussed] at one of the staff meetings earlier in the day, so I noted him, especially. He stuttered and stammered and usually exhausted the attention of the listeners before he had his message delivered. He wanted to hold Tiffany—and with all those greedy little hands and arms striving to grasp her, she had retreated into the folds of my vest and hidden her head. I said: "She is very shy. She is often afraid in strange places with people she doesn't know." Several of the children looked gravely at me, and this young boy said quite clearly: "I am like that." Several said: "So am I." It was a wonderful moment and as we talked, the children bragged about some of their "exploits" which were not affirmed by me, but there were several rays of therapeutic "hope" that were reinforced.

Meek asked for some feedback from a former WSU student there, and found that the staff had complained about the presence of the dog. She points out:

Old attitudes really die hard, and I ponder the possibility of staff jealousy. How would you like to work with hostile, recalcitrant teenagers every day — prying every word out of them — digging for grist for a relationship — to have one lady and one dog walk in and have a group session right there in the hall after a 2-second period of acquaintance and hear things that you have been digging for for weeks, maybe months?

Discussing Tiffany's personality and interpreting her moods has provided disclosures from Meek's patients:

One 12-year-old boy I was seeing asked: "Can I hold her?" I said: "She wouldn't like that." He said: "What if I picked her up anyway, would she bite?" I said: "No, she would just cry." He understood that and her lack of retaliation puzzled him — this was a child who struck out in anger whenever he was deeply hurt or afraid — a factor that may not have been discussed so quickly without this exchange.

Sometimes Tiffany's mere presence can provide some benefit. Says Meek:

I had been talking to the mother of an anorexic who was having difficulty pursuing therapy and who was showing a great deal of resistance to continuing in therapy. I made several suggestions to the mother about how I thought she could aid in the process and I also apologized for, so far, having been unable to establish a better relationship with her daughter. Her mother readily forgave me with the comment: "Listen, the first day she saw you, she came home with her eyes asparkle, and said:

'Mom, you'll never guess what she had in her office.'" The mother said: "Carroll, you keep bringing that dog to work with you, and I think you'll have a chance."

During the entire 7-year stint at WSU, Tiffany only had 2 "accidents," and even these were therapeutic material. "How many of us need to be reassured that, should we commit a gross social *faux pas*, we will be accepted and not sent to our rooms on 'permanent assignment,'" explains Meek.

The presence of a dog also provides needed distraction and diversion for the therapist. "Many of our patients fear that their troubles will inundate their therapist," says Meek. "The presence of the little dog seems to reassure them that they never will."

And the little dog was not above providing humor. Meek recalls:

When I worked at the Counseling Center at WSU, Tiffany always went into the waiting room and found her next customer. She always recognized a former visitor to my office and she would sit next to their feet and wait with them. It was always a source of amusement to me that when I (by chance) did not have a "next patient" and, by luck, had a "free hour," she still went into the waiting room and when she did not recognize her next "customer," would "pick" a likely candidate and wait next to his or her foot and watch me with an expectant look on her face which seemed to say: "Can we see this one? This looks like a good one." One day I walked into the pharmacy. There sat a prim older lady with white gloves and a pillbox hat, waiting for the pharmacist to fill her prescription. Tiffany was sitting next to her foot with the same expectant look on her face and I knew what she was up to. The lady, of course, had no idea what was going on, but I must say that provided me with several chuckles during the course of an otherwise hectic day.

Tiffany's presence has also had a comforting effect on victims of crime and trauma. While at WSU, Meek worked closely with campus police helping the officers identify psychological problems in the public, particularly among victims. The officers routinely recommended victims of violent crime, particularly rape, to confer with a counseling psychologist about their experience. But, as Meek points out:

> Although these officers became quite adept and sensitive to making these referrals, many victims of violent crime felt that the officer thought they must be inadequate, psychologically "flawed" or worse. I think that one might expect this reaction from many people referred to a psychologist, regardless of the circumstances. On at least two occasions (so there are probably more), the officers who escorted a victim in to see me reported to me later that when they saw "that counselor and that little dog" [the victim] experienced immediate relief and said to [the officer], "Hey, I'm not crazy after all!" I think the existence of the little dog indicated to them that these were very human services and that they did not have to expect that they were going to be given another examination under some sort of microscope as though they were some sort of bug.

Summarizing the effect of Tiffany on her practice, Meek says:

> Some clients ignore her presence in my office after the initial introductions. She has been taught to be as unobtrusive as possible. Some talk to her. Some have been calmed by her presence. The emphasis in our society of people-people interactions has been somewhat overestimated. My understanding of Tiffany and her understanding of me has led me to affirm in my own mind that "animals" are sold "far short" because we, as human beings, lack in the observational capacity department. We miss so much because we are simply unaware this is not only in our personal relationships but in the realms of our environment as well. Perhaps increasing our awareness is one of the most important avenues of exploration in psychotherapy.
>
> My husband, when he was in private practice in psychiatry in Anacortes, Washington, had two Irish wolfhounds in his office. One day, he reports, a woman sat sobbing in her chair. One of the wolfhounds got up, walked over to her, sat down in front of her (his head, therefore, in equal height to hers,

seated) and with one deft lap engulfed her entire face with one sweep of his tongue.

Sometimes we, as human beings, need a little help to see — really see — the immensity with which we assign importance to the trivial. On a different occasion, during a particularly difficult point in one of [my husband's] sessions with a patient, an eagle soared by the window within feet of the occupants struggling within. My husband and she both watched this magnificent creature soar past and out of view. It was a wondrous and touching moment for both of them, and maybe both might say it was a "turning point" in therapy.

Most of the patients who come to counseling have been alienated somewhere along the way by other people. Some desperately need to relate to a companion who will accept them for who they are and ask for nothing in return. During the years I have been conducting psychotherapy with Tiffany, the benefits have been many. I will even venture to say that I would be unwilling to work without an animal in my office again. My experiences with Tiffany tell me that use of "one other" in the therapy setting can provide a wealth of information about my clients — their ways of relating to me, to the world, to their needs.

REFERENCES

1. Meek, L. (1984, April & August). Personal communication.

2. Meek, L. (1982, summer). Dog presence proves salutary in university counseling service. *The Latham Letter*, p. 22.

3. Warren, (1982, December 18–19). Carroll Meek: Helping people recapture the magic in their lives. *Palouse Woman*. (Suppl. to *Idahonian/Palouse/Empire News.*)

CHAPTER 13

Prison Pets

In the past I never had that really deep-down compassion-type feeling for any kind of animal, reports an inmate from Lima State Hospital:[1]

> As a boy I used to go hunting quite a lot and shoot rabbits such as this. I never really thought that they were animals, it was just something to do in the fall. Now, after seeing the birds and the guinea pigs and the hamsters and the gerbils and the rabbits on the ward and coming close to them, you really understand the necessity of feeling for these animals and not harming them. It's really changed my attitudes toward all animals in general.

Robert Stroud, "The Birdman of Alcatraz," is probably the most famous example of the effect of animals on prisoners. Stroud's devotion to his charges was so complete that he eventually became a world expert on the diseases of birds and their treatment. In fact, *Stroud's Digest on the Diseases of Birds* is still in demand by aviculturists today.

Stroud's case became such a cause célèbre that it was recounted in a movie in which the single-minded aviculturist was portrayed by Burt Lancaster. Prison authorities, however, overlooked the rehabilitative nature of Stroud's work and eventually removed all the birds in what Arkow[2] describes as ". . . a classic case of bureaucratic bumbling."

Since the celebrated Stroud case a few prison facilities, recognizing the positive effect that animals have on morale, have allowed prisoners to care for pets. In 1958 Joseph Flaherty[3] wrote about Pete, a kestrel (sparrow hawk) that had been critically injured by a hunter's bullet. As a result of his injuries, the small raptor lost a wing and a leg, and return to the wild was not possible. Inmates at the Massachusetts State Prison nursed the bird back to health and even built him an outdoor cage. Pete never became socialized and frequently bit the hands that fed him, but it mattered little to the prisoners, who seemed content just to care for the injured creature.

The need of incarcerated individuals to care for something living has been recognized by prison officials. H. R. Swenson, who was a warden at the Missouri State Penitentiary, said:[4] "I have worked in various prison capacities for the past 31 years and I know there is a universal urge among inmates to acquire the affection of something alive. Inmates, in turn lavish their love on the object of affection."

Swenson told of an incident illustrating the depth of emotion surrounding the animals:[5]

> I went inside the prison early one morning to observe the breakfast meal. On my way, an inmate told me a foreman had filled a hole in the yard with concrete while a mother cat and her kittens were inside the hole. I was again stopped by several other inmates who told me about the cat and kittens. I went to the place where the concrete had been poured, then to the office of the chief engineer and told him to have a crew remove the concrete immediately. Sure enough, out came a mother cat and five kittens.

> I firmly believe that if I had not gone into the prison that morning or had not answered to the inmates, we could have had real trouble. As it was, however, I received several "thank you" notes from inmates following the rescue of the pets.

Arkow[6] reports that the California Institute for Women at Frontera allows inmates to keep aquariums in individual cells and that the California Institution for Men at Chino tolerates stray cats in the minimum security facility. They are, however, occasionally removed by the staff.

But not all facilities have been as tolerant. In 1976 officials at the California State Prison at San Quentin removed pet cats kept by prisoners. According to the prison's information officers, the cats had reached unmanageable numbers (hundreds) and had become objectionable. Although they admitted that many prisoners received therapeutic benefits from the animals, many others, they said, did not like the cats. Rather than risk an incident, they decided to remove the animals instead. The cats' welfare was also a consideration, said the authorities, who cited lack of proper food, sanitation, and vet care as further reasons for disallowing pets in prison.[7]

LIMA STATE HOSPITAL

Thus, until relatively recently, the use of pets as therapeutic agents for prison inmates has been informal and scattered. Astute officials who recognize the ability of animals to improve morale and inspire cooperation have overlooked regulations prohibiting pets in institutions, but are quick to remove them if the situation appears to be getting out of hand or interfering with the routine of prison life.

But in 1975, David Lee, a psychiatric social worker at the Lima State Hospital for the Criminally Insane initiated a program that has since become one of the most discussed and noteworthy projects in pet-facilitated therapy.[8]

The Lima State Hospital is an all-male, maximum-security facility that receives the misfits, notably inmates showing signs of depression, mental illness, and suicidal tendencies, from other Ohio prisons. Inmates there have few visitors, and social interaction in the population is limited. Lee observed they spent much of the time pacing the halls, preoccupied with their own emotional problems.

What they needed, he decided, was an interest beyond themselves. With the approval of an admittedly skeptical administration, he cautiously introduced an aquarium and 2 parakeets to the dayroom of one ward. The results are pet-facilitated therapy history.

"It just snowballed," said Lee. "The guards became accustomed to birds flying around. Nobody broke the aquarium. Nobody strangled the birds. It was considered a minor experimental success. And other wards saw that this ward was getting something that they liked."

The program expanded and presently involves approximately 175 animals, including courtyard creatures such as goats, ducks, deer, and rabbits (which are kept in fenced-in yards outside each ward and are cared for collectively by the ward residents) and personal pets such as birds, a lizard, and a cat, which are kept by the individual prisoners. The hospital budgets $100 a month for maintenance of the group pets, and there is space in a greenhouse for injured wildlife. Prisoners themselves defray some costs through car washes and the sale of greenhouse plants. Six of 10 wards are currently active in the program; excluded are those wards containing men who have histories of violence and assault.

Recently, Lee[9] conducted a 1-year comparison study between two honor wards with 28 patients each. "The only difference in treatment," he says, "is that one had pets and the other did not. During that year the ward without pets had 12 fights and 3 suicide attempts, while the ward with pets had 1 fight and no suicide attempts." Lee also found that patients with pets needed fewer drugs than those without them.

Says Lee:[10]

> The program's philosophy is simply to help depressed and suicidal patients help themselves. The use of pets as therapeutic catalysts is done to achieve the following goals:
>
> 1. improving self-esteem
> 2. providing nonthreatening, nonjudgmental affection
> 3. stimulating a responsible attitude within the pet caretaker
> 4. catalyzing communication
> 5. improving the atmosphere of the ward
> 6. providing a new focus of attention
> 7. providing a necessary diversion from hospital routine
> 8. providing needed companionship

That 175 animals can live peacefully within the walls of a maximum-security prison might be considered success enough, but the case histories are even more dramatic. When one man, for example, imprisoned for assault, came to Lima, he was withdrawn, reclusive, and deeply depressed. Recently the now-sociable inmate, anticipating a new start outside the institution, completed work for an Associate's Degree with a 4.0 average. He credits his two Amazon parrots with changing his outlook. "They helped bring me out of my shell, and now I reciprocate with the other patients. They seem to help alleviate the loneliness and give me motivation to get up and go,'' he said.[11]

Another man, dubbed "Killer" because he once killed a fellow inmate, is the proud owner of Babe, a cockatoo. "I used to argue with the attendants because there was nobody else to get mad at. Now I just come in and talk to the bird, and I just don't yell at anyone anymore."[12]

Says Lee:[13]

> Many patients who have taken care of a pet on a one-to-one basis have improved remarkably. In one instance, a patient who had not spoken a word in 4 months and who failed to respond to regular treatment began to speak when a cockatiel was given to him as his pet. Shortly after, he began to interact with humans. Eventually the patient and his beloved pet cockatiel were discharged together.

Some patients were so bonded to their pets that they were reluctant to leave the State Hospital. That problem has fortunately been greatly alleviated. Since Lee's pet therapy program has received widespread and highly favorable publicity, many Ohio area mental institutions that receive former Lima inmates will accept their small pets as well. Collective pet ownership with the courtyard animals also depersonalizes the actual ownership. According to Lee:[14]

> Caretaking is often the responsibility of more than one client so there would not be eventual feelings of total ownership by any one client. If the attachment [is such that] it might affect the patient to lose the pet, [the pet] can be discharged with its caretaker upon parole or can be transferred to [that person's] family. A recent emphasis toward farm animals assists greatly in depersonalizing actual ownership.

The welfare of the animals, however, is a primary concern as well. Local veterinarians and a pet shop owner help the inmates learn about the needs of the pet, and according to Robert White,[15] a representative of the American Humane Association: "The pets in that hospital receive better care in most instances than pets in a normal home.''

Says Lee:[16]

>The abuse of animals that might initially have been expected has not been a problem because we screen closely and monitor constantly. Since our pets are used only with depressed and suicidal patients, not with acute short-term or assaultive cases, any likelihood of maltreatment is reduced.

The program begins with a referral system that includes questions about past pets and pet preferences. Next, a pre-evaluation reviews potential problem areas, goals sought, and the particular pet to be used. An addendum that will be updated weekly and monthly is drawn up for the treatment team's approval. Upon discharge, accomplishments and recommendations are noted. Additionally, the program allows the inmate to participate in a pet caretaker group that discusses pet-related problems, sets new policies, monitors hygiene, and develops printouts on the care and feeding of the pets for the new patients. Patients can participate during the day, in the evening, or on weekends, and this flexibility insures that the pet therapy program does not interfere with any existing therapeutic programs.

Staff for the pet therapy project include the coordinator, who monitors the program daily, assisted by attendants, social workers, activity personnel, and school teachers, who assist on a volunteer basis. The Lima project also enlists the aid of outside volunteers (at present, these include three veterinarians and a pet store owner).

The program is extensively monitored to include:

1. daily rounds by the coordinator
2. daily rounds by attendant and nursing staff
3. weekly documentation in nursing notes
4. monthly meetings with project coordinator and client case manager
5. monthly update in client's chart
6. weekly meeting (caretaker club) with all residents involved
7. monthly update to program director

8. monthly update to nine national humane societies
9. periodic review from various media.[17]

Since the program is relatively young and many of its participants have long sentences to serve, it is too soon to determine if the benefits of the pet therapy program will have long-term effects on the inmates once they are released. Lee can point with pride to at least one individual who became so involved with animals that upon his release he got a job at the Atlanta Humane Society. But Lee claims no miracles for the program:[18]

> Having a pet brings with it instant responsibility and companionship. The pet's total dependency tends to cause the patient to react and this reaction when monitored properly is usually positive, giving the patient a new focus for his attention. Hopefully the unique bond between patient and pet will have overall positive results and be therapeutically beneficial.

PURDY TREATMENT CENTER'S PRISON PARTNERSHIP

No dogs are used in the Lima project because of state health requirements and, as Lee points out, "The welfare of the animals is paramount, and a prison is no place for a dog." At the Purdy Treatment Center, (Washington State's maximum-security prison for women), however, a unique new program is ensuring exemplary animal care while providing inmates with an opportunity to learn dog grooming and training skills.

The Prison Partnership is the latest outreach of the People-Pet-Partnership-Program, in Pullman, Washington. The wide-based PPPP has extended the concept of pet therapy to the community at large, and sponsors numerous projects including equestrian therapy, the placement of hearing dogs with the hearing impaired, humane education in the schools, and the placement of pets with senior citizens. The Prison Partnership, which began in 1982, is the newest in a lengthy and impressive list of achievements.

The concept of uniting women inmates and area canines for their mutual benefit began with Kathy Quinn, a Tacoma-based free-lance photographer, and was implemented by Leo Bustad, dean of Washington State's Veterinary School, and Linda Hines, coordinator of PPPP. The pilot program began with three professional dog trainers from Tacoma State College and veterinary support from Washington State University's College of Veterinary Medicine, but no funds. Following publicity about the program, the only one of its kind in the country, an anonymous donor provided the essential: a kennel with large, fenced runs and a grooming room.

Under the supervision of the program's director, Steve Kelley, specially selected inmates are chosen to learn vocational skills of dog grooming and training. Dog owners in the community are encouraged to bring their pets to be groomed or to learn obedience, and the fees help to defray the costs of the program, which continues to be underfunded. In addition to providing job skills to the inmates and a service to the community, the Prison Partnership has another goal: to train dogs as companions for the physically disabled. And Burt Pusch, who received the program's first graduate, Glory, couldn't be happier about it.

Pusch is the manager of the independent living program at Good Samaritan Hospital in Puyallup, Washington, and has a congenital disability that affects the movement in his arms and legs. Glory is a medium-sized Australian Shepherd that was donated to the program and that has a mind of her own and a natural herding instinct. According to the female inmate who channeled the dog's energy and enthusiasm into useful tasks that include about 60 retrieving or fetching functions: "She wants to do things her way, and you have to convince her your way is better."[19]

The inmate has taught Glory a number of tasks, and the dog's training was so successful that she was dubbed "Wonderdog" by staff and inmates alike. Glory opens and closes doors, carries packs, answers the telephone, and fetches needed items such as the television tuner. She can even retrieve a coin from the floor.

Pusch sees his new friend as providing three things:[20]

> First is companionship, I live alone. Second, she's opened a world of normality for me. I'm very independent, and I can do just about anything anyone else can do. But what Glory can do in five seconds may take me 15 minutes and I may expend two

to three times as much energy to do it. Finally, Glory will be a demonstrator dog. We hope to do some traveling to show people with disabilities what dogs can be trained to do.

First, however, Pusch and his canine companion will realize a cherished ambition. "I hope to go camping with her," he said, "something I've never done in my life."[21]

But Pusch and Glory are not the only individuals who have benefitted from the program. For the inmate, who is serving a life term for murder, training Glory has provided a new-found confidence and self-esteem, as well as skills that she hopes someday she will use in a life outside of prison walls.

"I've gained a new sense of responsibility," she said. "The dogs love us unconditionally, regardless of what's in our past."[22]

"The dogs don't understand that some of these women are murderers or drug addicts," said Quinn, who started the program:[23]

> Dogs respond to positive attitudes, feelings and senses. And these girls have all of those things. But this program isn't all fun and games. Not only are the girls learning about dogs, they are also learning how to get along with each other. The program keeps them out of trouble and they find new friends.
>
> But most importantly, almost all of these girls will be back into the community someday. Maybe some of the positive attitude changes that are occurring will carry through in their lives when they are released. And this gives them something to do . . . other than getting into more trouble when they get out.

The head trainer, Dawn Jecs said:[24]

> When we were approached by Kathy we didn't know if we wanted to give it a try. We were very suspicious of the program and thought it might even be dangerous. What did we know? We had never been in a prison before. We were kind of apprehensive about using our own dogs, too. But the dogs turned out to be a real bridge. Since the start it's been very enjoyable and educational, and we haven't had the slightest problem communicating and working with the girls.

Steve Kelley, who overseas the project, confirms that the dog program has produced a cooperation and camaraderie among the inmates selected, even friendships between individuals who previously had disliked one another. "The dogs have produced a warmth and caring that's unbelievable," he said.[25]

Currently, the Prison Partnership has eight dogs scheduled to become companions of physically disabled individuals. Training takes from 6 months to 1 year at a cost of $1800-$2500 per animal, depending on the special needs of the handicapped individual. Kelley says there is a waiting list of inmates who want to join the program and a waiting list of individuals who want the dogs. Quipped Jecs: "We've got waiting lists for just about everything except contributors to financially support the program."[26]

But with Glory's training successfully completed, the value of Prison Partnership is evident, and this innovative program could serve as a model for institutions throughout the world. At the graduation ceremony, at which time the kennel was dedicated, Pusch said: "We are not dedicating a kennel, but dedicating a seed."[27]

ATTITUDES OF CRIMINALS TOWARD ANIMALS

The affinity toward animals displayed by both the Lima State Hospital and Purdy Treatment Center inmates is not isolated to these cases, but appears to reflect a widespread craving for animal companionship among prisoners, according to ten Bensel and his colleagues from the Center to Study Human-Animal Relationships and Environments, at the University of Minnesota in Minneapolis.

The researchers compared the experiences of inmates who have committed violent crimes with the experiences of a matched control group. They asked questions concerning type of pets, special pets, reactions to loss of pets, and sexual experiences with animals (bestiality).

Ten Bensel and his colleagues found that although both the control and the inmate populations valued pets for the same reasons — companionship, love and affection, protection and pleasure — more than 80% of the offenders (compared to only 39% of the control group) wanted a pet now. This, they say, ". . . may suggest something about the deprivation of imprisonment and the therapeutic implications of having pets in prison."[28]

The researchers found that the violent offenders were more likely to have dogs in their homes while growing up, compared with the control group, which had more animals as pets other than dogs and cats. The inmates, however, had larger and more atypical pets, such as a baby tiger, a cougar, and a wolf pup.

More than 86% of criminals and 75% of the controls reported a special pet, but fewer of the offenders were willing to identify their specific special pet. More than 60% of both groups had lost their pets through death or theft. More inmates' pets had died of gunshots, and the offenders were more likely to be angry rather than sad or hurt over the death of their pets. The inmates were also more likely to have exhibited violence toward their own pets, which the researchers suggested could be a reflection of the more violent environments in which they had lived.

According to the researchers' personal communication with Lenoski and Disbrow, their findings do not corroborate that of prior work in the field. Lenoski[29] noted that a mere 3.7% of abusing parents had a significant pet as a child; however, in the ten Bensel et al. study, 86% of the criminals reported a special pet.

Disbrow[30] found that pets were less likely to be part of an abusing family than of a nonabusing family. Abusive parents also more often reported a bad attachment to a pet. This, too, was not supported by the ten Bensel research.

Nor does the ten Bensel group's study support the Peele and Brodsky[31] contention that a pet can become an addiction and take the place of other emotional needs, say the researchers, nor did they find evidence of what Peele and Brodsky hypothesized as "emotional abuse of a pet."

Although 3.9% of the control group in the ten Bensel et al. study admitted to having sex with animals, none of the inmates acknowledged this; in fact, the question, say the researchers, aroused strong emotional statements, in one case a page being torn out of the questionnaire.[32]

REFERENCES

1. Arkow, P. (1982, August). *Pet therapy: A study of the use of companion animals in selected therapies* (p. 28). Colorado Springs, CO: The Humane Society of the Pikes Peak Region.

2. Ibid.

3. Flaherty, J. A. (1958, July-August). Jail bird. *The National Humane Review*.

4. Tabscott, J. (1970, January-February). Lady of the cages. *The National Humane Review*, pp. 4–6.

5. Ibid.

6. Arkow, P. (1982). op. cit. p. 29.

7. Ibid.

8. Goldenberg, S. (1983, March 24). Pets are their therapy. *The Journal-Gazette*, Fort Wayne, IN.

9. Lee, D. (1983, March). Personal communication.

10. Ibid.

11. Foster, K. G. (1982, December 5). A means of escape: Pet therapy in prison. *Columbus Dispatch*, Columbus, OH.

12. Ibid.

13. Lee, D. (1983, March). Personal communication.

14. Ibid.

15. Ibid.

16. Ibid.

17. Ibid.

18. Ibid.

19. Rhodes, E. (1983, May 26). Pooch program perks up prison. *The Seattle Times*.

20. Ibid.

21. Stewart, M. (1983, September 28). Glory is first graduate of prison's dog program. *The Peninsula Gateway*, Washington State.

22. Brown, C. (1983, September 28). Prison-bred "wonderdog" to aid disabled man. *The Seattle Times*.

23. Koehler, T. (1983, March 31). Prison dogs. *Pierce County Herald*, Washington State.

24. Ibid.

25. Brown, C. (1983). op. cit.

26. Ibid.

27. Stewart, M. (1983). op. cit.

28. ten Bensel, R. W., Ward, D. A., Kruttschnitt, C., Quigley, J., & Anderson, R. K. (1984). Attitudes of violent criminals toward animals. In R. K. Anderson, B. L. Hart, L. A. Hart (Eds.), *The pet connection* (pp. 309–318). Minneapolis: University of Minnesota Press.

29. Lenoski, E. F. Personal communication with ten Bensel et al. as reported above in reference 28.

30. Disbrow, M. Personal communication with ten Bensel et al. as reported above in reference 28.

31. Peele, S. & Brodsky, A. (1974). *Love and addiction*. New York: Taplinger Press.

32. ten Bensel et al. op. cit.

CHAPTER 14

The Veterinarian as Human Psychologist

When we think of the role of the veterinarian in pet-facilitated therapy, we envision a knowledgeable and caring professional treating the physical, behavioral, and even emotional problems of the therapy pet or, perhaps, playing a pivotal role in its selection. Certainly these functions are vital, and no pet therapy project is complete without them.

However, even without participating in a formal pet-facilitated therapy project, the veterinarian performs the important therapeutic function of serving as a human psychologist and bereavement counselor when the pet is euthanized or dies from other means.

Even before the tremendous interest in the human-animal bond and pet-facilitated therapy, the veterinarian's role as human psychologist had been emphasized in the professional literature.

In 1964, Speck[1] observed that in cases of emotional or mental illness, the roles of the individual, the family, the pet, and the veterinarian are often interlocked. By understanding the client's relationship to the pet, the veterinarian may glean insights into the client's family life since many aspects of animal behavior are direct reflections of the behavioral patterns in the owner's family unit.

Antelyes[2,3] cautioned that the normal relationship between a pet and its owner is disrupted when the animal becomes ill, and a practitioner who is concerned solely with the pet's physical disorder will not be able to deal effectively with the distraught owner. Since the pet often serves as an emotional outlet for its owner, every successful veterinarian is, to some extent, a psychologist as well.

The expanding role of the veterinarian is a result of the changes in the pet-owner relationship, according to Levinson.[4] Pets have become privileged, valued, and protected members of the family. Additionally, they are used to satisfy our psychological needs and, thus, may not only mirror and localize our emotional illnesses, but may function as therapeutic agents as well. Levinson noted that veterinarians can become valuable members of the human health care team by being alert to signs of mental illness in pet owners.

For example, Rynearson[5] points out that the pet-owner relationship becomes pathological when the human-pet bond becomes more important than bonding with other people. Possibly, this sort of aberration would first be noticed by the veterinarian.

Odendaal[6] identifies two factors that cause people to keep pets: the hectic pace of city life, which inevitably results in broken relationships, and our alienation from nature. Our highly specialized and technical society inundates us with stress and frustrations, he says, and often the place where they all come together is the home. The result is a strain on personal relationships.

The second factor is the urban dweller's alienation from nature, and a pet may be the perfect medium through which some of this lost contact can be regained. Michael Fox[7] observes that for city dwellers, the pet may be the sole link with something authentic. Owners of several pets have in a sense created another world or reality. They belong to this other social group, in which they can play a more meaningful role than the one in which they must participate during the day.

Clients may seek veterinary help for their own psychological reasons as well as the pet's medical problems. Often anthropomorphism is evident in that the owner's needs can be projected onto the pet and reputedly human needs can be seen as real needs of pets. For example, Antelyes[8] reports on a survey that suggests that the manner in which the pet is fed and the frequency of feedings indicate the emotional closeness of the pet and owner. Nine out of 10 owners supplement their pets' meals with table scraps because they believe that human tastes are reflected in the tastes of the pet.

Andrysco[9] describes a case in which a wealthy, elderly woman brought in a pet dog for treatment of nail biting. After a physical examination, he found a perfectly healthy, if somewhat overweight, pet that exhibited no signs of nail biting. He observed, however, that the owner had fingernails bitten to the quick. He proceeded quite diplomatically, suggesting some techniques to abate the dog's "problem." A follow-up several weeks later revealed no change in the dog but a dramatic improvement in the hands of the owner, who was convinced that the problem was solved. Andrysco points out that the relationship between dog and owner was an especially intimate one, with the animal accompanying the owner everywhere, sharing in the woman's bonbons, and even wearing jewelry similar to hers.

When the veterinarian is consulted because of a real medical need for the pet, the consultation is a positive one based on the owner's concern for and responsibility toward the pet. But the two categories of consultations may overlap. Clients who usually consult a veterinarian only for a real medical need may at times use the veterinarian as a stress outlet. And clients who predominantly arrange visits for psychological reasons will also consult the veterinarian for medical reasons.

Odendaal[10] stresses sympathy and understanding for both types of clients:

> Clients who use their pets as a means of stress release will project all sorts of minor complaints onto their pets. These complaints may be used to compensate for the owner's own feelings of guilt, loneliness, lack of communication or frustration.

Odendaal cautions that the veterinarian must consider the needs of the animal patient as well as of the human client, particularly if an examination reveals no pathology in the pet. Treatment should not harm the pet, he stresses, although a placebo may be considered to please the client.

Odendaal urges his colleagues to be firm yet sympathetic toward clients who consult veterinarians for their own psychological reasons: "One should keep in mind that all people cannot handle stress equally well and that some pet owners will inevitably project more of their own anxieties onto their pets."[11] Oftentimes, he points out, the client may be unaware of the real reasons for the visit. However, if the veterinarian is too indulgent, such a client could disrupt the routine of the practice.

He concludes:[12] "The veterinarian renders a professional service to people, and because the pet plays an ever more important role as a stress conductor in modern society, the veterinarian will not be able to escape his responsibility in this regard."

Some areas in which psychological problems arise:

1. Men, in general, exhibit extreme reluctance to neuter a male animal, but have few problems with spaying a female animal. Women, in general, seem more willing to alter an animal of either sex. This may reflect castration anxiety or be an indicator of the powerful psychological (though not necessarily biological) link between potency and fertility. Women, however, are more conditioned to accept the end of their childbearing years. With millions of unwanted animals destroyed annually, this is an area that should not be ignored.

2. Odendaal, who practices in South Africa, reports the end-of-the-month visitors — elderly pensioners whose pets develop a minor ailment on the 28th of each month. In the United States, timing would more likely be at the beginning of the month, when Social Security checks are mailed. The trend also extends to restaurants: Ask any waiter or waitress about the influx of senior citizens at that time. Odendaal suggests placebos, if necessary, for the animal and time given to the owner who has come to fix attention on himself.

3. "Feelings of guilt are often projected on pets," says Odendaal:[13]

> When the owner puts the pet on the consultation table he immediately begins to apologize that the pet has not been bathed or that routine inoculations have been neglected. All sorts of apologies are made for things which have no bearing on the present consultation. Actually they feel guilty over something quite different but they now attempt to apologize for something they have neglected with regard to their pet.

In addition to seeing perfectly healthy pets as projections of their owner's neurosis, a veterinarian may also see animals whose abnormal behavior or illness reflects the pathology of an individual or family. Several researchers have remarked that the behavior of pets of schizophrenic families directly reflects the fluctuations within the family mood (see the section "Pets in Dysfunctional Families" in Chapter 10). Friedman[14] reported a family whose social phobia was so pronounced that the pets were reluctant to go outside.

A pet that suffers persistent injuries may indicate a violent family. A recent study that examined the role of pets in 53 child-abusing families found that although the pattern of pet ownership was similar to the pattern in normal families, 88% of the abusive families had pets that were abused as well.[15] Veevers[16] points out that the veterinarian on the lookout for chronically injured animals may be the first professional to suspect a problem. Unfortunately, as in child abuse, the abusers may not seek medical treatment for the victims until severe and prolonged damage has been done.

Finally, veterinarians may wish to consider the impression they are making on their future clients, youngsters. In their survey of 300 children, Kidd and Kidd[17] found that one third of each age group surveyed said that the veterinarian hurt or frightened their pets. Several young children blamed the veterinarian for the death of a pet. Only 2 youngsters, a 3-year-old and a 5-year-old, were unequivocally positive about veterinarians.

This is a disturbing finding, particularly since — unlike the human medical profession, which has a distinct Jekyll and Hyde image — veterinarians are consistently portrayed in a positive manner both in literature and on the screen, James Herriot perhaps being the most notable example. The generally negative attitude that children have of them then must be either based on an actual or perceived negative experience or the reflection of the attitude of parents.

Youngsters believe that pets feel pain and discomfort much the way they do. The attitude may reflect the child's painful experience with a human doctor, and it would be most interesting to see how these same youngsters perceive people doctors. A child, for example, who gets a painful injection or has to take bitter medication could assume the pet feels the same way. Perhaps when youngsters are present, veterinarians should take more time to explain that procedures are not painful and that often a pet's reaction is the result of surprise or anxiety in the unfamiliar situation rather than pain.

Also, some of these negative feelings no doubt reflect a past euthanasia that was handled poorly by the veterinarian and/or the parents. The next chapter offers suggestions for dealing with this extremely stressful decision.

REFERENCES

1. Speck, R. V. (1964). Mental problems involving the family, the pet, and the veterinarian. *Journal of the American Veterinary Medical Association, 145,* 150–154.

2. Antelyes, J. (1968). Group therapy in the veterinary office. *Veterinary Medicine/Small Animal Clinician, 63,* 975–976.

3. Antelyes, J. (1967). The petside manner. *Veterinary Medicine/Small Animal Clinician, 62,* 1155–1159.

4. Levinson, B. M. (1965). The veterinarian and mental hygiene. *Mental Hygiene, 49,* 320–323.

5. Rynearson, E. K. (1981). The veterinarian's nightmare. *Archives of the Foundation of Thanatology, 9*(2), 16.

6. Odendaal, J. S. J. (1983, spring). The veterinarian as animal clinician and human psychologist. Paper excerpted in *The Latham Letter,* (p. 10–11).

7. Fox, M. W. (1975). Pet owner relations. In R. S. Anderson (Ed.), *Pet animals and society* (pp. 8–17). London: Bailliere Tindall.

8. Antelyes, J. (1967). The psychology of pet feeding. *Veterinary Medicine/Small Animal Clinician, 62,* 249–251.

9. Andrysco, R. M. (1985, summer). Pet behavior reflects owner behavior. *The Latham Letter,* pp. 12–14, 16.

10. Odendaal, J. S. J. (1983). op. cit.

11. Ibid.

12. Ibid.

13. Odendaal, J. S. J. (1984, April). Personal communication.

14. Friedman, A. S. (1965). The "well" sibling in the "sick" family: A contradiction. In A. S. Friedman (Ed.), *Psychotherapy for the whole family in home and clinic.* New York: Springer.

15. DeViney, E., Dickert, J., & Lockwood, R. (1983). The care of pets within child abusing families. *International Journal for the Study of Animal Problems, 4,* 321–329.

16. Veevers, J. E. (1985). The social meanings of pets: Alternate roles for companion animals. In M. B. Sussman (Ed.), *Pets and the family* (pp. 11–30). New York: The Haworth Press.

17. Kidd, A. H. & Kidd, R. M. (1985). Children's attitudes toward their pets. *Psychological Reports, 57,* 15–31.

CHAPTER 15

The Death of a Pet

Of the many experiences we will share with a pet, none is more dreaded or less escapable than death. The possibility of a human death is, of course, ever present; but somehow it seems more remote than the death of an animal companion. We expect our peers and mates to travel to old age with us, and we fully expect our children to outlive us. From its first moment of puppyhood or kittenhood, however, we are faced with the fact of our pet's life expectancy. Accidents aside, we can expect an upper limit of 18–20 years for a cat, 12–15 for a dog, and considerably less with a small mammal such as a rabbit or rodent.

In addition to the problem of unequal life spans, the pet-owner relationship is also plagued by another specter. The owner may be called upon to make the ultimate decision: to decide if the quality of the pet's life is worth continuing. For the most part, we are not faced with this wrenching decision in our human relationships; human life and death is, as a rule, out of our hands. With a pet, however, we can, quite literally, be asked to play God. And since the veterinarian is the professional who usually advises and performs the euthanasia, his role during and after the process is critical.

Until relatively recently grief response following the loss of a pet was ignored by professionals and society alike. One could expect support and sympathy from the immediate family and perhaps the neighborhood eccentric who kept 20 cats. Poets like Lord Byron could eulogize their dead animals in verse or epitaph, but that was different: that was literature. Ordinary mortals were expected to replace or not replace the pet and resume life as if nothing had happened, certainly nothing that would suggest the magnitude of a major family loss. More likely we grieved in silence, unwilling or unable to expose our innermost feelings to the ridicule or apathy of our fellows.

Fortunately, with the growing acceptance of the human-animal bond, more and more professionals are taking another look at pet loss and finding ways to help the owner compensate for and adjust to the animal's death.

PET DEATH
DURING LIFE'S STAGES

Fenner[1] observes that there is a denial of the reality of death by society in general, causing people to be less aware of the dying process and the expression of grief. In today's urban society, the pet's loss may be an individual's first contact with death and may thus provide the important health benefit of forcing the person to learn how to cope with grief.

This is particularly true for children. Says Levinson:[2]

> The death of a pet may prepare a child emotionally for greater losses yet to come. When a parent dies, a pet may become the temporary crutch that helps the child hold on to life until the void is filled. The pet is a sympathetic, nonjudgmental listener with whom a child can openly display his grief and other emotions.

But the death of a pet is not merely a "dress rehearsal" for more significant events to come; it is an intense, deeply moving experience itself, and is affected by age and emotional development as well as such factors as degree of attachment to the pet and manner in which the pet died. Nieburg and Fischer[3] report that children under 5 years of age perceive the pet's death as a temporary absence. Children between 5 and 9 years old do not yet accept the inevitability of death and view their pet's demise as something that could have been avoided. During adolescence, however, youngsters experience the most profound feelings. They have learned that death is permanent and final, and because of their strong attachment to the pet, they often undergo a lengthy grieving process.

Veterinarian Mary Stewart[4] analyzed the essays of 135 school-age children, 65 between the ages of 6 and 11, and 70 between the ages of 12 and 17. Interestingly, 78% of the younger children told of the death of an animal, but only 20% of the older children mentioned such an experience. More than half of those children who had lost a pet reported being upset or very upset by it. The older children were most affected, many expressing anger that their parents were unwilling to get another pet. Only 7% of the younger group and none of the older group reported having had support during their grief. Stewart found that getting a new pet definitely helped the youngsters' bereavement.

The small percentage of older children who reported the death of a pet probably to some degree reflects society's denial of the validity of grieving for a pet. Robin and ten Bensel[5] remark that children are often surprised and embarrassed by the intensity of their grief for an animal and may feel the need to hide this grief from others.

But the very young child has special vulnerabilities, too. Death can be viewed as a form of punishment to which the child himself might be subject.[6]

Death may also be perceived as an unreal or impermanent state, and death wishes toward the pet (or parents or other adults for that matter) are not uncommon. If the death actually occurs, however, the child may experience intense guilt and even terrifying nightmares about the pet.[7]

Pioneer pet bereavement counselor Jamie Quackenbush[8] of the University of Pennsylvania compares the death of a pet to the death of a spouse or family member, both of which are associated with increased mortality. ". . . If older pet owners have only their pets as household companions and social affiliates, an owner's emotional and/or physical health may be compromised when the pet dies," he says.

Quackenbush surveyed 138 bereaved persons who had been involved in the death or euthanasia of a pet. There were 61 elderly persons in this group. He compared their data to data about a group of non-bereaved pet owners selected from another research project.

Quackenbush found that bereaved owners were older (average 46 years) than unbereaved owners (average 36 years). Elderly bereaved owners were also significantly more likely to live alone or with only one other person than the members of other groups.

The death of the pet considerably influenced the social behavior patterns of most elderly bereaved owners, reports Quackenbush. Ninety-seven percent of elderly bereaved owners and 91% of non-elderly bereaved owners reported experiencing some disruption in their daily routines: Most often, eating and sleeping schedules became erratic. Socialization diminished for 82% of the elderly bereaved owners and for 61% of the nonelderly bereaved owners. In both the elderly and nonelderly groups the bereaved owners tended to remain at home, to talk less, and to isolate themselves from family and friends more than usual. All of the working elderly bereaved owners experienced job-related difficulties after their pet's death, while 55% of the working nonelderly bereaved owners experienced similar difficulties. The difficulties for both groups consisted of missing several days work and being angered or upset by the insensitivity of colleagues to their grieving and mourning.

"The pet bereavement had an observable impact on the daily lives of the elderly," says Quackenbush.[9] "It affected their ability to work as well as their social interactions with other people significantly more than with non-elderly bereaved pet owners."

Particularly vulnerable were elderly female pet owners and those who lived alone or with one other person. "Perhaps as the human family size decreases, the social role and status of the companion animal tends to increase: animal-owner relationships become more dependent," Quackenbush observes.[10]

STAGES OF BEREAVEMENT

Many researchers have observed that the stages experienced in pet loss are similar to those experienced in human loss. As identified by Kübler-Ross,[11] the stages are denial, depression, anger, guilt, and acceptance.

Denial is often the first response, and as Cowles[12] notes, can serve as a delaying mechanism until the individual is able to cope with the appropriate painful responses. Although this stage can be frustrating and seem illogical to veterinarians and others not bereaved, Hopkins[13] advises allowing the owner time to work through this stage since refuting it will only heighten the client's defenses.

Cowles,[14] who interviewed 9 adult subjects regarding the death of their pets, found that the most frequently mentioned feelings were sadness, emptiness, and pain. Nieburg and Fischer[15] report that the death of a pet is a time of crying, sadness, grieving, mourning, and real depression. Additionally, bereaved owners may experience such physical symptoms of depression as loss of appetite, insomnia, and lethargy.

Too often the veterinarian is at the receiving end of the client's anger, says James Harris.[16] This stage, he points out, can last from 6 to 8 weeks, during which it is critical for the veterinarian to recognize that this is a defense mechanism on the part of the client and not respond in kind. Anger toward the veterinarian regarding the death of a pet may be one of the reasons so few children appear to have a positive image of these health professionals (see Chapter 14).

If children are involved, however, the anger can be directed to the parents as well. Hopkins suggests that euthanasia decisions should be made by the entire family.[17]

> When the animal is a family pet and there are children who are dependent upon the love of that animal, the veterinarian should recognize that [the children's] anger can be directed at family members who make the decision [for euthanasia]. This anger at parents "who had my dog put to sleep" can be remembered with intense feeling for the remainder of a child's life.

Feelings of guilt relating to the pet's death are common and, particularly where euthanasia is involved, can be overwhelming.[18] However, Cowles'[19] subjects reported neither guilt nor much anger of any kind. "There appeared instead to be a sense of satisfaction on the part of the subjects that they had made appropriate choices and that their choices had been pet-oriented, rather than self-oriented," she reports. The significant factor, says Cowles, may have been that all subjects had a strong support system both from veterinarians and the family.

Ideally, if all the grief stages are worked through therapeutically, the client will arrive at recovery. The process is of course, highly individual, and in addition to the above-mentioned casebook stages may involve shock, bitterness, resentment, anxiety, and idealization.[20] Katcher and Rosenberg[21] note that grief over pet death lasts an average of 10 months, during which time the bereaved owner is more susceptible to illness (just like bereaved persons who have lost a human companion). But the need for counseling may resurface later. Pet bereavement counselor Betty Carmack[22] reports a case of a woman seeking counseling after the death of a friend's dog rekindled memories of her own dog's death 7 years before.

Most pet owners do recover from their pet's death, but the experience may leave an indelible mark. One study reports that 15% of pet owners never own another pet because the pain of losing one is so great.[23] Wille[24] found that of 100 respondents to a survey of a retirement village in southern New Jersey, 53 of the sample were nonowners and most cited the pain of grief as the prime reason for not owning a pet. "Pet loss is only beginning to be recognized as a significant social problem," she says. "Loss of a close friend who is human is an occasion that draws sympathy, empathy and social support. Loss of a close friend who is a companion animal does not command this kind of sympathy and support."

EUTHANASIA: SPECIAL PROBLEMS

Some sources suggest that one of every 50 animal-patient contacts with the veterinarian ends with a completed euthanasia.[25] When the owner is asked to decide the life or death of his pet, the veterinarian's role is crucial. The veterinarian must use all of his or her resources and training to guide the owner through the decision and the resultant guilt, anger, and grief, and must be available for support after the animal has been put down.

Levinson[26] has observed that if an animal dies from natural causes the owner's reaction is usually similar to the reaction experienced when a person dies, but death through euthanasia may raise conflicts and fear of punishment. The most trauma, he believes, occurs when the pet's fate is unknown, as when it is lost or stolen.

Although approximately 2.5 million pets are euthanized annually, most veterinarians are unprepared to deal with the grief of their clients. Antelyes[27] attributes this to the general cultural taboo against talking about death and the fact that scientists are supposed to be objective and unemotional.

Yet, as Cowles notes, a support system, including strong veterinary input, is vital for the client's recovery. Crow[28] conducted a telephone interview study of grief after the death of pets, the majority of which died of cancer about a year before the call. All owners said they felt great personal loss at the death of their pets. Nearly all the owners remembered exactly when their pet died, and two thirds felt that the treatment their pets received from veterinarians had helped them deal with their pets' illnesses. Stewart[29] found that the feelings adults had about their pets' deaths were strongly influenced by the veterinarian. She points out that this professional has a particular responsibility to provide support to those individuals who lack family or other social links.

Several factors can ease the euthanasia process and avoid the painful second-guessing (Why wasn't the sickness seen sooner? Should another vet have been contacted?) noted by Hopkins and others. Kelly[30] advises stressing that euthanizing the dying pet was an act of kindness and love. In addition to stressing the positive aspects of euthanasia, Burt[31] advises discussing any and all alternatives to that procedure so the pet owner can make an informed decision about the fate of his companion. Quackenbush[32] cautions that allowing a pet to go home to suffer a slow and painful death may result in even more pain and guilt for the owner. However, Cowles[33] makes a valid point when she notes that for those pet owners who believe euthanasia is morally wrong, there is no decision. These clients must be given emotional support, as well as medical assistance, in caring for the ill pet at home.

Once the decision for euthanasia is made, several other decisions follow, such as which individuals will take the pet to the veterinarian, whether they will be present at the time of euthanasia, whether they will need time with the pet immediately prior to euthanasia, whether they will need time with the body after euthanasia, and how will they dispose of the body.

Allowing the client to be present during euthanasia is one of the more controversial issues surrounding pet death. In a survey of 50 small animal hospitals in the San Diego area, veterinarian Alice De Groot[34] found that only 12 offered their clients a choice to stay with an animal during euthanasia:

> The one area of veterinary medicine in which owners of cherished pets have the most vital stake of all is the arena of death for those pets. In that instance of denial, veterinarians rob pet owners and themselves of an opportunity to participate in a highly significant life cycle. They are robbed of a moment of intimate sharing which transcends to a new dimension of communication with the capability of enriching their lives. No other area of veterinary medicine is fraught with such a potential for client frustration, intimidation, and alienation than is this area concerning death and dying of the patient, planned or otherwise.

Most of the literature agrees with de Groot. Harris[35] says:

> Part of the grief process, part of the recovery process, involves what is called psychologically "closure" [closing a chapter in life]. . . . Seeing the body is often a very necessary and helpful process to allow closure. Being present at the euthanasia is often very helpful in facilitating closure. It used to be considered taboo to ever let a client in the room when you euthanized a patient. I suggest to you that it was an excuse to protect our own guilt and grief.

Part of the problem veterinarians have in dealing with their clients' grief, he says, is their absorption in their patients:[36]

> At times of terminal illness, our efforts tend to be directed toward our patients, in the areas of medical support, relief of discomfort and pain, and often euthanasia. Efforts toward our clients, all of whom grieve, are often totally lacking or at best deficient. It is as though the contract is abruptly terminated upon the death of our patient.

A special problem can arise when the pet, usually old or very sick, has been at the veterinarian's office for several days and the decision is made to euthanize. The owner anticipates the death and may have begun to separate from the pet. In a situation like this, the veterinarian may be tempted to advise the owner against further contact with the animal, but I believe this is a mistake. The two sentiments that continually recur with this situation are a feeling of deserting the pet ("I felt like I left him to die with strangers") and a need for resolution ("If only I had seen him, talked to him, held him once more. . . .") Admittedly, there is never "enough" time left for a dying loved one, human or animal. Sometimes with our pets we are luckier, we are able to spend those final moments together. It won't be any easier, and it may be a good bit harder if we are denied them.

Clients who do not wish to be present should be given the opportunity to spend time alone with the body afterward. "I even leave them alone for as long as they like," says Hopkins.[37] "Judging from the letters I've received, this indulgence is greatly appreciated by clients."

If the animal is a family pet, children should be involved in the decision of euthanasia as much as their age and emotional development permits to prevent unresolved anger and guilt. Time alone to say goodbye to the pet is preferable to being present at the euthanasia: a burial or ceremony—even planting a tree, as Harris suggests—is helpful. What is important is that the process be one in which the entire family feels comfortable and can vent their feelings of loss and sadness.[38] Cowles[39] points out that the ritual can be as simple as sharing family photographs and memories of the pet. Stewart[40] has also observed the value of a "formal" burial, but remarks that religion, often so comforting in human death, appears to be of little solace in an animal's death.

Body disposal, burial arrangements, fees, and paperwork should all be worked out prior to the actual euthanasia, and Harris[41] advises that the veterinarian send his condolences, either in a written note or a phone call.

FACTORS INFLUENCING
PET BEREAVEMENT

In addition to life stage and the decision of euthanasia, if applicable, other factors influence the duration and intensity of bereavement. These include attachment to the pet, the owner's social structure, and the special significance the owner attaches to the pet.

Since a pet is perceived as a family member, its loss disrupts the family group and its functioning, says Carmack,[42] who has identified four special areas of loss. First, pets are family members, often occupying the role of a child. Thus, illness and subsequent euthanasia have intense effects on the pet's "parents."

Second, some pets are perceived as having special qualities, usually unexplainable to others ("you have to know her to understand"), that make them unique from pets previously owned and utterly irreplaceable. The third area of loss is intimacy, which involves talking with pets and touching them. Pet owners come to depend on the verbal and nonverbal communication they enjoy with their pets. Often this intimacy is much greater than that shared with human friends and family members. Being needed is the fourth loss described by Carmack. Often the dead pet is one either perceived as or actually dependent on the owner. Carmack reports that 15% of her clients had pets who were ill for a lengthy time, thus heightening the attachment and grieving process. Because of the deep and intimate attachment people share with their pets, owners may grieve more for their animals than for relatives, including spouses.

Stewart[43] found that for individuals who are very dependent on their pets, the death of the animal can be an "earth stopper," producing physiological symptoms such as withdrawal, anorexia, and depression. Harris[44] describes such overdependence as the "nonconventional human/animal bond" and has observed such intensity in almost 40% of his clients. To these individuals the pet is a substitute for human companionship, and they can experience severe stress when the animal dies. Sometimes the grief can be pathological, even precipitating suicide in the pet's owner.[45]

Two phenomena tend to confound the progression from one grief stage to another, says Holcomb,[46] anticipatory grief, as identified by Kübler-Ross, and the rebound effect.

In anticipatory grief the client, aware of the pet's impending death, begins to separate from it. The same phenomena occurs with humans and appears to ease the pain of death of loved ones. But it is probably vital here that separation does not occur too quickly, or the pet owner may feel guilt later.

The rebound effect is the wave of remembering that occurs when you visit a favorite place (a park, for example) or engage in a favorite activity. The rebound effect may be the operative mechanism in owners who change veterinarians after a pet dies. For some individuals, returning to the same veterinarian is simply too painful.

Holcomb has also identified six characteristics that make individuals more susceptible to stressful bereavement. These are:

1. The owner has a strong attachment to the pet.
2. The owner is in a personal crisis at time of pet's death.
3. The owner is emotionally immature.
4. The owner has a poor psychological support system.
5. The owner is younger than 20 or older than 50.
6. The owner is female.

However, Holcomb also advocates four treatment strategies that should be utilized by the veterinarian to facilitate the recovery process:

1. *Empathy:* Give the clients the feeling that you understand their emotional state.
2. *Active listening:* Listen to the concerns behind the concerns.
3. *Stage management of euthanasia:* Set the stage for the procedure as much as possible in accordance with the client's wishes. Suggest a means for ritualized mourning, if appropriate.
4. *Time:* Give the client as much time as possible to talk about the significance of the loss.

REPLACING THE PET

Just as a human being is irreplaceable, a new animal can never take the place of a beloved pet. What can be filled, however, is the space and the role the pet occupied. Widows and widowers remarry, parents who have lost a child enjoy other children, so pet owners usually find a new animal friend to share their lives.

The question then is how soon, and there are no hard and fast answers. Stewart[47] found that, particularly for children, the presence of a second pet was definitely comforting. The multipet family would thus have some built-in supports during bereavement. Quackenbush[48] says that the death of a pet disrupts the social system of the owner and that the grief response is due to the loss of these interactions with pets on which the owners have come to depend. The presence of other pets provides these interactions and helps preserve the continuity of the owner's life.

There are individuals who, anticipating the eventual death of a pet, get a second pet when the older one reaches a certain age or stage of infirmity. Although some might think this is emotionally cruel to the established pet, it does not have to be as long as the old pet is given as much time and love and special attention as the newcomer. In fact, there are many stories of aged, infirm pets rejuvenating and getting a "second wind" when an energetic youngster comes to the house.

Quackenbush[49] advises against getting a new pet too soon because the owner may not have had enough time to get over the death of the old pet. The owner may also feel guilty because a new pet implies the dead pet is replaceable. One small study found that of 25 short-term pet replacements, 72% were the same breed of dog or cat and 72% the same sex. Fifty-two percent of all replacements were an identical breed and sex of the animal that died.[50] A second study looking at replacement cats found that replacement time was much shorter if the new cat was similar to the cat that died. Cats of the same color replaced the former pet in 13 days, compared with 174 days for a cat of a different color. Cats of the same sex replaced the former pet in 56 days, compared with 219 days for different sex cats.[51] Says Messent:[52]

> It seems that owners may adopt a strategy of trying to find a replica of their dead pet, especially if replacement is rapid. With a longer gap before replacement, owners are less inclined to opt for a pet that is very similar to their last one.

Some owners never replace the pet: on the other hand, I know a woman who made sure a new kitten was home waiting for her when she returned from her 16-year-old cat's euthanasia. Most pet owners fall between these two extremes. Usually someone who has been a responsible pet owner and who has worked through his or her grief will eventually opt for another animal.

Many pet owners need only a little prodding and support to take the plunge again. And why not? We are no more limited to loving one pet than we are limited to loving one person. In fact, in defiance of the laws of physics, it often seems the more love we give, the more we have available to give. There are not enough good pet homes for all the animals who need them: what a pity if a kind, caring home is lost because the grieving owner has no support or solace during bereavement or has a mistaken idea of loyalty to a dead pet. I think that the opportunity to provide a loving home, good care, even a chance at life for another pet is the most fitting tribute to the deceased animal. It is a living memorial; it is a way of saying thank you to the lost animal for all that has been shared and learned.

REFERENCES

1. Fenner, W. R. (1981). Caring for a pet as a model for caring for a human. Paper presented at the Symposium on Veterinary Medical Practice: Pet Loss and Human Emotions, New York, N.Y. 1981. *Archives of the Foundation of Thanatology, 9*(2), 31.

2. Levinson, B. M. (1967). The pet and the child's bereavement. *Mental Hygiene, 51,* 197–200.

3. Nieburg, H. A. & Fischer, A. (1982). *Pet loss: A thoughtful guide for adults and children.* New York: Harper Row.

4. Stewart, M. (1983). Loss of a pet – loss of a person: A comparative study of bereavement. In A. H. Katcher & A. M. Beck (Eds.), *New perspectives on our lives with companion animals.* Philadelphia: University of Pennsylvania Press.

5. Robin, M. & ten Bensel, R. (1985). Pets and the socialization of children. In M. B. Sussman (Ed.), *Pets and the family* (pp. 63–78). New York: The Haworth Press.

6. Cowles, K. V. (1985). The death of a pet: Human responses to the breaking of the bond. In M. B. Sussman (Ed.), *Pets and the family* (pp. 135–148). New York: The Haworth Press.

7. Levinson, B. M. (1972). *Pets and human development.* Springfield, IL: Charles C. Thomas.

8. Quackenbush, J. E. (1984). Pet bereavement in older owners. In R. K. Anderson, B. L. Hart, & L. A. Hart (Eds.), *The pet connection* (pp. 292–299). Minneapolis: University of Minnesota Press.

9. Ibid.

10. Ibid.

11. Kübler-Ross, E. (1969). *On death and dying.* New York: Macmillan.

12. Cowles, K. V. (1985). op. cit.

13. Hopkins, A. F. (1984). Pet death: Effects on the client and the veterinarian. In R. K. Anderson, B. L. Hart, & L. A. Hart (Eds.), *The pet connection* (pp. 276–282). Minneapolis: University of Minnesota Press.

14. Cowles, K. V. (1985). op. cit.

15. Nieburg, H. A. & Fischer, A. (1982). op. cit.

16. Harris, J. M. (1984). Understanding animal death: Bereavement, grief, and euthanasia. In R. K. Anderson, B. L. Hart & L. A. Hart (Eds.), *The pet connection* (pp. 261–275). Minneapolis: University of Minnesota Press.

17. Hopkins, A. F. (1984). op. cit.

18. Harris, J. M. op. cit.

19. Cowles, K. V. (1985). op. cit.

20. Holcomb, R. (1985, spring). Psychological dimensions of pet loss. Paper presented at the 1984 Annual Meeting of the Delta Society, abstracted in *People-Animals-Environment, 3*(1), 10–11.

21. Katcher, A. H. & Rosenberg, M. A. (1979). Euthanasia and the management of the client's grief. *Compendium on Continuing Education,* 1, 887–891.

22. Carmack, B. J. (1985). The effects on family members and functioning after the death of a pet. In M. B. Sussman (Ed.), *Pets and the Family* (pp. 149–162). New York: The Haworth Press.

23. Pet Food Institute. Cited by Hopkins, A. F. (1984). op. cit.

24. Wille, R. (1985, spring). A comparative study of the relationship between loneliness and pet companionship in a retirement community. *The Latham Letter,* p. 16.

25. McCulloch, M. J. (1983). Incidence of euthanasia and euthanasia alternatives in veterinary practice. In A. H. Katcher & A. M. Beck (Eds.), *New Perspectives on our lives with companion animals.* Philadelphia: University of Pennsylvania Press.

26. Levinson, B. M. (1981). Human grief on the loss of an animal companion. Paper presented at the Symposium on Veterinary Medical Practice: Pet Loss and Human Emotions, New York, N.Y. 1981. *Archives of the Foundation of Thanatology, 9*(2), 5.

27. Antelyes, J. (1981). When the pet animal dies — Attitudes and behavior of the veterinarian. Paper presented at the Symposium on Veterinary Medical Practice: Pet Loss and Human Emotions, New York, N.Y. 1981. *Archives of the Foundation of Thanatology, 9*(2), 6.

28. Crow, S. E. (1981). Pet owner grief in a university hospital. *Archives of the Foundation of Thanatology, 9*(2), 23.

29. Stewart, M. (1983). op. cit.

30. Kelly, J. A. (1984, summer). Facing the loss of a family pet. *The Latham Letter,* p. 1–3.

31. Burt, M. R. (1981). The euthanasia decision: An analytical model. Paper presented at the Symposium on Veterinary Medical Practice: Pet Loss and Human

Emotions, New York, N.Y. 1981. *Archives of the Foundation of Thanatology,* 9(2), 14.

32. Quackenbush, J. (1985). *When your pet dies.* New York: Simon & Schuster.

33. Cowles, K. V. (1985). op. cit.

34. DeGroot, A. (1984). Preparing the veterinarian for dealing with the emotions of pet loss. In R. K. Anderson, B. L. Hart, & L. A. Hart (Ed.), *The pet connection* (pp. 283–291). Minneapolis: University of Minnesota Press.

35. Harris, J. M. (1984). op. cit.

36. Ibid.

37. Hopkins, A. F. (1984). op. cit.

38. Harris, J. M. (1984). op. cit.

39. Cowles, K. V. (1985) op. cit.

40. Stewart, M. (1983). op. cit.

41. Harris, J. M. (1984). op. cit.

42. Carmack, B. J. (1985). op. cit.

43. Stewart, M. (1983). op. cit.

44. Harris, J. H. (1982). A study of client grief responses to death or loss in a companion animal veterinary practice. *California Veterinarian, 36,* 17–19.

45. Katcher, A. H. & Rosenberg, M. A. (1979). op. cit.

46. Holcomb, R. (1985). op. cit.

47. Stewart, M. (1983). op. cit.

48. Quackenbush, J. (1982). The social context of pet loss. *Animal Health Technician, 3,* 333–336.

49. Quackenbush, J. (1985). op. cit.

50. Payence, P. (1982, March). La Mort et les familiers. Paper presented at the meeting of the Society for Companion Animal Studies, Paris. Cited by Messent, P. R. (1984) below in reference 52.

51. Spencer, A. (1983, March). Replacement cats. Paper presented at the meeting of the Society for Companion Animal Studies, London. Cited by Messent, P. R. (1984) below in reference 52.

52. Messent P. R. (1984). Correlates and effects of pet ownership. In R. K. Anderson, B. L. Hart, & L. A. Hart (Eds.), *The pet connection* (pp. 331–340). Minneapolis: University of Minnesota Press.

CHAPTER 16

Pet-Facilitated Therapy
for the Physically Challenged

No discussion of pet-facilitated therapy would be complete without a brief review of the ways in which animals can act as physical extensions of ourselves, compensating for congenital or accidental loss of senses, limbs, or motor functions. This chapter in no way attempts to be a complete overview of this field; that would take several volumes in itself. However, I would like to discuss two specific treatment strategies, equestrian therapy and the use of service dogs, to give the reader a sense of the immense and multiple benefits animals offer to the physically challenged.

EQUESTRIAN THERAPY

Although formal equestrian therapy is a relatively recent technique, the use of the horse as an aid in human recovery from illness is not new. The early Greeks prescribed riding to improve the morale of persons who were otherwise untreatable.[1] In the 1600s, Thomas Sydenham recommended daily riding for gout, and in the 17th century, August Tissot insisted the sport alleviated the symptoms of tuberculosis.[2]

Therapeutic riding, in its present application, originated in Europe in the 1950s. Considerable interest in this form of therapy for disabled individuals arose with Liz Hartel of Denmark, who, though wheelchair-bound, won a silver medal in dressage at the 1952 Olympics in Helsinki. Later, Elsbet Bodtker of Norway began using her own ponies to provide riding sessions for victims of polio and cerebral palsy, thus initiating the treatment in her country.[3]

Such programs now exist throughout the world. In the United States there are currently more than 160 accredited institutions that give physically handicapped children a chance to ride and associate with horses.

According to psychiatrist Michael McCulloch,[4] these programs offer psychological, social, and physical benefits. For children confined to a wheelchair, the horse, for once in their lives, allows them to sit higher than their peers, giving their self-image a needed boost. With the aid of the animal physically disabled children can compete with other children in sports events. Finally, the physical condition required to ride provides an incentive for the youngsters to continue their tedious therapeutic regime with weights and pulleys.

According to Karen DePauw,[5] of Washington State University, equestrian therapy is a multifaceted treatment that has three main components: medicine, psychology-education, and horsemanship, each of which includes several sub-divisions. The medical component encompasses hippotherapy and riding therapy. Hippotherapy refers to passive riding, in which the patient sits on the horse and is placed in different positions, thus accommodating himself or herself to the swinging motions of the animal. The success of hippotherapy has been demonstrated by X rays and electromyographs, and the transference of the swinging motions from horse to patient has been verified by scientific films.[6]

In riding therapy the patient not only is passively exercised by the horse, but also performs exercises such as those for relaxation, stretching, strengthening, equilibrium, reflex, and coordination. Riding therapy is individually prescribed and usually complements other physical therapy treatment.[7]

The psychology-education component includes therapeutic remedial education riding and vaulting. Therapeutic remedial education riding utilizes education methods incorporating the horse and has effected positive changes in youngsters with both physical and behavioral problems. Natalie Bieber conducted a study at the handicapped unit of the Village School in North Haven, Connecticut. Bieber's subjects ranged in age from 6-17 years and were afflicted with such disabling disorders as spina bifida and cerebral palsy. The program consisted of 1 day of riding on a gentle horse or in the pony cart and 2 days in the classroom using horse and horse-related material as an incentive for learning. Staff who evaluated the children found that most benefited significantly from the program. One retarded child who was also withdrawn demonstrated beginning signs of communication prompted by a picture of a horse.[8]

Vaulting is the performance of gymnastic exerises on horseback, and has value in correcting behavior problems, diminishing anxieties, building up trust and concentration, improving self-esteem, providing stimulation for the sensorimotor system, and increasing social interaction and friendship.

Horsemanship includes riding for rehabilitative purposes, explains DePauw,[9] and is valuable both in enhancing physical functioning and in uplifting mental attitudes. In athletic competition, the horse is the great equalizer that allows the disabled to compete with able-bodied peers.

Research into the value of therapeutic horseback riding can be traced back to 1875, when the French neurologist Chassaignac found that the physical movements of the horse improved patients' posture, balance, joint movement, and muscle control. He also noticed an improvement in morale and said that riding was most beneficial to paraplegics and patients with other neurological disorders.[10]

Webb[11] reports on a 1969 study at Queen Mary's Hospital near London. After only a few weeks, 6 riders (3 who were mentally retarded and 3 who were physically impaired) showed dramatic improvements in behavior, language, communication, and motor function, resulting in the almost immediate expansion of the program.

Rosenthal[12] evaluated horseback riding as a form of "risk exercise," which he says increases self-confidence, courage, and motivation. He studied 102 children in therapeutic riding centers in England, Ireland, Wales, Canada, and the United States, and found that the children had significantly improved in mobility, motivation, and courage. Morale boosts ranging from elation to euphoria were also common.

Renaud[13] has identified several physiological reasons that account for the rehabilitative value of therapeutic riding:

1. improved neuromuscular control of head and trunk
2. maintenance of symmetry and physiological posture
3. improvement of muscular control of hip joints
4. inherent motivation factor
5. increased coordination in voluntary muscular action
6. continuous challenge and stimulation to the vestibular system
7. considerable amount of sensory stimulation reaching cerebral cortex, which may account for increases in attention span and concentration

According to research presentations at the Fourth International Congress on Therapeutic Riding in 1982, hippotherapy was found to be effective supplementary treatment for patients suffering from scoliosis (curvature of the spine). Using electromyography, Bausenwen[14] found that therapeutic riding normalized muscle tone and improved coordination. DePauw[15] reports on a riding therapy program for the physically and mentally handicapped in Washington, D. C. The program was evaluated on a yearly basis since 1975, incorporating input from teachers, parents, and the students themselves. In summary:

1. Average gain in motor skills ranged from 7% to 31%.
2. Eighty-eight percent of the participating children were found to have improved language skills, with the average gain between 9% to 29%.
3. Average gains of 6% to 19% were found in emotional control, social awareness, peer relations and self-concept.
4. Seventy percent of the children showed notable improvement in work skills, with an average gain of 17%.
5. Eighty-seven percent of the parents commented upon their child's improved self-confidence. There was a 52% decrease in the number of negative statements by the child.
6. Teachers' overall evaluation of the effectiveness of the program was "very good" or "excellent."

Rehabilitative horseback riding can also benefit those with language disorders, according to a study by Ruth Dismuke, of Therapeutic Horsemanship of New Mexico.

Dismuke selected as subjects 30 children who ranged in age from

6 to 10 years old and were classified as moderately to severely language disordered. The 30 children were matched for age, type, and degree of language disorder, and were randomly assigned to the treatment of control group.

All subjects received language therapy for three 1 hour sessions per week for 12 weeks. The control group received therapy in a public school therapy setting; the experimental group was treated in a structured horsemanship program in which the speech and language pathologists were also professional riding instructors. Independent testers who were unaware of the children's group placement evaluated their improvement through tape-recorded conversations.

The results indicated that the horsemanship program facilitated the language therapy. Although both treatment groups demonstrated more complex sentence structure following therapy, the experimental group demonstrated an increased frequency of the number of intelligible, analyzable utterances, as well as more complex use of phrase and clause structure.

Explains Dismuke:[16]

> The [experimental] subjects showed great improvement not only in the ability to use more complex language structure, but also in the ability to use their language in an efficient and appropriate manner. Although the control group made some significant gains in language complexity, these gains do not reflect the development of a more mature language system. The use of the structured horseback riding setting as a medium for language therapy appears to have facilitated more productive development of language skills. Further, the experimental group demonstrated significant gains in the supplemental areas of muscle strength, sensorimotor integration, and self-esteem.

DOGS FOR THE
PHYSICALLY CHALLENGED

Canines, because of their seemingly infinite versatility, have for centuries functioned as extensions of their human companions. Keen smell, sharp hearing, agility, and mobility have enabled the dog to fulfill virtually any role asked of it. Guide dogs for the blind are the most well-known service animals. Recently dogs have been functioning as ears for the hearing impaired and as arms and legs for the physically disabled.

But these dogs function as far more than prostheses. Perhaps even more important, they provide tremendous psychological support to their companions, who often find social and emotional barriers far more difficult to surmount than physical ones.

Alysia Zee,[17] of the University of Pennsylvania, surveyed 44 guide dog owners and found that the dogs not only offered their human companions greater mobility, but also gave them an increased capability to cope with their blindness. The positive aspects of guide dog ownership include acceptance of life and risk taking, expression of feelings, assertiveness, personal achievement, orientation to the present, relaxation, improved body image, security, self-control, self-awareness, and opportunities for social outlets.

Hearing dogs to assist deaf and hearing impaired persons are currently being trained by various organizations around the country. The dogs respond to the telephone, the doorbell, the fire alarm, and such specialized needs as the timer on a microwave oven or a crying baby. Owners of the dogs report a decreased dependency on hearing people and a newfound freedom that may allow them to live alone or free the hearing spouse from anxiety when he or she has to leave the impaired spouse.

The dogs also help their owners realized cherished dreams. Canine Companions for Independence (CCI), a California-based organization, trains Signal dogs (to act as ears for the deaf), Social dogs (who become institutional mascots and cotherapists), and Service dogs (to function as limbs for the handicapped). One placement gave a young woman the courage to start a family. The woman's husband had normal hearing but worked a late shift, and she feared she would be unable to hear her baby's cries in the night. With a signal dog, alert and trained to respond to the slightest sound, she could put her mind at ease. Another signal dog, whose owner has a dental laboratory, alerts his master to all the timers and sounds of the electronic equipment.

The first official helping hand dog may have been Thunder of the Mountain, later dubbed the "Wonder Dog," a German Shepherd dog that belonged to Len and Betty Cohen of New Jersey. Betty was born without arms. Len was born with only one arm, yet, in spite of having had no special instruction, he trained the dog himself. Len gives all the credit to Thunder, who, he says, instinctively seemed to know what was asked of him.

Thunder's skills seemed endless: He turned the lights on and off, delivered the bank deposit, brought the vacuum cleaner and its attachments, and cleared the dinner table and put the dishes in the sink. He answered the phone and opened the door. He could carry a soda can upstairs without spilling a drop. Thunder even played Parcheesi, but had a penchant for rolling the dice out of turn.

Thunder became so celebrated that he and his owners traveled throughout the United States and Canada demonstrating his prowess. He even visited the White House and met then-president Richard Nixon.

Thunder died in 1981, but not before his example showed how valuable and helpful a specially trained dog can be. Says Len Cohen:[18] "I understand there are now some 5,000 dogs trained to help the handicapped who are doing things for their owners similar to what Thunder did for us. Thunder paved the way for these dogs. He was the first."

Part of Thunder's legacy are surely the superbly trained service dogs of CCI. Bonnie Bergin, who along with her husband Jim founded CCI in 1975, got the inspiration for her organization during an overseas teaching assignment in Asia, where she noticed animals used by the disabled to accomplish daily tasks.

The Bergins' first puppy was Abdul, a Labrador/Golden Retriever mix that found a home with Kerry Knaus. Since infancy, Knaus has been the victim of an incurable, crippling muscle disease. Her condition was so severe that she was not expected to live beyond early childhood. She defied the odds and, although confined to an electric wheelchair, at the age of 16 she moved away from her parents, determined to make a life for herself.

Knaus trained Abdul herself and graduated at the top of her obedience training class. The dog responds to over 100 commands: He turns lights off and on, picks up items that Knaus needs, opens doors, helps her with the shopping. He wears a backpack that is actually her purse and briefcase, and when she needs a particular item, he positions himself in such a way that, in spite of her limited mobility, she can easily get it. Abdul even turns on the heater in the specially designed van that Knaus drives. In fact, he fetches her pillow and places it behind her back.

Because of Abdul, Knaus can manage with only a part-time human attendant, a financial savings that could amount to $90,000 within 10 years. But Abdul's worth is far beyond money. With Abdul as her constant companion, ready to do her every bidding, Knaus, who works full time as the placement coordinator for CCI, no longer has to depend on someone else for her needs and wishes. She has control over her life in a way she never thought possible. And in learning to control the willful puppy, the strength of her own personality has emerged. Once passive, unassuming, even shy, the young woman has blossomed into a forceful spokesperson for CCI and its potential for the disabled. "She has gone from a soft-spoken yes-person to an assertive, even aggressive, knowledgeable dog-person," says Jim Bergin.

The canine companion can open social doors as well as physical ones. Jim Bergen recalls the poignant story of Kathy, a young quadriplegic with a severe speech impediment. Someone had just donated a collie, and although Bonnie Bergin had some misgivings about Kathy's ability to groom the dog's luxurious silky coat, she decided to give it a try. Intrigued when his wife said how well the sessions were going, Jim decided to see for himself:[19]

> Bonnie had talked with Kathy for awhile about how things were going and they started to walk toward town to do some training. I walked behind and heard Kathy's unrecognized utterance at which time the dog promptly sat at the side of her wheelchair. Obviously, he understood Kathy better than I did. The next sound I heard was one that anyone could understand. No language barriers could have contained the pure golden timbre of the laugh of Kathy's success.
>
> A little later, as we walked toward town, Bonnie had dropped back to let Kathy work the dog on her own when some kids came up to Kathy and started asking questions about the dog. At first I thought they were a problem because they were interfering with her training, but it didn't take long to

realize that what was happening was an invaluable social interaction with people who never would have stopped to talk with
Kathy if it hadn't been for the dog at her side. The fact that she
had control over this dog intuitively told the kids that Kathy
was okay, no matter how different she looked or sounded.
Kathy was elated.

Fortunately, Kathy's experiences are not unique. A study of the
socializing effects of service dogs found that individuals in wheel-
chairs reported a significantly higher number of social encounters
when accompanied by the dog than without the animal. As a bonus,
the individuals increased their evening outings after obtaining the
dog. "For disabled people who yearn for increased social contact,
prescribing a service dog may be a specifically targeted socializing
device," say the researchers.[20]

ADDITIONAL THOUGHTS

It might be a therapist's pipe dream to place an animal specially
trained to meet the needs of every physically challenged individual.
This is neither probable nor desirable. Helping hand pets are a tremendous asset and valuable addition to an ongoing therapy program, but they are not a panacea, nor are they suitable for all patients.

Some individuals are so impaired mentally or physically that they
are not able to provide minimal care for an animal. In these cases
animals can be used only with constant supervision. Dogs have so
far been unsuccessful as aids to people who are both blind and deaf
because the lack of reinforcement causes their training to be extinguished rapidly.

The unique Capuchin Monkey Project[21] headed by Mary Joan
Willard is currently training these small primates to perform various
tasks for quadriplegics. The capuchins, which are best known as
organ grinders' performers, are being bred especially for the project. In fact, taking a page from guide dog programs, Willard is
looking for loving homes to rear the babies for the first 2-1/2 years
of their lives so that they will be sociable, affectionate, and amenable to the extensive training. To date, the animals placed seem ca-

pable of a dazzling variety of tasks. They may be far more suitable for the confines of a small apartment than a dog, and they certainly don't require walking. They do not eliminate the need for part-time human aides. They do, however, help ease the terribly lonely hours many quadriplegics face and, like their canine counterpart, facilitate social communication. One young woman reports that before she got her monkey "Henry" (short for Henrietta) people would stare at her and turn away. Her primate companion, however, has inspired many pleasant and humorous encounters. People are so curious about Henry that they forget about her disability.

We take such simple human interactions for granted and seldom realize how vitally important they are to someone who is "different" and isolated from others because of that difference. The despair and isolation of many disabled individuals has led to suicide or suicidal thoughts. Could such individuals find additional enrichment and meaning in their lives with a companion animal? As previously noted, no current study has correlated pet ownership and suicide; however, some intriguing preliminary studies from Hungary suggest that where a close human-pet relationship exists, suicide will not occur. Not a single case of suicide of a blind person with a dog has been reported.[22] Sometimes the objection is raised that the ongoing cost, supplies, and veterinary care of keeping a dog may be prohibitive for some individuals. This is the weakest of the objections since as the story of Kerry Knaus illustrates, the service dog can, by reducing the cost of human care, be immensely cost-effective. Additionally, donation of a service dog is an area ripe for development by charities. Many community and civic groups sponsor seeing eye and hearing dog placements and would likely be just as willing to place a helping hand dog.

No, a helping hand pet is not for everyone, nor will it take the place of a human care giver. On the other hand, however, sometimes the role of the animal is so vital, so unique that a human cannot take its place either. This final example comes from ABC's "World News Tonight." Roger Caras[23] reported on Sheba, a dog trained by Sue Miller at the Purdy Treatment Center (see Chapter 13). Sheba was trained to be the companion of a young adolescent, Angie, who has suffered from chronic seizures since childhood. The seizures come several times a day; sometimes Angie stops breathing. Before Sheba came, the young woman could not even wash her hair without supervision for fear she would have a sudden attack. But Sheba "knows" when Angie is about to have a seizure, she makes the young woman lie down so she won't injure herself in a fall and then monitors her breathing during the attack. Sheba has given Angie a sense of freedom and enriched her life in a way that her people, no matter how loving and caring, could not. That's pet-facilitated therapy at its best.

REFERENCES

1. Mayberry, R. P. (1978). The mystique of the horse is strong medicine: Riding as therapeutic recreation. *Rehabilitation Literature, 39,* 192–196.
2. DePauw, K. P. (1984). Therapeutic horseback riding in Europe and North America. In R. K. Anderson, B. L. Hart, L. A. Hart (Eds.), *The pet connection* (p. 141). Minneapolis: University of Minnesota Press.
3. Ibid. p. 142.
4. McCulloch, M. (1983). Pet facilitated psychotherapy. In A. H. Katcher & A. M. Beck (Eds.), *New perspectives on our lives with companion animals.* Philadelphia: University of Pennsylvania Press.
5. DePauw, K. P. (1984). op. cit., p. 142.
6. Timm, C. (1983, spring). Fourth international congress for therapeutic riding. *People-Animals-Environment,* 1(1), 21–22.
7. DePauw, K. P. (1984). op. cit., pp. 141–153.
8. Bieber, N. (1983). The integration of a therapeutic equestrian program in the academic environment of children with physical and multiple handicaps. In A. H. Katcher & A. M. Beck (Eds.), *New perspectives on our lives with companion animals.* Philadelphia: University of Pennsylvania Press.
9. DePauw, K. P. (1984). op. cit., pp. 141–153.
10. Bain, A. M. (1965). Pony riding for the disabled. *Physical Therapy, 51,* 263–265.
11. Webb, K. (1982, August). Four good legs. *Therapeutisches Reiten '82. Proceedings of the Fourth International Congress on Therapeutic Riding.* Cited by DePauw, K. P. (1984). op. cit., p. 145.
12. Rosenthal, S. R. (1975). Risk exercise and the physically handicapped. *Rehabilitation Literature, 36,* 144–149.
13. Renaud, R. E. (1982, August). Horseback riding for the disabled: A review of some physiologic concepts. *Theraputisches Reiten '82. Proceedings of the Fourth International Congress on Therapeutic Riding.* Cited by DePauw, K. P. (1984). op. cit., p. 146.
14. Bausenwein, I. (1982, August). Electromygraphische untersuchungen zur objektivierung des therapeutischen reitens bei serbalparetikern. *Therapeutishes*

Reiten '82. Proceedings of the 4th International Congress on Therapeutic Riding. Cited by DePauw, K. P. (1984). op. cit., p. 147.

15. Ibid.

16. Dismuke, R. P. (1984). Rehabilitative horseback riding for children with language disorders. In R. K. Anderson, B. L. Hart, & L. A. Hart (Eds.). *The pet connection* (pp. 131–140). Minneapolis: University of Minnesota Press.

17. Zee, A. Guide dogs and their owners: Assistance and friendship. Paper presented at the International Conference on the Human Companion Animal Bond. (1981, October). Philadelphia, PA.

18. Cusack, O. & Smith, E. (1984). *Pets and the elderly: The therapeutic bond* (p. 68). New York: The Haworth Press.

19. Cusack, O. (1984, August). The amazing dogs at Bonnie Bergin's. *Ladies' Circle.*

20. Hart, L. A., Hart, B. L., & Bergin, B. (1985, October). Socializing effects of service dogs for people with disabilities. Paper presented at the annual meeting of the Delta Society, Denver, CO.

21. Salvatore, D. (1986, May). A very special love story. *Ladies' Home Journal.*

22. Pethes, G. (1983, October). Some aspects of the human-pet relationship in Hungary. Paper presented at the International Symposium on the Occasion of the 80th Birthday of Nobel Prize Winner Prof. Dr. Konrad Lorenz. Vienna, Austria.

23. Caras, R. (1986, February 12). *ABC World News Tonight.*

CHAPTER 17

Closing Thoughts

Although general definitions of "pet therapy" and the related terms "pet-facilitated therapy" and "animal-facilitated therapy" (which at this stage of the discipline's development are mostly interchangeable) are given at the beginning of Chapter 1, nowhere in the course of this book do I define them precisely. This is not an oversight but a deliberate effort not to impose limits in this exciting new field.

Pet therapy is not a single treatment or strategy. It may be as simple as stroking a pet cat to relax or as complex as training an animal to function as a person's eyes, ears, or limbs. I disagree with critics who insist that the recreational use of animals (as in institutional visiting pet programs) is not strictly a form of "therapy." I prefer to consider therapy in its broadest sense for it is only by looking at all possibilities that we can begin to understand the impact that animals make in our lives.

Kidd and Kidd[1] note four traditional definitions of therapy:

1. treatment and its techniques
2. subjecting a person to an action or influence
3. an effort to ameliorate an undesirable condition
4. an attempt to help a person attain better health or psychological adjustment

By these definitions, play and leisure activity with animals certainly qualify.

Can we say that just placing a pet in a room with a person constitutes a form of therapy? Of course not; something else must occur, and that something else is an interaction between the person and the pet. It may be passive, such as watching fish in an aquarium, or it may be active, such as petting a dog or cat. Implied in this interaction is that the relationship between the person and pet is a positive one. In the case of an active interaction, the relationship is symbiotic, that is, beneficial to both parties. Pet animals certainly thrive on our love as much as we thrive on theirs.

The therapeutic effect, then, appears to be an outgrowth of the human-animal bond, that often elusive attachment between a person and a pet that transcends species barriers and even logic. Many recent studies demonstrate that the significant factor in pet-owner relationships is the degree of attachment to the pet. Strong attachment correlates with improved morale, increased happiness, and optimism, whereas low or no attachment is related to unhappiness and the perception of the pet as a burden.

What determines attachment to a pet? There are no hard-and-fast rules. Research by Kidd in the United States and Serpell in Great Britain (see Chapter 4) indicates that childhood experiences with pets appear to be an important factor in adult pet ownership. Other research by Kidd (see Chapter 4) points out differences between people that like dogs or that like cats or that like both equally. It is not clear, however, if certain psychological traits predispose attachment to a certain animal or if interacting with the animal actually enhances or nurtures these traits.

Does everyone benefit from human-animal interactions? Populations that appear to benefit range from nonviolent criminals to chief executive officers. Studies have so far identified only two groups for whom pets appear to be a liability: men who belong to service organizations (see Chapter 2) and rural, low-income elderly women (see Chapter 11). Certainly there are individuals — dangerous criminals for example — who should not have access to an animal. There are others whose severe mental impairment demands that any pet keeping be carefully supervised. Potentially everyone could benefit, but not everyone does. This distinction is one of the challenges facing pet therapy researchers.

In addition to determining who benefits, we also need to learn exactly "how" one benefits. Yes, interacting with a pet definitely lowers blood pressure, so spending time with an animal friend can be an effective relaxant. However, can daily and ongoing human-animal interaction achieve prolonged blood pressure reduction? Can we prescribe, for example, 10 minutes petting King or Fluffy three times a day as an effective technique to combat hypertension? Do high-bond pet owners have lower overall blood pressure than low-bond pet owners or nonowners? These are questions that have not yet been answered.

Aside from physiological responses, what behavioral effects can we reasonably expect from pet therapy? Critics have charged that an increase in smiling, for example, does not constitute a valid therapeutic benefit. Perhaps not, but it usually is indicative of a positive psychological state, however transitory. Perhaps too much is expected from a once-a-week, 1-hour group visit. Yet some studies (see Chapter 11) found definite improvement in a variety of behaviors after these visits, and sometimes the improvement persisted long after the visit had ended. Various other studies cited have demonstrated a decrease in aggression, hostility, and depression in groups with access to a pet. These variables, however, were measured during the course of the respective studies, and there is no way to know if the improvement was permanent. Still other studies found little or no improvement between pet and nonpet groups.

Another major question facing researchers is "why" pets have the effect they do. Pet therapy is badly in need of a theoretical framework in which to begin to design experiments and postulate hypotheses. Currently, human-animal bond and pet therapy studies are pieces of a giant jigsaw puzzle. Certain parts interlock to reveal small, tantalizing sections — the physiological studies, for example. Other puzzle parts don't fit, and whole portions are still missing. But even more exasperating, the puzzle comes in a plain brown box, and we have, as yet, no idea what the complete picture will look like. Theories about our need to return to nature or to feel one with the earth are attractive and feel intuitively correct, but they are generally too broad and vague to be tested experimentally. In contrast, Brickel's distraction model (see Chapter 4), though highly testable, is applicable only to certain facets of human-animal interaction.

Until more of these questions have been answered, can we — should we — endorse pet therapy so enthusiastically? Critics have charged that if the costs and risks of pet therapy are to be justified, this treatment must work better than existing therapies or must ben-

efit groups of individuals who have not been helped by more conventional means.[2] Let's examine these charges in detail.

Critics who wish to look at the cost-benefit of pet therapy compared to existing therapies have complained about the lack of financial data from existing pet therapy programs. This is a petty criticism. Pets are simply not that expensive. Even high estimates of
food, grooming, and veterinary costs average about $300–400 year
for a medium-sized dog, $500–700 for a large dog, and $150–200
for a cat. These costs can be further reduced if, for example, the pet
is groomed by the owner and pet food coupons are used. If the
facility housed 100 patients, costs would range from $1.50 per pa-
tient per year up to $7.00 per year. This is the cost of a few boxes of
letter paper or a few skeins of yarn, hardly exorbitant. Care of the
pet can easily be incorporated into the duties of an aide, and perhaps
can even be performed by the patients so that an extra staff member
need not be hired. Of course, a visiting pet program conducted by
volunteers is entirely free.

The costs of placing a pet with an individual can be offset by
careful selection of a low-upkeep animal, support from the humane
society, and veterinary support. Many shelters have such placement
programs for unwanted animals and senior citizens, and the cost to
the individual is extremely low. In addition, people who receive
these pets are usually high-bond individuals who have expressed a
strong desire to have a pet. These are the very people who would
stand to benefit the most from them.

Concern about possible pet-related health risks, particularly with
elderly, frail, and susceptible individuals, is a valid consideration,
but facts indicate that fears in this regard are largely unfounded. In
fact, a major Minnesota study found that people pose more of a risk
than pets (see Chapter 11). Regular veterinary care, common sense,
and proper sanitation can make pet therapy as close as possible to
being risk free.

Once cost and health risks are eliminated, there seems to be no
reason to deny pets to the many persons who enjoy them. For most
residents of institutions, an animal is a pleasant, entertaining morale
booster. Even if one does not want to consider this "therapy," the
amusement factor certainly enhances and enlivens the institutional
environment. There are many examples of recreational therapy:

dance, music, arts and crafts, for example. To my knowledge none of these therapies has been subjected to the same scrutiny and criticism as pet therapy. They are available to patients with the understanding that they will at least temporarily provide entertainment, improve morale, and alleviate boredom for some, not necessarily all, individuals. Even the harshest critics of pet therapy programs have to admit that the sessions with the animals do this.

Are patients reacting to the placebo effect? Do they feel better because they are expected to feel better? Even if part of the therapeutic process involves a placebo effect, this should not be discounted. We are learning that the mind's influence on our body is more powerful than we ever imagined. A recent Harvard study, for example, demonstrated that a combination of relaxation and imagery could boost the immune system.[3] Some practitioners advocate imagery and visualization are used in combination with other therapies to fight cancer and other diseases. This research may add a new dimension to the concept of the placebo. Do those who believe in the efficacy of pet therapy reap greater benefits than those who do not? It is certainly a concept worth examining.

Pet therapy, thus, meets the minimal requirements for therapeutic benefit at little cost and low risk. But there is still another consideration that must be discussed and that is the well-being of the cotherapists, the animals, themselves.

After the 1983 human-animal bond conferences at the Universities of Minnesota and California-Irvine, a purist animal rights organization, Citizens United for Animal Rights, put out a scathing denunciation of the entire bond and pet therapy concepts. They viewed this new field as another way for animal researchers to get grant monies, and saw immense potential for animal abuse in, for example, nursing homes and prisons.

Unfortunately, any activity that involves animals has potential for abuse. We can no more guarantee the welfare of every animal therapist than we can guarantee the welfare of every household pet. But pet therapy programs do have some safeguards that should minimize the potential for abuse.

First, in order to be therapeutically effective, the animal must be healthy, happy, and loved. Nothing can be gained with a sick or fearful pet. When the media first reported about the health benefits of companion animals, a correspondent of mine grumbled about people getting pets just to reduce their blood pressure. I assured her it would not happen. People do not even stay with medically-recommended diets or exercise programs; some don't even take their medication. So they are not going to take on the responsibility of a pet simply because it may have health benefits. And I doubt if stroking a pet would have a beneficial effect on someone who perceived it as a chore or a burden. Those of us who love our pets seek them out as friends and companions. We relish the time we spend with them and look upon the disagreeable aspects of pet ownership as simply a small price to pay for all the joy we receive.

Visiting pet programs are as close as possible to being abuse-proof. They are usually conducted through humane societies or dog clubs and involve volunteers with exemplary motives. These individuals are giving up leisure time to perform a service for no payment and sometimes little thanks, except the internal satisfaction that comes from helping others. And the animals, many of them former show dogs that are social and people-oriented, seem to enjoy the visits as much as the patients. In addition, these programs are "media darlings," and the group that wants to take its members and pets to local hospitals or geriatric facilities is usually assured a nice story and photographs in the paper or a feature on the local TV news. Although critics have complained that this media attention lauds pet therapy beyond its current scientific validity, it does provide a safeguard for the animals involved.

Mascot pets in institutions, of course, are another matter. Horror stories surface regularly about conditions in prisons and nursing homes. How can these facilities properly care for a pet if they cannot properly care for their patients? Of course, they can't, but these facilities are unlikely to have an animal in residence. Again, the role of the media emerges. The last thing a poorly run facility wants is public scrutiny to expose its deplorable conditions. Why get involved in a novel therapy that will surely attract the attention of some journalist? The very institutions that are enlightened enough to want to adopt a mascot pet are those that invite publicity to show off their facilties. And why not? Favorable publicity makes sound economic sense. Furthermore, a mascot pet is often the aftermath of a successful pet visiting program and may even be placed directly by one of the volunteers or a veterinarian. This provides an additional safeguard for the institutional pet.

Finally, pet therapy is usually initiated by someone who genuinely likes animals and often supervises or directly takes responsibility for the care of the new mascot. Patient abuse of pets, even in prisons, has not been a problem to date, primarily because of careful selection of the inmates involved and strict supervision of the programs (see Chapter 13). In open settings such as nursing homes the animals seem instinctively to avoid patients who do not like them, and there is some evidence that peer pressure may act as a deterrent to a potentially abusive patient. Two problems that have been reported are obesity (the result of too much love in the form of treats) and canine burnout, the result of too little rest time. Obesity can be treated by sensible diet and supervision of treats, and burnout can be avoided by providing the pet with a place of its own away from all the bustle of institutional life and by giving the pet an occasional weekend at the home of a willing staff member.[4]

Pet therapy programs, which often utilize shelter animals, offer a second chance for life for some of the millions of dogs and cats euthanized every year. We all know persons, often elderly, who have had to give up their pets because of apartment restrictions. Widespread acceptance of the role that pets play in the health of their owners may forestall or at least slow down the growing trend toward no-pet housing. It will give legislators and the public alike a potent weapon to use on behalf of their animal friends.

Pet therapy is indeed good for people and good for pets, but perhaps its greatest impact may be to help alter the perception of animals in our society. Traditionally animals have been regarded as tools for human use, and too often our so-called stewardship of the earth and its creatures has been a synonym for exploitation. Now there is a growing body of evidence to suggest that this view of animals is not in our best interests.

Individuals promoting the welfare and humane treatment of animals have been in the mainstream of our culture for some time, but a new animal rights movement has taken concern for animals much farther. Whether or not one agrees with the ideology (which, in its purest form, champions all sentient species) or the methods (which may condone the destruction of property and the liberation of the captive animals), the animal rights movement has, by its passion and commitment, demonstrated that many humans can and do include nonhumans within their arena of moral concern. By highlighting the deep rapport and mutual benefit of bonding between man and animal, pet therapy has dramatically pointed toward the validity of that moral concern.

Human-animal bond and pet therapy studies may finally dissolve that chasm between us and the beasts. If we accept animals as potential healers, as major contributors to our health, happiness, wellness, and vitality, can we in good conscience continue indiscriminately to exploit them and dispose of them at will? I think not. To do so is not only moral hypocrisy, but self-destructive folly. Albert Schweitzer once said that we need a new and wiser concept of animals. With the acceptance of the human-animal bond and the therapeutic value of pets, we may at long last get it.

REFERENCES

1. Kidd, A. H. & Kidd, R. M. (1984, fall). Dr. & Mr. Kidd respond to JAVMA article on PFT. *The Latham Letter*, pp. 16–17.

2. Beck, A. M. & Katcher, A. H. (1984). A new look at pet-facilitated therapy. *Journal of the American Veterinary Medicine Association, 184*(4), 414-421.

3. Silver, N. (1986, July–August). Cold virus: Surrender. *American Health*.

4. Cusack, O. & Smith, E. (1984). *Pets and the elderly: The therapeutic bond* (pp. 81–83). New York: The Haworth Press.

5. Dixon, D. (1982). Real furs: Ranching and trapping—An energy waste. (Available from The Fund For Animals, 140 W. 57th Street, New York, NY 10019.)

6. Singer, P. (1975). *Animal liberation* (pp. 50–51). New York: Avon Books.

Bibliography
and Selected Readings

Allen, L. D. & Burdon, R. D. (1982, fall). The clinical significance of pets in a psychiatric community residence. *American
Journal of Social Psychiatry, 2*(4), 41–43.

Amatora, Sr., M. (1960). Expressed interests in later childhood.
Journal of Genetic Psychology, 96, 327–342.

Anonymous. (1984). A Siamese survival kit. *Buffet Cat Club
News, 1*(7), 5.

Andrysco, R. M. (1982). Companion Animal Services, Inc. Proposal prepared for the Columbus Foundation, Columbus, OH.

Andrysco, R. M. (1982, spring). Pet facilitated therapy in an Ohio
nursing community. *The Latham Letter,* pp. 9–10.

Andrysco, R. M. (1985, summer). Pet behavior reflects owner behavior. *The Latham Letter,* pp. 12–14, 16.

Antelyes, J. (1967). The psychology of pet feeding. *Veterinary
Medicine/Small Animal Clinician, 62,* 249–51.

Antelyes, J. (1967). The petside manner. *Veterinary Medicine/
Small Animal Clinician, 62,* 1155–1159.

Antelyes, J. (1968). Group therapy in the veterinary office. *Veterinary Medicine/Small Animal Clinician, 63,* 975–976.

Arkow, P. (1980). How to start a pet therapy program. Colorado
Springs, CO: The Humane Society of the Pikes Peak Region.

Arkow, P. (1977). A study of the use of companion animals in
selected therapies. Report to the American Humane Education
Advisory Committee, Denver, CO.

Arkow, P. (1980, September). Puppy love at the humane society.
Senior Beacon.

Askins, J. (1979, June 30). Man's best friend his best therapy? *San
Jose Mercury News.*

Atkinson, D. (1985). Nothing more precious. *Social Work Today,
16*(46), 13-14.

Bain, A. M. (1965). Pony riding for the disabled. *Physical Therapy, 51*, 263-265.

Bandura, A., Grusec, J., & Menlove, F. (1967). Vicarious extinction of avoidance behavior. *Journal of Personality and Social Psychology, 5*, 16-23.

Bandura, A. & Menlove, F. (1968). Factors determining vicarious extinction of avoidance behavior through symbolic modeling. *Journal of Personality and Social Psychology, 8*, 99-108.

Banzinger, G. & Roush, S. (1983). Nursing homes for the birds: A control-relevant intervention with bird feeders. *The Gerontologist, 23*, 527-531.

Beck, A. M. & Katcher, A. H. (1984). A new look at pet-facilitated therapy. *Journal of the American Medical Association, 4*, 414–421.

Bedell, J. W. (1971-1972). Role reorganization in the one-parent family: Mother absent due to death. *Sociological Focus, 5*(2), 84-100.

Blair, B. (1976, September 27). Pets brighten life for sick, lonely. *Detroit News*.

Brickel, C. M. (1979). The therapeutic roles of cat mascots with a hospital-based geriatric population: A staff survey. *Gerontologist, 19*(4), 368-372.

Brickel, C. M. (1982). Pet-facilitated psychotherapy: A theoretical explanation via attention shifts. *Psychological Reports, 50*, 71-74.

Brickel, C. M. (1984). The clinical use of pets with the aged. *Clinical Gerontologist, 2*(4), 72-75.

Bridger, H. (1976). The changing role of pets in society. *Journal of Small Animal Practice, 17*, 1-8.

Brown, C. (1983, September 28). Prison-bred "wonderdog" to aid disabled man. *The Seattle Times*.

Brucke, W. F. (1903). Cyno-psychoses: Children's thoughts, reactions, and feelings towards pet dogs. *Journal of Genetic Psychology, 10*, 459-513.

Burke, M. (1978, April). The humane society—People who care. *Denver Magazine*, p. 34.

Bustad, L. K. (1977-1978). The peripathetic dean. *Western Veterinarian, 16*(5), 2-3.

Bustad, L. K. (1978, September-October). Pets for people therapy. *Today's Animal Health*, pp. 8-10.

Bustad, L. K. (1979). Profiling animals for therapy. *Western Veterinarian*, *17*(1), 2.

Bustad, L. K. (1979). People-pet partnership. *Western Veterinarian*, *17*(3), 2-4.

Bustad, L. K. (1979, September). How animals make people human and humane. *Modern Veterinary Practices*, pp. 707-710.

Bustad, L. K. & Hines, L. M. (1981, March). People-pet-partnership-program. *Scientists Center Newsletter*, *3*(1).

Bustad, L. K. (1981-1982, winter). Bethel—An institution without walls. *The Latham Letter*, pp. 4-5.

Butz, G. (1980, July). Dogs for the elderly. *Dog World*, p. 131.

Christy, D. W. (1974, April). The impact of pets on children in placement. *The National Humane Review*.

Cooper, J. E. (1976). Pets in hospitals. *British Medical Journal*, 1, 698-700.

Corson, S. A. & Corson, E. O. (1978). Pets as mediators of therapy. *Current Psychiatric Therapies*, *18*, 195-205.

Corson, S. A. & Corson, E. O. (1979, December). Pet assisted psychotherapy. *Mims Magazine*, pp. 33-37.

Corson, S. A. & Corson, E. O. (1977). Pets as socializing catalysts in geriatrics: An experiment in nonverbal communication therapy. In L. Levi (Ed.), *Society, stress and disease: Aging and old age* (pp. 1-47). Oxford, England: Oxford University Press.

Corson, S. A. & Corson, E. O. (1981). Companion animals as bonding catalysts in geriatric institutions. In B. Fogle (Ed.), *Interrelations between pets and people*, pp. 146-174. Springfield, IL: Charles C. Thomas.

Corson, S. A., Corson, E. O., O'Leary, D., DeHass, G. R., Gunsett, R., Gwynn, P., Arnold, E., & Corson, C. (1976). The socializing role of pet animals in nursing homes: An experiment in nonverbal communication therapy. Ohio State University Department of Psychiatry.

Corson, S. A., Corson, W. L., Gwynn, P. H., & Arnold, E. L. (1977). Pet dogs as nonverbal communication links in hospital psychiatry. *Comprehensive Psychiatry*, *18*, 1.

Curtis, P. (1979, May 20). Animals that care for people. *The New York Times*.

Cusack, O. (1982, February). Therapy dogs international. *Pure-bred Dogs American Kennel Gazette*.

Cusack, O. (1982, April 4). Phila the therapy dog specializes in love. *Grit*, p. 2.

Cusack, O. (1983, February 24). Therapists: Pets who heal. *Hillside Times*, Hillside, NJ.

Cusack, O. (1983, summer). Why we love our pets. *Orion Nature Quarterly*, pp. 35-43.

Cusack, O. (1984, August). The amazing dogs at Bonnie Bergin's. *Lady's Circle*, pp. 32-33, 55-56.

Deeb, B. (1984, spring). War's impact on the people-pet bond. *People-Animals-Environment*, pp. 17-18. Also in *Pure-bred Dogs American Kennel Gazette* (1985, August), pp. 60-63.

DeVinney, E., Dickert, J., & Lockwood, R. (1983). The care of pets within child abusing families. *International Journal for the Study of Animal Problems*, *4*, 321-329.

Doll, M. (1977, July 31). Little pets with big hearts provide therapy of love. *The Denver Post*.

Doll, M. (1979, May 22). Young, old share joy. *The Denver Post*.

Douglas, M. (1977, November). Getting Billy to talk. *American Humane Magazine*.

Doyle, M. C. (1975). Rabbit—Therapeutic prescription. *Perspectives in Psychiatric Care*, *13*, 79-82.

Editorial. (1969, September-October). Old folks need their pets. *The National Humane Review*.

Editorial. (1983, fall). PAW/Latham radiocasts. *The Latham Letter*, p. 10.

Editorial. (1972, November). Pets by prescription—A novel program of Minnesota Humane Society. *Colorado State Department of Public Health News*, Public Veterinary Section.

Editorial. (1973, November). Pet therapy: A boon for the golden age. *National Humane Review*, pp. 10-11.

Editorial. (1973, December). Canine visits to nursing homes reinforce pet therapy theory. *Animal Shelter Shoptalk*.

Editorial. (1974, August). It's a cat's world. *The National Humane Review*.

Editorial. (1974, December). Pet placement program involves senior citizens. *Animal Shelter Shoptalk.*

Editorial. (1975, November). Canine therapist sparks interest at nursing home. *Animal Shelter Shoptalk.*

Editorial. (1976, May). Pet day at the Falls Nursing Home. *Animal Shelter Shoptalk.*

Editorial. (1979, October). Dogs help humans regain health. *Dog World*, p. 50.

Editorial. (1979, November 8). Dogs, other pets, used to treat emotionally ailing. [Norristown, PA] *The Times Herald.*

Editorial. (1980, March). Allowing pets in nursing home opens new practice opportunities. *D.V.M. Magazine.*

Editorial. (1980, summer). Senior pets for senior citizens. *Brief Paws—News of the Humane Society of the Willamette Valley,* Vol. 15(3).

Editorial. (1980, September 23). No-pet rule a killer? *Philadelphia Daily News.*

Editorial. (1983, fall). Profiles. *People-Animals-Environment,* *1*(1), 9.

Editorial. (1985, March 24). Pets as co-therapists: Idea gaining respect. *Los Angeles Times.*

Fales, Jr., E. D. (1960, March). Can pets help people get well and stay well? *Today's Health.*

Felthous, A. (1980). Aggression against cats, dogs and people. *Child Psychiatry and Human Development,* *10,* 169-177.

Flaherty, J. A. (1958, July-August). Jail Bird. *The National Humane Review.*

Foster, K. G. (1982, December 5). A means of escape: Pet therapy in prison. *Columbus Dispatch,* Columbus, OH.

Francis, G. & Odell, S. (1979). Long-term residence loneliness: Myth or reality? *Journal of Gerontological Nursing,* *5*(1), 9-11.

Francis, G., Turner, J. T., & Johnson, S. B. (1982). Domestic animal visitation as therapy with adult home residents. Unpublished paper.

Francis, G. (1981, March). Animals and nursing: A neglected affair. *Nursing Outlook.*

Franti, C. E., Kraus, J. F., Borhani, N. O., Johnson, S. L., & Tucker, S. D. (1980). Pet ownership in rural northern California.

Journal of the American Veterinary Medical Association, *176*, 143-149.

Friedmann, E., Katcher, A. H., Meislich, D., & Goodman, M. (1979). Physiological response of people to petting their pets. *American Zoologist*, *19*, 327.

Friedmann, E., Katcher, A. H., Lynch, J. J., & Thomas, S. A. (1980). Animal companions and one year survival of patients after discharge from a coronary care unit. *Public Health Reports*, *95*, 307-312.

Friedmann, E., Katcher, A. H., Thomas, S. A., Lynch, J. J., & Messent, P. R. (1983). Social interactions and blood pressure: Influence of animal companions. *Journal of Nervous and Mental Disease*, *171*, 461-465.

Gantt, W. H. (1972). Analysis of the effect of person. *Conditioned Reflex*, *7*(2), 62-73.

Gaunt, J. (1975, December). A snowball's chance. *The National Humane Review*.

Goldenberg, S. (1983, March 24). Pets are their therapy. *The Journal-Gazette*, Fort Wayne, IN.

Grundy, P. (1979). Patient progressing well? He may have a pet. *Journal of the American Medical Association*, *241*, 438.

Hall, G. S. & Browne, C. E. (1904). The cat and the child. *Journal of Genetic Psychology*, *11*, 3-29.

Harris, J. H. (1982). A study of client grief responses to death or loss in a companion animal veterinary practice. *California Veterinarian*, *36*, 17-19.

Hayman, H. L. (1975, December). Dogs serving the community. *Off-Lead*, pp. 9-13.

Heiman, M. (1965). Psychoanalytical observations on the relationship of pet and man. *Veterinary Medicine/Small Animal Clinician*, *60*, 713-718.

Hellman, D. & Blackman, N. (1966). Enuresis, firesetting, and cruelty to animals: A triad predictive of adult crime. *American Journal of Psychiatry*, *122*, 1431-1435.

Helsing, K. & Monk, M. (1985). Dog and cat ownership among suicides and matched controls. *American Journal of Public Health*, *75*(10), 1223-1224.

Horn, J. & Meer, J. (1984, August). The pleasure of their company. *Psychology Today*, 52-57.

Hutton, J. S. (1982, November). Social workers act like animals in their casework relations. *Society for Companion Animal Studies Newsheet 3*.

Jernigan, J. (1973, November). Pet therapy brings happiness to the lonely. *The National Humane Review*.

Justice, B., Justice, R., & Kraft, I. A. (1974). Early warning signs of violence: Is a triad enough? *American Journal of Psychiatry*, *131*(4), 457-459.

Katcher, A. H. & Rosenberg, M. A. (1979). Euthanasia and the management of the client's grief. *Compendium on Continuing Education*, *1*, 887-891.

Kearny, M. (1977, May-June). Pet therapy. *Massachusetts SPCA Animals*, *110*(3).

Kellert, S. R. (1979). *Public attitudes toward critical wildlife issues*. Washington, DC: U.S. Government Printing Office, Number 024-020-00-623-4.

Kelly, J. A. (1984, Summer). Facing the loss of a family pet. *The Latham Letter*, p. 1.

Kerilowski, A. C. (1958). Animals help them get well. *Modern Hospital*, *91*, 105-106.

Kidd, A. H. (1981-1982, winter). Mills college psychology professor explores aspects of H/CAB. *The Latham Letter*, p. 18.

Kidd, A. H. & Feldman, B. M. (1981). Pet ownership and self-perception of older people. *Psychological Reports*, *48*, 867-875.

Kidd, A. H., Kelley, H. T., & Kidd, R. M. (1983). Personality characteristics of horse, turtle, snake and bird owners. *Psychological Reports*, *52*, 719-729.

Kidd, A. H. & Kidd, R. M. (1980). Personality characteristics and preferences in pet ownership. *Psychological Reports*, *46*, 939-949.

Kidd, A. H. & Kidd, R. M. (1984, fall). Dr. & Mrs. Kidd respond to JAVMA article on PFT. *The Latham Letter*, pp. 16-17.

Kidd, A. H. & Kidd, R. M. (1985). Children's attitudes towards their pets. *Psychological Reports*, *57*, 15-31.

Kidd, A. H. & Martinez, R. L. (1980). Two personality characteristics in adult pet-owners and non-owners. *Psychological Reports, 47,* 318.

King, K. (1983, fall). Green chimneys. *People-Animals-Environment, 1*(1), 10-11.

Koehler, T. (1983, March 31). Prison dogs. *Pierce County Herald,* Washington State.

Lawson, D. (1981, Autumn). Pets vital to the health, happiness of the elderly. *Montgomery County SPCA News,* Pennsylvania.

Lehman, H. C. (1927). The child's attitudes towards the dog versus the cat. *Journal of Genetic Psychology, 34,* 62-72.

Levinson, B. M. (1962). The dog as co-therapist. *Mental Hygiene, 46,* 59-65.

Levinson, B. M. (1964). A special technique in child psychotherapy. *Mental Hygiene, 48,* 243-248.

Levinson, B. M. (1965). Pet psychotherapy: Use of household pets in the treatment of behavior disorders in childhood. *Psychological Reports, 17,* 695-698.

Levinson, B. M. (1965). The veterinarian and mental hygiene. *Mental Hygiene, 49,* 320-323.

Levinson, B. M. (1966, April). Some observations of the use of pets in psychodiagnosis. *Pediatrics Digest, 8,* 81-85.

Levinson, B. M. (1967). The pet and the child's bereavement. *Mental Hygiene, 51,* 197-200.

Levinson, B. M. (1968, September). Pets—A way to help disturbed children. *Parents Magazine.*

Levinson, B. M. (1969). Pets and old age. *Mental Hygiene, 53,* 364-368.

Levinson, B. M. (1970, July-August). Nursing home pets: A psychological adventure for the patient. *The National Humane Review.*

Levinson, B. M. (1970, September-October). Nursing home pets: A psychological adventure for the patient (part two). *The National Humane Review.*

Levinson, B. M. (1973, January). Pets and modern family life. *The National Humane Review,* pp. 5-9.

Levinson, B. M. (1978). Pets and personality research. *Psychological Reports, 41*(2), 1031-1038.

Levinson, B. M. (1983, summer). Green chimneys seminar of plants, pets, people presents fresh perspectives. *The Latham Letter*, p. 15.

Lynch, J. J., Fregin, G. F., Mackie, J. B., & Monroe, R. R., Jr. (1974). Heart rate changes in the horse to human contact. *Psychophysiology*, *11*(4), 472-478.

Lynch, J. J. (1980, June 20). Warning: Living alone is dangerous to your health. *U.S. News and World Report*, p. 47.

Mayberry, R. P. (1978). The mystique of the horse is strong medicine: Riding as therapeutic recreation. *Rehabilitation Literature*, *39*, 192-196.

McCulloch, M. J. (1982, February). Talking with . . . *Redbook Magazine*.

Meek, C. L. (1982, summer). Dog presence proves salutary in university in university counseling service. *The Latham Letter*, p. 22.

Miller, H. (1979, April). Cro-Magnon's best friend. *Dog World*, p. 24.

Miller, H. (1979, February). Pets as lifesavers. *Dog World*, p. 12.

Millsap, M. (1980, August 7). Pets for the elderly. *Colorado Springs Sun*.

Mugford, R. A. & M'Comisky, J. G. (1975). Some recent work on the psychotherapeutic value of cage birds with old people. In R. S. Anderson (Ed.), *Pet animals and society: Proceedings of the symposium of the British Small Animal Veterinary Association*, pp. 54-65. London: Bailliere Tindall.

Muschel, I. J. (1985). Pet therapy with terminal cancer patients. *The Latham Letter*. pp. 8-11, 15.

Odendaal, J. S. J. (1983, spring). The veterinarian as animal clinician and human psychologist. *The Latham Letter*, pp. 10-11.

Ory, M. G. & Goldberg, E. L. (1982). Pet possession and well-being in elderly women. Unpublished paper.

Ory, M. G. & Goldberg, E. L. (1983). Pet ownership and attachment: An analysis of demographic, health and social interaction correlates in the elderly. Unpublished paper.

Pets Are Wonderful Council. (1985, summer). Survey links career Success with childhood pet ownership. *Family Pet*, p. 2.

Pines, M. (1978). Invisible playmates. *Psychology Today*, *12*(4), 38-42.

Price, E. (1978, August). Canine club. *Dog World*, p. 61.

Quackenbush, J. (1982). The social context of pet loss. *The Animal Health Technician*, *3*, 333-336.

Quinn, K. (1979, September). Dogs for therapy. *Pure-Bred Dogs American Kennel Gazette*, pp. 38-41.

Rhodes, E. (1983, May 26). Pooch program perks up prison. *The Seattle Times*.

Rice, S. R., Brown, L. T., & Caldwell, H. S. (1973). Animals and psychotherapy: A survey. *Journal of Community Psychology*, *1*, 323-326.

Robb, S. S. (1982). Pilot study of pet-dog therapy for elderly people in long-term care. Unpublished paper.

Robb, S. S., Boyd, M. & Pristash, C. L. (1980). A wine bottle, plant and puppy: Catalysts for social behavior. *Journal of Gerontological Nursing*, *6*(12), 722-728.

Robb, S. S. & Stegman, C. E. (1983, June). Companion animals and elderly people: A challenge for evaluators of social support. *The Gerontologist*, *23*(3), 277-282.

Rosenthal, S. R. (1975). Risk exercise and the physically handicapped. *Rehabilitation Literature*, *36*, 144-149.

Ross, G. (1974, July). Chum — A turtle with a mission. *The National Humane Review*.

Rothman, I. (1970). Animal communication. *Voices* (special issue).

Ruby, J. (1982, summer). Images of the family: The symbolic implications of animal photography. *Photography*, III, 2G, pp. 2-7.

Rynearson, E. K. (1978). Humans and pets and attachment. *British Journal of Psychiatry*, *133*, 550-555.

Salmon, I. M. & Salmon, P. W. (1982). A dog in residence: A companion-animal study undertaken in the Caulfield Geriatric Hospital. Report from JACOPIS (Joint Advisory Committee on Pets in Society). Melbourne, Australia.

Salomon, A. (1982). Montreal children in the light of the test of animal infinities. *Annales Medico-Psychologiques*, *140*, 207-224.

Salvatore, D. (1986, May). A very special love story. *Ladies' Home Journal*, pp. 54-61.

Santostefano, P. G. (1984). The effect of a pet therapy on the aggressive behavior of institutionalized adolescents. Unpublished paper.

Schneider, R. & Vaida, M. L. (1975). Survey of canine and feline populations: Alameda and Contra Costa counties, California. *Journal of the American Medical Association*, *166*, 481-486.

Schowalter, J. E. (1983). Clinical experience: Use and abuse of pets. *Journal of the American Academy of Child Psychiatry*, *22*, 68-72.

Sease, M. S. (1980, May). Pets for the elderly. *Pure-bred Dogs American Kennel Gazette*, p. 113.

Serpell, J. A. (1981). Childhood pets and their influence on adults' attitudes. *Psychological Reports*, *49*, 651-654.

Serpell, J. A. (1983, spring). Pet psychotherapy. *People-Animals-Environment*, pp. 7-8.

Sifford, D. (1986, April 13). A sharing of cancer's pain. *The Philadelphia Inquirer*.

Speck, R. V. (1964). Mental problems involving the family, the pet, and the veterinarian. *Journal of the American Veterinary Medical Association*, *145*, 150-154.

Stewart, M. (1983, September 28). Glory is first graduate of prison's dog program. *The Peninsula Gazette*, Washington State.

Summit, R. (1983). The child abuse accommodation syndrome. *Child Abuse and Neglect*, *7*, 181.

Tabscott, J. (1970, January-February). Lady of the cages. *The National Humane Review*, pp. 4-6.

Tapia, F. (1971). Children who are cruel to animals. *Child Psychiatry and human development*, *2*, 70-77.

Timm, C. (1983, spring). Fourth International Congress for Therapeutic Riding. *People-Animals-Environment*, pp. 21-22.

Van, J. (1978, January 6). Pet therapy for hospitals and prisons? *Chicago Tribune*.

Walster, D. (1982, summer). Pets and the elderly. *The Latham Letter*, pp. 1-3, 14, 16.

Warren, K. (1982, December 18-19). Carroll Meek: Helping people recapture the magic in their lives. *Palouse Woman*, pp. 5, 7.

Warren, K. (1982, December 18-19). Carroll Meek: Helping people recapture the magic in their lives. *Palouse Woman*, pp. 5, 7.
Weaver, P. (1978, February). Pet therapy bringing shut-ins out of their shells. *The Washington Post*.
Whitaker, H. (1979, December). Dogs for therapy. *Dog Fancy*.
White, D. C. (1976). Pets for therapy. *Friskies Research Digest*, *3*(4), 1-7.
White, K. (1980, May). Dogs make excellent pets. *Dog World*, p. 142.
Wille, R. (1982, spring). Rutgers report on pet ownership and health stresses value of H/CAB for healthy population. *The Latham Letter*, pp. 10-11.
Wille, R. (1985, spring). A comparative study of the relationship between loneliness and pet companionship in a retirement community. *The Latham Letter*, p. 16.
Wolff, E. (1970). A survey of the use of animals in psychotherapy in the United States; A report to The American Humane Association. Women's SPCA of Pennsylvania.
Wood, D. (1980, September 1). Animals find a home at nursing home. [Minneapolis] *Tribune*.
Yates, J. (1980, May). Pets help us love and live. *Prevention*, 85-98.

BOOKS ON PET THERAPY
AND THE HUMAN-ANIMAL BOND

Anderson, R. K., Hart, B. L., & Hart, L. A. (Eds.). (1984). *The pet connection*. Minneapolis: University of Minnesota Press.
Anderson, R. S. (Ed.). (1975). *Pet animals in society*. New York: Macmillan.
Arkow, P. (1982). *"Pet therapy": A study of the use of companion animals in selected therapies*. Colorado Springs, CO: The Humane Society of the Pikes Peak Region. (Available for $10.00 from P. Arkow, P. O. Box 187, Colorado Springs, CO 80901.)
Arkow, P. (Ed.). (1984). *Dynamic relations in practice: Animals in the helping professions*. Alameda, CA: The Latham Foundation.
Bustad, L. K. (1980). *Animals, aging and the aged*. Minneapolis: University of Minnesota Press.

Corson, S. A. and E. O. (Eds.). (1980). *Ethology and nonverbal communication in mental health*. New York: Pergamon Press.

Cusack, O. & Smith, E. (1984). *Pets and the elderly: The therapeutic bond*. New York: The Haworth Press.

Fogle, B. (Ed.). (1981). *Interrelations between people and animals*. Springfield, IL: Charles C. Thomas.

Fogle, B. (Ed.). (1983). *Pets and their people*. New York: The Viking Press.

Hines, L. M. (1980). *The people-pet-partnership program*. Alameda, CA: The Latham Foundation. (Available for $5.00 from the Latham Foundation; see Appendix.)

IEMT: Austrian Academy of Sciences. (1983). *The human-pet relationship*. (Proceedings of the International Symposium on the Occasion of the 80th Birthday of Nobel Prize Winner Prof. Dr. Konrad Lorenz.) Vienna, Austria.

Katcher, A. H. & Beck, A. M. (Eds.). (1983). *New perspectives on our lives with companion animals*. Philadelphia: University of Pennsylvania Press.

Kay, Nieburg, H. A.; Kutscher; & Fundin (Eds.). (1985). *Pet loss and human bereavement*. Ames: Iowa State University Press.

Lee, R. L., Zeglen, M. E., Ryan, T., & Hines, L. M. (1983). *Guidelines: Animals in nursing homes. California Veterinarian* (Suppl.). (Available for $3.00 from the People-Pet-Partnership Program or the California Medical Veterinary Association; see Appendix.)

Levinson, B. M. (1969). *Pet-oriented child psychotherapy*. Springfield, IL: Charles C. Thomas.

Levinson, B. M. (1972). *Pets and human development*. Springfield, IL: Charles C. Thomas.

McLeod, C. (1981). *Animals in the nursing home – Guide for activity directors*. Colorado Springs, CO: McLeod. (Available for $6.50 from the author at P.O. Box 9334, Colorado Springs, CO 80932.)

Neiburg, H. A. & Fischer, A. (1982). *Pet Loss: A thoughtful guide for adults and children*. New York: Harper Row.

Quackenbush, J. E. (1985). *When your pet dies*. New York: Simon & Schuster.

Sussman, M. B. (1985). *Pets and the family*. New York: The Haworth Press.

Veterinary medical practice: Pet loss and human emotion. *Archives of the Foundation of Thanatology*, 9(2) (1981).

White, B. & Watson, T. (1983). *Pet love: How pets take care of us*. New York: William Morrow.

Yates, E. (1973). *Skeezer: Dog with a mission*. New York: Harvey House.

Appendix:
Organizations Involved in
Pet Therapy and Research
into the Human-Animal Bond

AMERICAN HUMANE ASSOCIATION (9725 East Hampden, Denver, CO 80231) has available a bibliography of pet therapy.

CALIFORNIA VETERINARY MEDICAL ASSOCIATION (1024 Country Club Drive, Moraga, CA) publishes *Guidelines: Animals in Nursing Homes* (order file no. 3758, PO Box 60000, San Francisco, CA 94160).

CANINE COMPANIONS FOR INDEPENDENCE (P.O. Box 446, Santa Rosa, CA 95403) trains social dogs for pet therapy in institutions, signal dogs for the hearing impaired, and service dogs for the physically challenged.

COMPANION ANIMAL SERVICES, INC. (For more information, contact Robert M. Andrysco, 1339–2 Presidential Drive, Columbus, OH 43212.)

DELTA SOCIETY (212 Wells Avenue South, Suite C, Renton, WA 98055; 206–226–7357) is the international society formed to investigate the human/animal bond. It publishes *People-Animals-Environment,* and the *Journal of the Delta Society*.

THE LATHAM FOUNDATION (Latham Plaza Building, Clement and Schiller Streets, Alameda, CA 94501) publishes *The Latham Letter*, a quarterly journal that contains many articles of interest on the human-animal bond and related topics, and has available a bibliography and a series of films for rental.

NORTH AMERICAN RIDING FOR THE HANDICAPPED ASSOCIATION (PO Box 100, Ashburn, VA 22011) publishes information and a list of sources on equestrian therapy.

PETS ARE WONDERFUL COUNCIL (PAW) (500 North Michigan Avenue, Suite 200, Chicago, IL 60611) publishes information on PAW Pals and related programs.

Index

Abandonment, of pet 45
Abasement 147
"Abdul" 203-204
Abuse, of pet 109-110,110-111,124-125, 166,171,179,213-214
Abused Children 122-125,128,171
Abusive Families 109-110,122-124,128, 171,179
Accidents, in nursing homes 146-147
Activity, effect of pets on 53,56,140, 142,144
Actualizing Relationship 111
Adolescents, animals as therapy for 107-117,156-157
Advertising 40
Affection, pets provide 11,81,139,164, 171
Aggression 27,43,113-114,211
  in Prisons 163,166
Alcoholics 75,142
Allen, L.D. 80-83
Allergy, to animal 53, 146-147
Alzheimer's Disease 143
Amatora, Sr. M. 92
American Association for the Advancement of Science 6
American Humane Association 5,8,165
American Humane Education Society 98-99
American Psychological Association 3
American Psychiatric Association 63
Amphibians 2
Anderson, L.J. 121-122
Anderson, R.K. 71,108-109,146-147
Androgeny 10
Andrysco, R.M. 16,134-135,140, 176-177
Angina Pectoris 10

Anima 27
Animal husbandry 100
Animal Rights 213-216
Animal Study Center 16
Animation, as catalyst for social behavior 75,142
Animus 27
Anorexia 157
Antelyes, J. 175-176,187
Anthropomorphism 31-33,40,48-49,115
Anticipatory Grief 190-191
Anxiety, pets decrease 4,10,42,45-47, 63-72,137
Aquarium (see also Fish) 48,65-66, 137-138,163,209
Aquinas, St. Thomas 109
Archetypes 27-28
Arkow, P. 6,121,162
Association for Children With Learning Disabilities 102
Asthma 19
Atkinson, D. 83-84
Atlanta Humane Society 167
Attachment
  to pets 30-31
  among the elderly 138,149
  mechanisms 82
Australian Shepherd 168
Autism 85-87,96
Autogenic Relaxation Phrases 69

"Babe" 165
Background Pets 84
Baking, as therapy 112-114
Bandura, A. 41
Baun, M.M. 67-69
Banzinger, G. 140
Beall, N. 146-147
Beck, A. 65-66,76-78

Conditioning 40-45
Connell, C.M. 148
Constancy 12,14-15
Contact Pets 84
Cooperation, effect of pets on 144
Cornell Companion Animals Program
 145-146
Cornell University 145-146
Corson, Elizabeth O'Leary 3-4,75
Corson, Samuel 3-4,52,75,81
Cost/benefit, of pet therapy 352-354
Cowles, K.V. 184-185, 187,189
Cows 44
Criminal Behavior, predictors of 109
Criminally-insane patients 122,163-167,
 210
Crow, S.E. 187
Cruelty, to pets, *see* Abuse of pet
Culturally-disadvantaged children 96

Dachshunds 53
Daniel, S.A. 144
Davis, Simon 1
Daydreams, of pets 92
Deaf patients *see* hearing impaired
Death
 denial of 182
 of pet 181-193
 stages approaching 58
 wish 183
Deeb, B. 69-71
Deer 163
De Groot, A. 188
Delinquents 109-114
Delta Society 4
Delusions 140
Dental Surgery 65-66
De Pauw, K.P. 198-199
Depression 51-60,80,82,117,128-129,
 141-142,155,163-164,166
Diarrhea 19,120
Dietary Preferences 36,44
Disbrow, M. 122,171
Dismuke, R.P. 200-201
Divorced People 120
Dogs *see* breed of interest
 ancestry 29,30-31

as companions, archaeological
 evidence of 1
clubs 214
domestication of 1
for the Handicapped 201-205
Dolphin Plus Project 86-87
Dolphin Therapy 85-87
Dominance 43
Douglas, M. 97
Dow, S. 121
Doyle, M.C. 79
Drawing, as therapy 114-117
Dr. Doolittle 20-22
Dreams, of animals 26-28,92
Dressage 197
Ducks 163
Dufour 17

Eagle 160
Eating Behavior 141
"Ebunyzar" 97-98
Elderly Patients 3-4,16,19,133-150,212
Elderly Pensioners 136,178
Emotionally-disturbed children 98-102
Empathy 111
Enemy, pet as surrogate 121
Entin, A.D. 126
Enuresis 109
Epileptics, animals as therapy for 2
Equestrian Therapy 2,167,197-201
Euthanasia 121,181-182,186-190
Exercise, pets as incentive to 11
Exotic Pets 171
Extinction (learning theory) 44-47

Fairy Tales 26
Family Support Center, Indianapolis 102
Farm animals, as adjuncts to therapy 2,
 99-102,163-165
Farming, as therapy 99-102
Feeding pets 119,139-140
Feldman, B.M. 147
Felthous, A. 109
Fenner, W.R. 182
Finches 76-78,84
Firesetting 109
Fischer, A. 182,185

Quigley, J 108-109
Quinn, K. 167-170

Rabbits 79-80,91,97,111-114,161,164
Rape victims 158
Reality Orientation 139
Rebound Effect 191
Recreational Therapy 212-213
Reinforcement
  negative 42,45-47
  positive 42,45-47
Relationships
  Between Institutionalized Patients
    138-140
  Between Patients and staff 138-140
Relaxation 108,137,210
Reminiscence therapy 54,146
Renaud, R.E. 199-200
Replacement pet 14-15,183,191-193
Reptiles 2
Resistance to therapy 108
Respiration, effect of pets on 67-69
Responsibility, pets effect on 164,167,
  169
Reverie 66
Rice, S.R. 5
Riddick, C.C. 137
Risk Exercise 199
Risks, of Pet Therapy 146-147,212
Robb, Susanne 75,142,149
Robin, M. 108-111,122,125,183
Rosenberg, M.A. 186
Rosenthal, S.R. 199
Ross, S.B. 100-102
Rothman, I. 13
Rotter's Locus of Control Scale 149
Roush, S. 140
Ruby, J. 126
Rynearson, E.K. 125,176

Safety 12,64-66,76-78
Salmon, I.M. and P.W. 120
Salomon, A. 92
San Francisco Recreation Center 79
San Francisco SPCA, 136
Santostefano, P.G. 79,111-114

Savishinsky, J.S. 27-28,34-35,145-146
Schizophrenics, pet therapy for 5,76-78,
  96,124,143
Schneider, R. 120
Scoliosis 200
Seaquarium 86
Searles, H. 114
Sebkova, J. 64
Segal H. 65-66
Seizure patients 206-207
Selective breeding 31
Self (Jungian psychology) 27
Self-care 135
Self-confidence 147
Self-esteem 117,164
Sentries, pets as 202
Separated People 120
Seraydarian, L. 76-78
Serpell, J. 17,44,47-49
Service Club Members 17
Service dogs 203-205
Sexual Inhibitor, pet as 126
Shadow (Jungian psychology) 27,36,
  43-44
"Sheba" 206-207
Shelton, S.H. 122
Shetland Sheepdogs 102
Shott, S. 122
Siamese Cat 57
Sifford, D. 60
Signal dogs, 47,203-205
"Significant Other" 111
Simon, L. 127
"Sixty Minutes" 6
"Skeezer" 97
Skinner, B.F. 41
Skin Temperature, effect of pets on 69
Skunks 97
Sleeping Practices of pet 14,119,123,126
Smiling, effect of pets on 144
Smith, B. 85-87
Smith, E. 136
Smith, S. 13
Snakes 26,28-30,39,41
Soares, C.J. 124